Global Environmental

Global Environmental Harm
Criminological perspectives

Edited by

Rob White

WILLAN
PUBLISHING

Published by

Willan Publishing
Culmcott House
Mill Street, Uffculme
Cullompton, Devon
EX15 3AT, UK
Tel: +44(0)1884 840337
Fax: +44(0)1884 840251
e-mail: info@willanpublishing.co.uk
website: www.willanpublishing.co.uk

Published simultaneously in the USA and Canada by

Willan Publishing
c/o ISBS, 920 NE 58th Ave, Suite 300,
Portland, Oregon 97213-3786, USA
Tel: +001(0)503 287 3093
Fax: +001(0)503 280 8832
e-mail: info@isbs.com
website: www.isbs.com

First published 2010

ISBN 978-1-84392-796-9 paperback
978-1-84392-797-6 hardback

British Library Cataloguing-in-Publication Data

A catalogue record for this book is available from the British Library

Project managed by Deer Park Productions, Tavistock, Devon
Typeset by GCS, Leighton Buzzard, Bedfordshire
Printed and bound by T.J. International, Padstow, Cornwall

Contents

List of abbreviations

catcon	catalytic converter
CCS	carbon capture and storage
CCTV	closed-circuit television
CDC	Centers for Disease Control (and Prevention) (US)
CEE	central and eastern European (countries – the former communist bloc)
CIA	Central Intelligence Agency (US)
CITES	Convention on International Trade in Endangered Species (of Wild Fauna and Flora)
DEA	Drug Enforcement Agency (US)
DEG	diethylene glycol
EC	European Commission
EIA	Environmental Investigation Agency
EPA	Environmental Protection Agency (US)
EU	European Union
e-waste	electronic waste (discarded computers, monitors, etc.)
FTA	Free Trade Agreement
GDP	gross domestic product
GMO	genetically modified organism
HSUS	Humane Society of the United States
IPCC	Intergovernmental Panel on Climate Change
IUCN	International Union for Conservation of Nature
MNC	multinational corporation
NAFTA	North American Free Trade Agreement
NGO	non-governmental organisation

PAH	polycyclic aromatic hydrocarbons
POP	(1) persistent organic pollutant; (2) problem-oriented policing
PVC	polyvinyl chloride
REDD	reduce emissions by decreasing deforestation
SARS	severe acute respiratory syndrome
SCCP	Scientific Committee on Consumer Products (European Commission)
SCP	situational crime prevention
SUV	sport utility vehicle
TAM	traditional Asian medicine
UN	United Nations
UNICRI	United Nations Interregional Crime Research Institute
WHO	World Health Organisation
WWF	World Wildlife Fund

List of figures and tables

Figures

Tables

List of contributors

Tim Boekhout van Solinge studied human geography at the University of Amsterdam (The Netherlands) and the University of Paris–Sorbonne (Paris IV). From 1995 to 2000, he worked for the University of Amsterdam, publishing on international drug control. Since 2000, he has been a lecturer and researcher in criminology at the Willem Pompe Institute for Criminal Law and Criminology, Utrecht University, The Netherlands. His dissertation at Utrecht (PhD conferred 2004) dealt with drug control in Europe. Since 2004, his main research area has been ecocrime and green criminology, in particular illegal tropical deforestation, including much fieldwork in rainforests, especially the Amazon.

Avi Brisman received a BA from Oberlin College (Oberlin, OH, USA), an MFA from Pratt Institute (Brooklyn, NY, USA), and a JD with honours from the University of Connecticut School of Law (Hartford, CT, USA). Mr Brisman is currently an adjunct assistant professor at CUNY/Kingsborough (Brooklyn, NY, USA), where he teaches courses in anthropology and sociology. He is also a PhD candidate in the Department of Anthropology at Emory University (Atlanta, GA, USA), where he is writing his dissertation on legal consciousness.

Diane Heckenberg is a PhD student in the School of Sociology and Social Work at the University of Tasmania, Australia. She has tutored in sociology and criminology, evaluated a post-release options project for prisoners, worked as a research assistant on the Australian Prisons

Project for the University of New South Wales, and is currently a casual researcher on environmental crime issues for the University of Tasmania's Criminology Research Unit. In 2010, Di will join a small team researching hazardous waste disposal in Australia. Di's key research interests include environmental harms and crimes, toxic harms and product harms.

Joe Herbig has been an associate professor in the Department of Criminology and Security Science at the University of South Africa, Pretoria, since 2007. Prof. Herbig previously lectured to students of nature conservation and fishery resource management at the Cape Technikon (now Cape Peninsula University of Technology) in Cape Town on a part-time basis for several years. He is passionate about environmental conservation crime and criminality research, and his recent articles published in *Acta Criminologica* include 'Conservation Crime: South African Concerns and Considerations from a Criminological Perspective' and 'Conservation Crime Causation – Towards Proactive Compliance Management'. His other interests include forensic psychophysiology (polygraphy) and offender risk and rehabilitation profiling as well as the compilation of presentence evaluation reports and victim-impact statements.

Rodney Kueneman is Associate Professor of Sociology at the University of Manitoba, Winnipeg, Canada. His current research and teaching interests include ecology and society, global political economy, and social and community reconstruction. He was active in policy-based research on human support systems in his early career, including youth justice, child welfare, and special education, but has increasingly turned his attention to the global political economic system that is generating massive social inequality and ecological destruction. He is currently working on a book proposing local community revitalisation as the only sustainable alternative to the global ecological dead end we are engineering.

Michael J. Lynch is a professor in the Department of Criminology at the University of South Florida (Tampa, USA). His recent publications include *Environmental Crime, Law and Justice* (2008, with R.G. Burns and P. Stretesky), *Racial Divide* (2008, with E.B. Patterson and K.K. Childs), *Big Prisons, Big Dreams* (2007), and *Primer in Radical Criminology* (2006, with R.J. Michalowski). He has been engaged in research on green and radical criminology since 1990.

Lorenzo Natali holds a PhD in criminal law and criminology and is currently a Research Fellow at the Department of Criminology of the University of Milano-Bicocca (Milan, Italy). His main fields of research so far have focused on violence as seen from an interactionist symbolic perspective, and the environment as examined from a criminological standpoint. His interests also comprise qualitative methodologies for social research, including visual techniques of investigation. With Adolfo Ceretti, he is co-author of *Violent Cosmologies. Criminal Life Stories* (2009; Cortina).

Yang Shuqin is an associate professor of sociology at Shanghai University of Engineering Technology, Shanghai, P.R. China. Her main research fields are cultural sociology and social work. Yang's recent books include *Jewish Culture* (2008; Beijing: Chinese Oriental Publishing House) and *Introduction to Sociology* (2009; Shanghai Jiaotong University Press).

Russell Smandych is Professor of Sociology and Criminology at the University of Manitoba, Winnipeg, Canada. His current research and teaching interests include global criminology and criminal justice, comparative legal history, and comparative youth justice. He is the editor or co-editor of seven books and has published widely in leading Canadian and international journals, including *Law and History Review, International Criminal Justice Review, Australian and New Zealand Journal of Criminology, Adelaide Law Review, Australasian Canadian Studies, Legal History, and Canadian Journal of Law and Society.*

Nigel South is Professor in the Department of Sociology, a member of the Human Rights Centre, and currently Pro-Vice-Chancellor for the Faculty of Law and Management at the University of Essex, Colchester, UK. He has previously taught in London and New York. His research interests include green criminology; drug use, health and crime; inequalities, crime and citizenship; and theoretical and comparative criminology. He has served on various editorial boards and continues to serve on the international editorial board of *Critical Criminology* and as an associate editor of the journal, *Deviant Behavior*.

Paul B. Stretesky is an associate professor in the School of Public Affairs at the University of Colorado Denver, USA. His recent publications include *Environmental Crime, Law and Justice* (2008, with R.G. Burns and M.J. Lynch) and *Guns, Violence, and Criminal*

Behavior: The Offender's Perspective (2009, with M.R. Pogrebin and N.P. Unnithan). His research interests include environmental justice, green criminology, and corporate crime.

Noriyoshi Takemura is a professor in the Faculty of Law at Toin University of Yokohama, Japan. He has researched and written extensively in areas such as crime and justice in Japan, organised crime, juvenile justice and Internet crime, human trafficking networks around Japan and East Asia, and green criminology. He lectures in the areas of criminal policy, criminology and criminal law, and is on the editorial board of the *Asian Journal of Criminology*.

Melanie Wellsmith is a senior lecturer in criminology at the University of Huddersfield, UK. Previously she worked as a research fellow at the University College London (UCL) Jill Dando Institute of Crime Science, and as a police crime analyst, as well as volunteering as a police special constable. Melanie's PhD research (at UCL) involves the analysis of spatial patterning of crime within facilities and the routine activities and practices of facility users. Her other research interests include crime analysis and policing, situational crime prevention and design, and environmental harms, particularly against non-human animals. Melanie has publications and conference presentations across these fields.

Rob White is Professor of Environmental Criminology at the University of Tasmania, Australia. He has published extensively in the areas of juvenile justice, youth studies, green criminology and crime prevention. His recent books that deal with environmental issues include *Controversies in Environmental Sociology* (2004); *Crimes Against Nature: Environmental Criminology and Ecological Justice* (2008); *Environmental Crime: A Reader* (2009); and *Crime, Criminality and Criminal Justice* (with Santina Perrone, 2010).

Introduction

Rob White

Issues such as climate change, disposal of toxic waste and illegal fishing have generated increasing attention within criminological circles in recent years. This book brings together original, cutting-edge work that deals with global environmental harm from a wide variety of geographical and critical perspectives.

In compiling this collection we wanted to cast the net as broadly as possible, and as part of this to include writers from many different parts of the world and at different points in their research careers. Aside from the usual regrettable omissions due to work pressures and personal calamities, the final selection involves writers from countries such as Australia, Canada, the USA, South Africa, Japan, China, The Netherlands, Italy and the UK. Together in our analyses, we cover most parts of the world in some way or another. Future collections can perhaps fill in the gaps from the point of view of the places and issues discussed, and the place of origin of the contributors.

Interestingly, each chapter tends to be written in its own particular cultural and (perhaps) national style, and each certainly frames the issues from a particular location and political viewpoint. Diversity of input is necessary to compiling a sophisticated and informed survey of issues that are of global environmental importance. We do not all see the world in the same way, and this is partly because we occupy that world in substantively different ways to begin with. Where we live, work and play, and where we travel, have important bearings on the shape of our thinking and on the content of our research and scholarship. So, too, the language of academic discourse – in this case, English – likewise impacts on how we re-present the world around us, with special difficulties and challenges for those from non-English-speaking backgrounds. Yet, the voices from around the globe need to be heard, and heard more often, if we are to develop a more profound and inclusive understanding of key issues, and to identify the significant sites for social intervention.

The topics covered in the book are global, regional and local in nature, although in each case there are clear transnational or global dimensions. There were three broad criteria that underpinned the inclusion of the specific contributions to this book. These were:

- That the contributions deal with *global or transnational* issues or processes. These have various definitions and dimensions that might be explored, relating to cross-national comparison and global studies through to more narrowly defined conceptual parameters pertaining to specific types of transnational crime.
- That the contributions deal with *environmental harm*. This, too, has various definitions and dimensions that might be explored, relating to conventional criminological notions of crime, through to wider ecological and green criminology notions of harm.
- That the contributions provide *original* and innovative understandings of important environmental issues. This includes different emphases:
  - *theoretical* – e.g. concepts of harm, transference of harm, nature and natural resources, crime, typologies of specific harms, different theoretical approaches
  - *methodological* – e.g. how to do and/or think about global research, alternative data sources, development of facts and statistics on specific harms
  - *substantive* – e.g. case studies of particular types or categories of harm, cross-border harms, what is going on in your region or country.

Moreover, in putting the book together, we felt that there is some urgency in producing specifically criminological contributions to global debates surrounding the environment. Criminologists need to shape as well as respond to the world political agenda.

As a whole, then, the chapters in this book explore topics that provide theoretical, methodological and substantive insights into the nature and dynamics of environmental harm, and the transference of this harm across regions and continents and globally. Specific topics include the criminal nature of global warming, an ethnographic study of pollution and consciousness of environmental harm, environmental destruction associated with huge industrial developments, chaos theory and environmental social justice, deforestation as a global phenomenon, illegal trade in endangered species, and transference of toxicity.

The book is divided into three sections. The first part, 'Global Problems', provides the geographical and conceptual context for trying to understand and map out the nature of global environmental harms. Chapter 1 by White outlines the importance of developing an ecoglobal criminology, and sets out a spatial agenda for the study of environmental harm. Boekhout van Solinge, in Chapter 2, discusses the harms associated with deforestation, both in South America and in Asia, and the activism that has grown up around such issues and harms. Heckenberg in Chapter 3, then defines and describes the concept of 'transference' as this pertains to environmental harm, using the movement of toxic materials around the planet as an illustration of general processes. In Chapter 4, Lynch and Stretesky provide insight into the issues that green criminology sees as important vis-à-vis global warming, and they identify a number of associated social, environmental and political issues that warrant our close scrutiny.

The second part of the book, 'Specific Issues', provides an opportunity for more detailed and in-depth study of particular issues. Chapter 5, by Smandych and Kueneman, provides a searing and penetrating critique of the tar sands development in Alberta, Canada, both in regards to its destruction of environments and in terms of the greenwashing campaigns used to justify this destruction. Herbig examines the illegal reptile trade in Chapter 6, and provides an overview of the various methods and dimensions of this trade in the South African context. In chapter 7, Wellsmith continues the discussion of the illicit trade in endangered species, by asking how crime prevention can be applied in the most effective ways to deal with this, and in ways that dovetail with a broad green criminology agenda. The question of pollution in China is the subject of Chapter 8 by Shuqin, and the pervasive negative role of the multinational corporation is a key target of her critique.

In the final section, 'Alternative Visions', the authors once again return to matters of perception, investigation, analysis and theoretical emphasis. In Chapter 9, Brisman questions why ecologically benign activities such as 'dumpster diving' and some other forms of recycling, and the use of pedicabs, are, in effect criminalised, especially in the light of generalised public concerns about the environment. Natali, in Chapter 10, examines a case of pollution in Spain in which residents both affirm and deny the problem, simultaneously, and he argues for a more nuanced and complex understanding of how people on the ground make sense of the world around them. The subject of Chapter 11, by Takemura, is likewise that of complexity. Here the concern is to explicitly acknowledge the non-linear nature of environments and issues, including unintended consequence, and to build chaotic thinking into our models of understanding and action. The final chapter by South provides a rounded and comprehensive overview of key issues facing us all as we collectively and individually come to grips with the ecocidal tendencies of late modernity.

The collection as a whole reinforces the importance of ecoglobal criminology as a dynamic paradigm for theory and action on environmental issues in the twenty-first century. The book features contributions from different parts of the world, each with its own unique perspective on and analysis of specific types of environmental harm. Global warming and the many environmental harms identified in this book are the vital issues of our age. Accordingly, the criminological perspectives presented herein are important both in discerning the nature and complexities of these harms and, ultimately, in forging responses to them.

Part I

Global problems

Chapter 1

Globalisation and environmental harm

Rob White

Introduction

Global environmental harm is not new. For many centuries humans have done things to the environment that have fundamentally transformed local landscapes and regional biodiversities. From bringing plants and animals from the 'homeland' to new parts of the world, to polluting rivers and seas with industrial outfall, to fire burning in particular local biospheres, ecological change has been part and parcel of how humans have worked with each other, and nature, for millennia. Not all such activities have been viewed as harmful, and the transformation of environments has not always been seen as a negative.

In ecological terms, however, there are, today, several areas of acknowledged harm that are garnering ever greater attention and concern from the scientific community and from the population at large. The main reason for this is a consensus that the relationship between human activity and environmental well-being is essentially toxic – we are killing the world as we know it. Thus, the last four decades have seen much greater international cooperation and sharing of knowledge among scientists, including social scientists, from many different areas of endeavour. One result of these efforts at collaboration and synthesis is a better sense of global ecological health. This is well documented, and baseline data are now available with which to measure the impact of human activity on all types of life on the planet (United Nations Environment Programme 2007). Basically, the message is that the human ecological footprint is too big to sustain us, and everything else, for much longer into the foreseeable future.

Briefly, there are three key problem areas of ecological harm (White 2008a). These are:

- the problem of *climate change*, in which the concern is to investigate activities that contribute to global warming, such as the replacement of forests with cropland
- the problem of *waste and pollution*, in which the concern is with activities that defile the environment, leading to such phenomena as the diminishment of clean water
- the problem of *biodiversity*, in which the concern is to stem the tide of species extinction and the overall reduction in species through application of certain forms of human production, including the use of genetically modified organisms.

Ecological understandings of harm view these matters in essentially trans-boundary terms; there is worldwide transference of harms. The bottom line is that, regardless of legal status, action must be taken now to prevent harms associated with global warming, further pollution and waste generation, and threats to biodiversity. The key issue is that of sustainability, and the division of social practices into benign and destructive, from the point of view of ecological sustainability. The imperative is ecological, and the goal is no less than that of human survival.

Within this context of increasing concern about environments and the ecological limits of human activity, there has emerged enhanced interest within criminology about conventional environmental crimes and more broadly defined environmental harms (White 2009a). Whether termed green, environmental or conservation criminology, this interest in environmental issues and ecological matters is reflected in a broad and expanding range of issues, and in the work of a small but growing network of scholars and researchers who are concerned about various aspects of the environment (e.g. Beirne and South 2007; White 2008b, Gibbs *et al.* 2009). Inevitably, some of this attention has also been directed at the transnational nature of the harm that is at the core of recent investigations, whether this is in relation to the illegal trade in ivory (Lemieux and Clarke 2009) or disposal of hazardous waste (White 2009b). Institutionally, efforts to combat international environmental crime have also been stepped up by Interpol, which has further professionalised its resources and general approach to pollution issues, and to issues pertaining to the illegal trade in flora and fauna (e.g. Interpol 2009).

Simultaneous with the increasing interest in environmental issues within criminology and criminal justice agencies, there has been growing interest in the development of a global criminology. This takes several different forms, from the publication of recent books explicitly concerned with global and comparative criminological issues (e.g. Aas 2007; Van Djik 2008), through to new international networks whose brief is expressly that of building transnational knowledge and colleague linkages. The latter include, for example, the International and Comparative Criminal Justice Network (functionally based at Leeds, UK, and Sydney, Australia) and the Supranational Criminology Group (based in Amsterdam, The Netherlands). There are also similar groups linked to Australia's Monash University (via the Prato campus in Italy) and in the USA to Old Dominion University (namely, the International State Crime Research Consortium). The shift to a global stage means that issues such as terrorism, national security, cybercrime and environmental harm are being dealt with in ways that transcend the usual parochialism of much mainstream criminology. It also poses special challenges from the point of view of conceptualisation and methodology (Larson and Smandych 2007; White 2009c).

Those who study global environmental harm have much to learn from this new movement that is stressing the importance of global scholarship. Likewise, global criminology can be enhanced by those pursuing their interest in environmental issues. In either case, it is clear that very often the issues of power, class, ethnicity and discrimination are at the heart of processes of both victimisation and criminalisation (including the lack thereof vis-à-vis corporate crime). Taking the perspective of the globe as a whole, it becomes hard not to discuss North–South relations, and to see social injustice as at the heart of much that is wrong in the world today (e.g. Pellow 2007). The continuing legacy of imperialism and colonialism is found in the racism and entrenched class inequalities in both the metropole and the periphery. It is also evident in the ways in which the voices from below, including those from the South (e.g. the indigenous, the Islamic, the poor), are marginalised in contemporary writings and substantive research, including and especially that on globalisation (Connell 2007).

Dealing with issues of global environmental harm, therefore, is a complex and multifaceted task. It involves not only turning one's gaze to specific incidents and events of environmental destruction, to learning about the ecological imperatives that demand more and more of our attention, and to hearing what the Other have to say about their socio-ecological worlds. It means forging new frameworks of seeing and acting on the world around us. Within criminology, one such framework or paradigm is that of ecoglobal criminology.

Ecoglobal criminology

Ecoglobal criminology refers to a criminological approach that is informed by ecological considerations and by a critical analysis that is worldwide in its scale and perspective (White 2009ab).

How we interpret and respond to global developments depends upon how we define environmental harm; how we envisage the protection of human, ecological and animal rights; and how we understand the power and interests that underpin recent trends and issues. For critical environmental criminology, there is no doubt that new typologies of harm have to be developed, new methodologies for global research instigated, and new modes of social control devised if we are to adequately address present issues.

The research agenda offered by an ecoglobal criminology is one that expresses a concern that there be an inclusive definition of harm, and that a multidisciplinary approach be adopted to the study of environmental harm. For example, there are a number of intersecting dimensions that need to be considered in any analysis of specific instances of environmental harm. These include consideration of who the victim is (human or non-human), where the harm is manifest (global through to local levels), the main site in which the harm is apparent (built or natural environment), and the time frame within which harm can be analysed (immediate and delayed consequences). Many of the key features pertaining to environmental harm are inherently international in scope and substance. Expanding our vision to incorporate the large and the small, the ecological and the social, the temporal and the spatial – these are essential to a theoretically informed analysis of contemporary environmental harms (White 2009b).

There already exists ample documentation of environmental harm across many different domains of human activity (White 2009a). One task of ecoglobal criminology is to name these harms as 'criminal', even if not considered illegal in conventional terms. Those who determine and shape the law are very often those whose activities need to be criminalised for the sake of planetary well-being.

Environmental harm is thus intrinsically contestable, both at the level of definition and in terms of visions of what is required for desired social and ecological change. The question of power is of vital concern to ecoglobal criminology.

This kind of work has ranged across a broad range of theoretical and substantive areas, including, for example, issues pertaining to ecojustice (which deals with transgressions against humans, non-human animals, and environments), disposal of waste (both legal and illegal), risk and the precautionary principle (and the contributions of crime prevention to addressing these), ecophilosophy and conceptualisations of harm (which relate to conventional, ecological, and green criminological theoretical and definitional concerns), and the opportunities and possibilities for global research into environmental harm (including considerations of whose views of the globe are heard or are most prominent in criminological investigations). Methods of investigation have involved document analysis, collation of statistics, interviews with key players and a mix of quantitative and qualitative methodologies.

As indicated, a crucial aspect of more recent work has been the need to shift the analytical and methodological focus toward global issues and international concerns. Consideration of scale and focus are implicit in the framing of research into transnational environmental harm, including climate change. There are at least three different ways in which transnational research can be approached (White 2009b):

1 global – refers to transnational harms, processes and agencies (*universal* effects, processes, agencies across the globe)

2 comparative – refers to differences between nation states, including 'failed states' (*particular* differences between nation states and regions)

3 historical – refers to epochal differences in modes of production and global trends (systemic differences *over time*, within and between different types of social formation).

The first approach focuses on globalisation as a far-reaching process in which harm can be traced in its movements across the world and its presence documented in many different locales. The second approach has a comparative focus, with a concern to study particular countries and regions, including failed states, in relation to each other. The nature of similarities and differences is fundamental to this kind of study. The third approach is based upon historical appreciation of social change and social differences. It views trends and issues in terms of major epochs, such as the transitions from feudalism to capitalism, or the shift from competitive capitalism to global monopoly capitalism.

Undertaking study of transnational harm is not only a matter of choosing one's focus (e.g. global, comparative or historical) or substantive subject (e.g. terrorism, torture or environmental harm). There are also epistemological issues at stake: we need to query whose knowledge, whose perspectives, and whose ideas come to dominate our understandings of the social world. This, too, needs to be borne in mind when considering how best to advance the agenda of ecoglobal criminology. Likewise, and especially in the context of this book, the question of scale becomes of vital importance.

Geographies of harm

To appreciate fully the nature of global environmental harm, for instance, it is useful to consider the physical location of harm within particular geographical contexts. This is an exercise that is simple to undertake, yet potentially confrontational in its impact.

Consider, for example, a political map of the world (Figure 1.1). This describes the planet as divided up into political entities – the nation state. On this map, it is possible to plot out a myriad of different types of harms, some of which are common across the surface of the

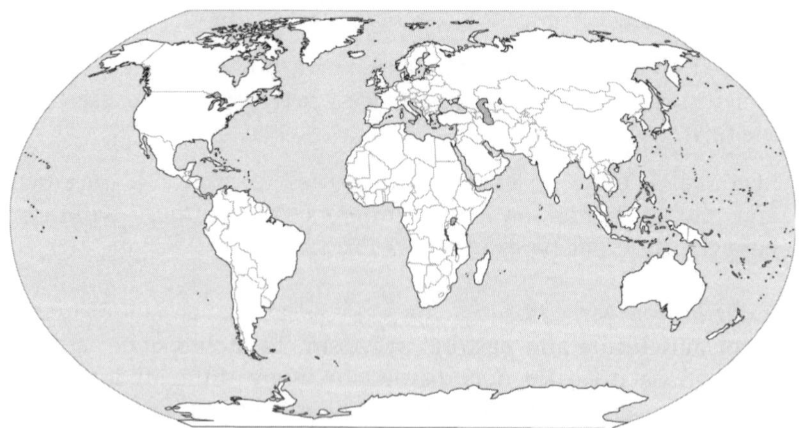

Johnomaps.comhttp://johomaps.com/world/worldblank_bw.html

Figure 1.1 Map of the world, by political divisions

globe, and others of which are specific to particular locales, regions and countries. Layer after layer of harm, present and potential, can be determined by, on the one hand, investigating ecological trends that involve degradation and destruction of environments (such as clear-felling of forests), and, on the other hand, by considering existing documentation of specific types of environmental crime (such as illegal international trade in flora and fauna). The harms so described are interconnected and intertwined in various ways: the 'butterfly effect' means that what happens at the local level has consequences for those on the other side of the planet. What happens in any one place is intrinsically important to what happens worldwide.

The local

The local basically refers to where we live, work and often play. It is what we are most familiar with, and yet at times least knowledgeable or questioning about. In Tasmania, for example, some communities have to boil their water before drinking it. The problem is local, and many of the locals do not think twice about doing something they have grown up to do. There is no 'environmental issue' as such, in that people have not framed the activity (yet) in this manner. Off the coast of Nova Scotia, many local people catch lobsters for personal use. Lobster poaching – that is, the illegal taking of lobster – is ingrained in long-standing popular culture, and for many there is no problem as such. In both cases, the activity and the response stem from how local people over time create their own spaces, their own routines, and their own sense of what is right and wrong, of the normal and the unusual. The cause and the consequence of each activity, however, may be far-reaching, both in terms of future viability (of humans, of lobster) and in ultimately leading to a widening of the search for clean, fresh water and more abundant crustaceans.

The national

Around the world different countries tend to have different types of environmental problems and issues. In New Zealand, for example, big questions have arisen over the use of pesticides and overuse of land for agriculture and pastoral purposes. Land and water are being contaminated through existing systems of production. By contrast, pressing issues of concern in Canada relate to the ecological impact of the huge oil tar-sands projects in Alberta, and to the impact of insect blights on the pine trees of British Columbia. In Palestine, Israel, Syria and Jordan, issues of water, for drinking and for agriculture, are at the top of the environmental agenda. Water is vital to life; perceived national interests dictate that its scarcity is in part generated by efforts to control it for some population groups over and above use by others. National context is important both in the objective nature of the problems at hand (e.g. pollution, deforestation, lack of adequate water) and in regards to subjective processes relating to the politicisation of issues (e.g. the role of social movements in shaping public consciousness and state action on specific issues).

The regional

Most countries of the world have borders with another country. Rivers flow, mountains soar, air currents weave their way through the atmosphere, and plants and animals cross artificial boundaries that, for them, do not exist. There are issues that are specific to particular regions of the world. Huge tropical forests are found in the Amazon, an area that encompasses several different countries such as Brazil and Peru. Such forests also cover parts of South-East Asia, spanning Indonesia, Malaysia, Thailand and Burma, among other countries. Africa is the home to elephants, reptiles, giraffes and other creatures that are unique to particular parts of that continent, and not the preserve of any one country. Desertification and drought are phenomena associated with the dry lands of northern Africa and the island continent of Australia. Meanwhile, cross-border pollution in Europe, and between China and Russia, is a matter that demands a regional rather than simply national response. Acid rain traverses provincial and state demarcations and can affect environments, animals and humans many kilometres away. A nuclear accident in the Ukraine makes its presence felt in Britain, as well as the immediate vicinity of Chernobyl.

The global

Changing weather conditions appear to be the harbinger of much greater changes to come. Climate change is something that affects us all, regardless of where we live, regardless of skin colour, income, ethnicity, religion and gender. How it does so is mediated by the power of some to ameliorate the worst effects of global warming, for themselves, often at the expense of others. Nonetheless, there are environmental issues that are intrinsically global in scope. Our oceans are filled with garbage, and huge gyres spin round and round collecting plastic from all over the planet, and killing sea life in the process. Satellites proliferate in the upper reaches of the atmosphere and a new junkyard is fast being created above our heads. Subterranean spaces are repositories for radioactive waste, and potentially for carbon emissions (as if these places are not alive too). Genetically modified organisms are distributed worldwide, with major potential to further diminish biodiversity through concentration of production into smaller numbers of species and products. Environmental harm comes in many different forms, and is sold to us in many different guises.

The transnational

The production of global environmental harm is partly determined through complex processes of transference. Harm can move from one place to another. Harm can be externalised from the producers and consumers in ways that make it disappear from their sight and oversight. The global trade in toxic waste (often under the cover of recycling), the illegal dumping of radioactive waste, carbon emission trading, and the shifting of dirty industries to developing countries constitute some of the worst aspects of the 'not in my backyard' syndrome. The result is a massive movement of environmentally harmful products, processes and wastes to the most vulnerable places and most exploitable peoples of the world. Tracking the movement of harm is as important as establishing its more fixed manifestations at the local, national and regional levels. In this vein, environmental degradation is not only about what is being done to local environments because of 'brown' issues such as pollution, but it also commands our attention in regards to the transfer of flora and fauna across borders and into new ecological habitats. Meanwhile, the Southern Ocean becomes the slaughterhouse that satisfies the palate of the Japanese for whale meat. If the harm cannot be done locally, then the transnational is the only way for it to occur.

For critical criminology that wants to address issues of environmental harm, a mapping of these harms is essential to furthering our understanding of how it occurs, where it occurs, and what might be done to respond to it. Such an exercise also reveals the strong connections between each of our own personal places in the world, and that of others close to and distant from us.

Climate change

While a myriad of specific environmental harms are evident, the most pressing and important international issue facing humanity today is that of climate change. As of yet, however, very little has been done in regards to this problem within criminology (by comparison, huge efforts are being made in the areas of international law, and environmental management, for example). From a specifically criminological point of view, there are several issues related to climate change that warrant immediate attention.

The first issue relates to existing and potential *social conflicts* surrounding global warming (White 2009d). In summary, these include:

- *conflicts over environmental resources*
  - e.g. water – anti-privatisation protests and diminished clean drinking water resources (Bolivia, South Africa, Israel, Palestine)
  - e.g. food – food riots particularly in relation to grain prices associated with tension between crops for food and crops for biofuel (Mexico, Haiti, Indonesia, Cameroon)
  - e.g. fish – competition between local fishers and commercial and industrial fishers, leading to 'war' over specific fisheries (Canada, Spain)

- *conflicts linked to global warming*
  - e.g. climate-induced migration of peoples – 'environmental refugees' (South Pacific Islands)
  - e.g. demographics – population size and profile (such as structural ageing) linked to distribution, availability and carrying capacity of land (China)
  - e.g. loss of territory and border disputes – receding coastlines and desertification (Egypt, Greenland, Canada, Russia, the USA)

- *conflicts over differential exploitation of resources*
  - e.g. indigenous people and biopiracy – theft of plants and indigenous knowledge and techniques under guise of legal patent processes (Brazil, Peru)
  - e.g. subsistence versus industrial production – uses of biotechnology such as genetically modified organisms (GMOs) and other forms of technology to increase yields beyond the norm and beyond precaution, for profit purposes (Zambia)
  - e.g. conflicts over energy supply – related to the concentration of the world's hydrocarbon reserves in specific regions (Iraq, Iran, Venezuela)

- *conflicts over transference of harm*
  - e.g. cross-border pollution – movement of pollutants through fluid medium such as water or air currents (China, Russia, Germany, Hungary)
  - e.g. transborder movement of toxic waste – corruption of companies and organised crime in redistributing waste to countries of least resistance, or the oceans and deserts of the world (Somalia, Ivory Coast, Nigeria)
  - e.g. circulation of pollution and waste – such as concentration of plastics in specific geographical locations and planetary sinks (ocean gyres, Antarctic ozone hole).

Issues of biosecurity and protection from environmental harms originating outside particular national boundaries will challenge criminology to be more global in scope and internationally sophisticated in its methods of analysis. National security agendas will increasingly be reflected in the interplay between how crime and sovereignty are socially constructed, and how the relationship between local, regional and global interests is construed within diverse social and political formations (e.g. the USA Russian Federation, European Union, Association of South-East Asian Nations, African Union). Conflict resolution will be at a premium, as will be devising suitable methods to minimise harm and prevent crime. Restorative justice strategies and community crime prevention methods are important resource areas to tap into as conflicts associated with climate change intensify.

A second pressing issue relates to the *criminalisation and regulation* of activities relating to carbon emissions. Two areas present themselves as of immediate interest to criminology.

Criminalisation of carbon gas emission

A recent Supreme Court ruling in the USA has determined that the Environmental Protection Agency has a legal duty of care to ensure that greenhouse gases do not continue to pose harm to human, animal and environments (see US Environmental Protection Agency 2009). The ruling is significant insofar as it is an explicit acknowledgement that greenhouse gas emission is a social and environmental harm, and that environmental law enforcers and regulators have a responsibility to protect others (including non-humans) from this harm. Criminalisation extends not only to carbon emissions; issues of water use and water theft, for instance, are also increasingly being posed in terms of the application of criminal sanctions against perpetrators who misuse or illegally 'steal' the resource.

Regulation of carbon emission trading

Insofar as one of the key proposed solutions to global warming is carbon emission trading, and the sequestration of carbon emissions (in the form of carbon emission storage, as well as in protection of the world's tropical and other old-growth forests), the introduction of a wide range of regulatory sanctions is inevitable. As with criminalisation processes generally, this will require concerted new forms of policing and enforcement, and compliance strategies that are flexible and multipronged (including, for example, restorative justice-based methods of restitution and conflict resolution). Collaborative policing efforts across national boundaries, and the further development of international institutions of justice (for instance, an international environment court or its equivalent), imply new areas of expertise, exchange of ideas and personnel, and strategic emphasis.

Issues pertaining to how harm and crime are conceptualised and institutionally addressed have major implications for the ways in which justice and governance are constructed at a material and ideological level. For the police, agencies such as Interpol will continue to grow in importance vis-à-vis leadership and the transfer of knowledge, information and skills. For the courts, new transgressions associated with carbon emission processes will demand new knowledge, new ways in which to view criminality and imaginative forms of jurisprudence.

Research is needed within criminology that critically examines the consequences of global warming for national security, societal peace, and social, species and ecological well-being. The urgency of engaging criminologists in climate change issues cannot be emphasised enough. Criminology's future is intertwined with the trajectory of climate change over the course of the next few years.

Developing global responses

One of the initial questions to be asked in responding to environmental crime – whether narrowly and legalistically defined or defined in regards to wider concepts of harm – is, who is actually going to take action on these matters and how will responses be framed? The answer to this is that it depends upon the country or jurisdiction in question.

For example, many jurisdictions have specialised agencies – such as environmental protection agencies – which are given the mandate to investigate and prosecute environmental crimes. The police may play an auxiliary role in relation to the work of these agencies. In other instances, the lead agency for environmentally related crimes – such as illegal fishing – may include specialist agencies such as a fisheries management authority. Personnel within these agencies are mandated to ensure compliance and enforcement as determined by legislation.

In some contexts and situations, members of a police service may be especially trained up to be environmental police, as with the 'green police' in Israel (White 2007). In other countries, such as The Netherlands, all police are trained and expected to actively deal with issues pertaining to environmental crime – it is built into the routines of everyday operational policing. In the UK, there are wildlife officers in most constabularies, and police in places such as Scotland are taking greater interest in environmental law enforcement, particularly as this relates to wildlife crime (Fyfe and Reeves 2009).

Within a particular national context, there may be considerable diversity in environmental standards, environmental law enforcement agencies and personnel, and the police will have quite different roles in environmental law enforcement depending upon the city or state/province within which they work. In a federal system of governance, for example, such as in the USA, Canada and Australia, there will be great variation in environmental enforcement authorities, ranging from police operating at the local municipal level (such as the Toronto Police Service) through to participation in international organisations (such as Interpol or Europol) (Tomkins 2005; White 2007).

Specific kinds of crime may involve different agencies, including civilian and police, and the transborder nature of much environmental crime – across state or provincial boundaries as well as international boundaries – means that often a local environmental law enforcement agency will necessarily have to work collaboratively with other local agencies, and with national agencies that, in turn, will have relationships with regional partner organisations (such as Interpol). As illustrated in Table 1.1, there are many diverse agencies engaged in some form of environmental law enforcement. Some of these are engaged in both regulation and enforcement, and individual agencies may be charged with either or both. Agencies dealing with environmental matters work in and across different jurisdictions and deal with a myriad of issues.

Table 1.1 Agencies at different tiers dealing with environmental issues: Australia

Examples of agencies	Examples at the operational level
Local	• Urban and metropolitan councils • Regional or rural (shires)
State	• Environmental protection agencies • Local government association • State police services
National	• Australian Fisheries Management Authority • Australian Federal Police • Australian Customs Service • Office of Consumer Affairs • Environment Australia
National/state bodies	• Australian Crime Commission • National Pollution Inventory • The Australian Environmental Law Enforcement and Regulators Network
International	• Interpol • International Network of Environmental Enforcement and Compliance

The plethora of players and laws demands an approach to environmental law enforcement and compliance that necessarily must be collaborative in nature. Dealing with global environmental harm will demand extraordinary efforts to relate to each other across distance, language and cultural borders; to understand specific issues; to coordinate actions; to enforce international laws and conventions; and to gather and share information and intelligence.

Among the many issues pertaining to the proliferation of agencies dealing with environmental crime and environmental harm is that each may be driven by different aims and objectives, different methods of intervention, with different powers, and exhibiting different levels of expertise and collaboration with others. Another issue relates to the need to distinguish between organisational affiliation (which may be formal and policy oriented) and interagency collaboration (which refers to actual operational practices and linkages). In some cases, there is a clear need for capacity building in order for collaboration and, especially, for rapid response, to be successfully institutionalised as part of agency normal practice. There can also be agency differences in defining and interpreting just what the crime is and how it should be responded to – as in the case of breaches versus crime, customs offences versus fisheries offences, and so on. Powers of investigation, particularly in relation to the gathering of suitable evidence for the specific environmental crime, will inevitably be shaped by state, federal and international conventions and protocols, as well as by the availability of local expertise, staff and resources.

Conclusion

The aim of this chapter has been to chart a broad canvas upon which issues pertaining to global environmental harm can be scrutinised and analysed. Fundamentally, environmental harm is about ecological damage, a process that frequently affects humans, specific biospheres and non-human animals in very negative ways. Analysis of environmental harm from a criminological perspective, therefore, must incorporate elements of an ecological consciousness – a sensitivity to how human action places stress on environments large and small. One mechanism by which to do this is adoption of an ecoglobal criminological approach to the study of environmental harm.

A key message of the chapter is that scale matters. That is, it is important to have a sense of the 'where' of environmental harm, as well as the 'how', 'why' and 'who'. Analysis of environmental harm ought to involve both spatial and temporal considerations, since place and time are integral to tracing the contours of environmental degradation and destruction in its many different forms and guises.

Dealing with environmental harm will necessarily also imply engagement of researchers, scholars, enforcers, advocates and regulators at many different levels of governance, again extending from the local through to the global. With climate change posing the central threat to humanity (and to specific environments and many other creatures inhabiting the earth), criminologists, too, are increasingly choosing to engage in cross-disciplinary, cross-cultural and global conversations that deal with this most important of survival issues. The challenges are clear; environmental issues are diverse and the time for action is now.

References

Aas, K. (2007) *Globalization and Crime*. Los Angeles: Sage.

Akella, A. and Cannon, J. (2004) *Strengthening the Weakest Links: Strategies for Improving the Enforcement of Environmental Laws Globally*. Washington, DC: Center for Conservation and Government.

Beirne, P. and South, N. (eds) (2007) *Issues in Green Criminology: Confronting Harms Against Environments, Humanity and Other Animals*. Cullompton: Willan Publishing.

Connell, R. (2007) *Southern Theory: The Global Dynamics of Knowledge in Social Science*. Sydney: Allen & Unwin.

DeSombre, E. (2006) *Global Environmental Institutions*. London: Routledge.

Fyfe, N. and Reeves, A. (2009) 'The Thin Green Line? Police Perceptions of the Challenges of Policing Wildlife Crime in Scotland', in R. Mawby and R. Yarwood (eds), *Policing, Rurality and Governance*. Aldershot: Ashgate.

Gibbs, C., Gore, M., McGarrell, E. and Rivers, L., III (2009) 'Introducing Conservation Criminology: Towards Interdisciplinary Scholarship on Environmental Crimes and Risks', *British Journal of Criminology*, 49: (advanced access 16 July).

Interpol (2009) *Environmental Crime Programme Newsletter*, No. 1, July.

Larsen, N. and Smandych, R. (eds) (2007) *Global Criminology and Criminal Justice: Current Issues and Perspectives*. Peterborough, Ontario: Broadview Press.

Lemieux, A. and Clarke, R. (2009) 'The International Ban on Ivory Sales and Its Effects on Elephant Poaching in Africa', *British Journal of Criminology*, 49(4): 451–71.

Pellow, D. (2007) *Resisting Global Toxics: Transnational Movements for Environmental Justice*. Cambridge, MA: Massachusetts Institute of Technology.

Petrisor, I. and Westerfield, W., III (2008) 'Hot Environmental and Legal Topics: Greenhouse Gas Regulation and Global Warming', *Environmental Forensics*, 9: 1–5.

Tomkins, K. (2005) 'Police, Law Enforcement and the Environment', *Current Issues in Criminal Justice*, 16(3): 294–306.

United Nations Environment Programme (UNEP) (2007) *Global Environment Outlook*. New York: UNEP.

United States Environmental Protection Agency (2009) Federal Register, Part III, Environmental Protection Agency, 40 CFR Chapter 1, Proposed Endangerment and Cause or Contribute Findings for Greenhouse Gases Under Section 202(a) of the Clean Air Act; Proposed Rule [online]. Available at: http://www.epa.gov/climatechange/endangerment/downloads/EPA-HQ-OAR-2009-0171-0001.pdf (accessed 28 November 2009).

Van Dijk, J. (2008) *The World of Crime: Breaking the Silence on Problems of Security, Justice, and Development Across the World*. Los Angeles: Sage.

White, R. (2007) 'Dealing with Environmental Harm: Green Criminology and Environmental Law Enforcement', Briefing Paper No. 5, November 2007. Tasmanian Institute of Law Enforcement Studies (TILES).

White, R. (2008a) 'The Criminalisation of Environmental Harm', *Criminal Justice Matters*, No. 74: 35–37. Magazine of the Centre for Crime and Justice Studies, King's College, London.

White, R. (2008b) *Crimes Against Nature: Environmental Criminology and Ecological Justice*. Cullompton: Willan Publishing.

White, R. (ed.) (2009a) *Environmental Crime: A Reader*. Cullompton: Willan Publishing.

White, R. (2009b) 'Toxic Cities: Globalising the Problem of Waste', *Social Justice*, 35(3): 107–119.

White, R. (2009c) 'Researching Transnational Environmental Harm: Toward an Eco-Global Criminology', *International Journal of Comparative and Applied Criminal Justice*, 33(2): 123–145.

White, R. (2009d) 'Climate Change and Social Conflict: Toward an Eco-Global Research Agenda', in K. Kangaspunta and I. Marshall (eds), *Eco-Crime and Justice*. Turin, Italy: UNICRC.

Chapter 2

Equatorial deforestation as a harmful practice and a criminological issue

Tim Boekhout van Solinge

An outbreak of violence in the Peruvian Amazon

In early June 2009, violent and deadly fights broke out between police and Amazon tribal groups on a jungle highway in northern Peru. It was the violent culmination of a 2-month-long campaign of peaceful rallies and blockades across Peru's Amazon region by indigenous groups. They protested against two decrees, passed in 2007 and 2008 as part of a free-trade agreement, that would allow exploitation of Peruvian rainforest, such as oil and gas concessions. As much of this area is on indigenous land, tribal groups argued the decrees would open up mineral and mining rights in a way that would threaten their ancestral lands and way of life.

On 5 June 2009, on a highway near the town of Bagua Grande, 1,000 km north of Lima, 2,500 Indians, many of them carrying spears and machetes, protested and blocked the road. Riots ensued when some 400 riot police tried to clear the roadblock, resulting in Peru's worst violence of the last decade. At least 31 people were killed, 22 tribesmen and nine policemen. Those nine were part of a group of 38 policemen who had been kidnapped, and nine of them were killed the next day when the army tried to free them. Twenty two escaped and seven were missing. The total number of casualties has remained unknown so far (late June 2009). Officials say at least 22 police and nine protestors died; protestors said 30 indigenous Indians were killed. According to some reports, the number of deaths is much higher, with a total of more than 100 indigenous protestors missing (BBC 2009).

Indigenous people said a demonstration escalated when police in helicopters opened fire on demonstrators. The authorities said the police were fired on first, and President Garcia accused the Indians of 'falling to a criminal level'. Indigenous leaders contradicted this version, and said they only carried traditional weapons. President Garcia, who had plans to open up communal jungle land for oil exploitation, logging, mining and large-scale farming, had declared earlier that 'all Peruvians should benefit from the country's natural resources, not just the people who happened to live in the areas concerned' (BBC 2009).

This conflict between indigenous people and the government, and, by extension, multinationals wishing to explore the natural resources of Peru's rainforest, attracted much international attention. Many (international) media reported widely about it (BBC 2009). In Peru itself, tribal groups had been protesting against a free-trade agreement with the USA since 2007, and the eruption of violence in 2009 made the government unpopular and divided the country over the issue. The government was blamed for its use of violence, and for not consulting native communities about a series of new laws which would affect them (BBC 2009). The approval rate of Peru's centre-right President Garcia consequently dropped to a low of 19 per cent, and some of Peru's neighbours also voiced criticism.

For the Peruvian government it meant bad public relations. Pictures, films, and eyewitness reports in the international media made this conflict in the Amazon rainforest an international affair. The criticism and negative publicity probably influenced the decision of the Congress of Peru, 2 weeks later (18 June 2009) to revoke the two controversial laws (BBC 2009). This decision was taken in the same period that the UN's Special Rapporteur for Indigenous People, James Anaya, visited Peru (17–19 June). Anaya said he had heard 'troubling allegations of abuse by security forces' and 'testimony of allegations of abuse that need to be taken seriously', and he asked for an investigation (BBC 2009).

Tropical deforestation and conflicts over land use

In many other rainforests around the globe, similar conflicts exist between forest inhabitants, in some cases indigenous people, and governments or multinationals wishing to explore rainforests. This exploration may take various forms: clearing forests for tropical hardwood, mining, or land conversion, transforming rainforest into agricultural land.

There appears to be a rise in the number of (violent) conflicts over land issues in many rainforests around the globe. What is rare, however, is that such a conflict in the middle of the Amazon should attract so much international attention. In this case, there happened to be photographs of the violent clashes, taken by eyewitnesses, two Belgians. Their eyewitness account and photographs was effectively made public by the UK-based non-governmental organisation (NGO) Survival International. Consequently, the Peruvian conflict quickly became visual news that went around the globe.

There are many other areas of rainforests, some of them very remote, such as, next to Peru, in the interior of the Brazilian Amazon, where images of conflicts between forest people and governments or commercial companies do not become global news. Most conflicts over land issues in rainforests hardly reach the international news media, or are never reported. Considering, however, the age of globalisation and the increasing accessibility of electronic equipment all around the globe (such as mobile phones that can film), it is becoming more likely that violent conflicts will be photographed or filmed and internationally transmitted by media.

Conflicts in rainforests over land use, like the recent one in Peru (so far to the advantage of the indigenous people), are an expression of the growing pressure on the tropical rainforests around the globe. Rainforests are cleared at the speed of several football fields a minute (such as in Brazil and Indonesia), for logging, mining or agricultural exploitation. Most tropical forests are inhabited by humans, who for their livelihood are at least partly dependent on them, and increased deforestation is leading to growing conflicts. As forest people and especially indigenous people are often found at the bottom in society, and considering the bad human rights records of some equatorial countries (or in the case of South America, a history of dictatorships and military rule that shaped violent and authoritarian societies), the rights of forest people are regularly abused. Representatives of law and order frequently commit crimes themselves, such as intimidation, abuse and extrajudicial killings.

Deforestation is obviously not only problematic to the people living in forests, but it also threatens animal and plant species. Tropical rainforests contain a very large number of animal and plant species and are the most biodiverse ecosystems (Wilson 2003). While representing no more than 6 per cent of the earth's surface (some sources say only 3 per cent), they house at least more than half, and maybe even two-thirds or more of all known species. As a result, rapid tropical deforestation poses a threat to the survival in the wild of many species.

Deforestation of tropical rainforests is often illegal (Boekhout van Solinge 2008a), and much of it could and should be considered criminal. Besides being often illegal, tropical deforestation is also harmful, considering its effects on humans, other living beings and ecosystems. The Amazon rainforest, for example, contains around 30 per cent of all known species. One hectare of Amazon rainforest has a larger variety of trees than is found in Europe. The Amazon contains approximately 20 per cent of the planet's river water, and some 5 per cent of the Amazon is flooded during part of the year, sometimes to several metres, creating a unique ecosystyem. The naturalist Alfred R. Wallace visited the Amazon prior to his later study, which resulted in his famous book, *The Malay Archipelago: The Land of the Orangutan and Bird of Paradise* (1869), dedicated to his friend and colleague Charles Darwin, who had published *The Origin of Species* (1859) 10 years earlier. After his visit to the Amazon, Wallace suggested that its diversity of animals and plants seemed to be determined by the many waterways, forming barriers that had, over long periods of evolution, led to a differentiation of species (Roosmalen 2008). Logically, therefore, deforesting an area almost automatically means that some species may be threatened.

As tropical deforestation is harmful to humans and non-humans, it is an area of research that fits well into the realm of green or environmental criminology. Although green or environmental criminology explicitly takes the harm principle as a starting point (Beirne and South 2007; Sollund 2008), this, of course, is not unique to this type of criminology. All criminology, and criminal law as well, looks at activities that are in one way or the other, at least by some people, considered harmful. Green or environmental criminology, however, such as in this chapter about tropical deforestation, explicitly addresses environmental or ecological harm, as well as the issue of ecological justice (White 2008): who has 'rights' to rich natural environments such as tropical rainforests?

The harm rapid tropical deforestation causes may be clear to many, but (illegal) tropical deforestation is a subject criminologists generally pay little attention to. Some research is being done, such as on illegal logging, but almost exclusively by NGOs. Some NGOs produce impressive studies on, for example, wildlife and the timber trade, based on difficult research, such as various studies by the

Environmental Investigation Agency (EIA) and Telapak (2004, 2005, 2006), but the attention from criminologists, so far, has been limited.

This chapter addresses tropical deforestation as a harmful and criminological issue. The main focus will be on the Amazon, the largest rainforest on the planet, found around the South American equator. Most deforestation in the Amazon is illegal and is harmful to its inhabitants, humans and non-humans, as well to the Amazon ecosystem. Moreover, conflicts over land use like the recent one in Peru regularly occur, including human rights abuses of forest inhabitants. In the much larger Brazilian Amazon, conflicts over land occur even more often, especially since more Brazilian than Peruvian rainforest has been cleared. The Brazilian deforestation case is different in the sense that logging and mining are no longer the main causes of deforestation. Land conversion, changing rainforest into agricultural land (in particular, cattle ranching), has been driving deforestation in the Brazilian Amazon for the last 15 years.

This research is an extension of earlier research and publications on tropical deforestation, such as the profitable international trade in 'conflict timber' (sold to fund conflicts) and illegal timber, and deforestation in west Africa and central Africa, as well as the South-East Asia islands of Sumatra, Borneo and New Guinea (Boekhout van Solinge 2008a–c). With the earlier case studies on the large equatorial rainforests of Africa (Congo basin) and Asia (Sumatra, Borneo and New Guinea), this study on the equatorial rainforest of the Amazon completes a series of publications addressing deforestation problems in the largest equatorial rainforests. In order of completeness, the final section of this chapter will address deforestation issues in equatorial Africa and Asia and make some comparisons with the Amazon, the main focus of this contribution.

The presented data of deforestation cases in the Amazon and on the island of Borneo are partly derived from (ethnographic) field visits and interviews. The Brazilian states Amazonas and Pará were visited in 2003 and 2009, and Indonesian Borneo (Kalimantan) in 2007. All other data are based on scientific literature, press articles and reports by NGOs.

Deforestation, conflict and crime in Amazonia

Over half of Peru is covered by rainforest. The Peruvian rainforest is the biggest stretch of the Amazon valley outside Brazil. The conflict in Peru between indigenous people and government forces was part of a longer-lasting process or rising conflicting interests over Peru's Amazonian rainforest.

In September 2006, indigenous communities of the Peruvian Amazon protested against oil companies. The Federation of Native Communities of the Corrientes river in the North of Peru (FECONACO) complained about pollution. FECONACO declared that for every barrel of oil there are nine barrels of contaminated water as a by-product – a total of more than a million barrels a day. The Achaur people, who have lived in the area for thousands of years, say the water contains high concentrations of hydrocarbons and heavy metals (lead, cadmium, mercury and arsenic) that is destroying the fragile ecosystem in which they live, killing the fish and wildlife and contaminating their water sources. A survey by Peru's Health Ministry that year indeed revealed that cadmium levels in the blood of more than 98 per cent of the Achuar exceeded safe levels. Robert Guimaraes, vice-president of another NGO, AIDESEP (Inter-Ethnic Association for the Development of the Peruvian Jungle), said that 'the oil companies, with the complicity of the state, are systematically violating our human rights' (BBC 2006). In October 2006, oil tappers in the Amazon were trapped as indigenous communities surrounded the three facilities to protest about the water pollution.

In 2007, this was followed by more protests, as the Peruvian government decided to auction off large swathes of the Amazon valley to oil and gas companies. This decision was denounced by environmental and human rights groups, who said the amount of Peruvian territory Amazon open to exploitation would increase from 13 per cent to 70 per cent. An area the size of California was already signed over for auction to oil companies. President Garcia said his policy was an investment shock in a country where more than half of the population live below the poverty line (BBC 2007). More protests followed in 2008, with indigenous protestors blocking roads and energy installations. Representatives of some 65 Amazon tribes said that when 70 per cent of the Peruvian Amazon is leased for oil and gas exploration, big energy companies could buy up the land, putting their lives and the biodiversity of the Amazon at risk (BBC 2008). A state of emergency was declared in 2008 after thousands of Amazonian tribespeople armed with spears and bows and arrows blocked roads and took over a hydroelectric dam and oil and gas installations in three provinces (Cusco, Loreto and Amazona). In Bagua province (where the later deadly violence occurred in 2009), 800 demonstrators clashed with police.

If we look at the recent history of conflict over rainforest land use in northern Peru, it becomes clear that the outbreak of violence in 2009 had a history of several years of growing tensions. Indigenous tribes have protested over current pollution and further rainforest exploitation, fearing this would mean a threat to their survival. After the declaration of a state of emergency in 2008, indigenous protests grew in size and intensity. In 2009, massive rallies involved some 30,000 people, with Indians blocking roads and bridges and occupying installations vital to the country's economy. By mid-May 2009, the Peruvian army was called in, resulting 2 weeks later in the violent escalation.

The conflict over Amazon rainforest in Peru is not unique. In different countries of the Amazon rainforest, similar conflicts are happening. In neighbouring Brazil, these types of conflicts also occur, seemingly on a larger scale, because of its much larger share of the Amazon. Sixty-seven per cent of the Amazon rainforest is found within Brazil's borders. The Peruvian share of the Amazon is much smaller – 10 per cent of the total Amazon basin (Goulding *et al.* 2003: 16). Brazil is the fifth largest country of the world, smaller than the USA and larger than Australia. In population terms, approaching 200 million inhabitants, it is also among the most populous countries. Brazil has many natural resources, which are exploited for its large internal market as well as export markets. Brazil is, for example, the largest iron producer of the world. Many of its natural resources are found and are being exploited in the Amazon basin. As part of the policy of economic growth, Brazil, just like Peru, intends to exploit many more of its natural resources.

Because 40 per cent of the Brazilian territory is formed by the Amazonian ecosystem, it is also a country with many forest inhabitants. Some 20 million people live in the Brazilian Amazon. In the last census (2005), 519,000 Brazilians classified themselves as indigenous. Other estimates put the number of indigenous peoples (of some 200 different tribes), depending on the definition, at 200,000 –700,000 – of a population that once counted several millions before Europeans arrived. Some 50 groups in the Amazon still do not have regular contact with the outside and keep away from it.

Since the 1970s, parts of the Brazilian Amazon have been opened up for further economic exploitation, such as by the construction of highways and dams. Logging for tropical timber is the best-known type of tropical deforestation. In the 1980s, (illegal) logging in the Brazilian rainforest led to international concern and criticism. The emphasis that is sometimes put on (illegal) logging as a cause of deforestation may distract attention from other, more important causes of deforestation. Mining, for example, is another important cause of deforestation of the Brazilian Amazon, and often has more devastating effects on the Amazonian ecosystem than logging.

By 2001, about 837,000 km^2 of Amazon rainforest had been cleared, with a 1990s gross rate of approximately 25,000 km^2 per year; 80 per cent of deforestation has been in Brazil. In 1988–2006, the deforestation in Brazilian Amazonia averaged 18,100 km^2 per year. It peaked in 2004 with 27,400 km^2, before gradually drecreasing to some 11,000 km^2 in 2007 (Malhi 2008: 169).

The process of clearing forests and converting them into mining projects and, increasingly, agricultural land, has led to an increase in conflict between forest inhabitants and those wishing to exploit and 'develop' the area. A very recent and still continuing conflict over a new mine project is taking place near the town of Juruti, in the middle of the Amazon, where Alcoa, the world's largest aluminium company, is digging a new, large bauxite mine. Communities living in forests that are planned to be deforested (in total some 9,000 people), protested at the Alcoa plant in Juruti in January 2009. Hundreds of protestors arrived by boats at the plant, which was protected by heavily armed police, who used teargas to drive away the protestors. So far, the protests of the forest communities near Juruti, who see their forests with important food and medicinal trees being destroyed, have not been successful. In the international press, reports about the new Alcoa plant in Brazil seem rather positive, and the protests did not get any international media attention at all. The protest leader from the forest communities who was met and interviewed (in Santarem, Pará, February 2009) had come to the city to get more attention for their case and managed to get an interview in a small local paper.

Pirate cows and soybean on former rainforest

Today, clearing forests for timber and mining is no longer the main cause of deforestation in the Amazon. Land conversion, transforming tropical rainforest into agricultural land, has become the main cause of deforestation since the 1990s. While the deforestation rate in the Brazilian Amazon had slowed down by the late 1980s (to an annual 10,000 km^2), it increased again until 1995 (27,000 km^2), mainly as a result of establishing cattle ranches on former rainforest soils. Cattle ranching has led to some 70 per cent of deforestation of the Brazilian Amazon (Malhi 2008: 169). With a growing cattle herd that today is over 200 million (more than the people), Brazil has become, since 2003, the world's largest beef exporter. The cattle numbers have grown especially in the state Mato Grosso (in the southern Amazon) and to a lesser extent in the state Pará (in the north-eastern Amazon). The expansion of cattle ranching in the Brazilian Amazon has even led to a new term, 'cattelization'.

The cattle ranches are often owned by big landowners, sometimes from the south of Brazil, who manage to get permits to clear an area, legally or illegally. It furthermore regularly occurs that more than the allowed 20 per cent of the area is being cleared, which means that the cows are there illegally. In Brazil, these illegally grazing cows are called 'pirate cows'. Illegal clearing, however, in general is not much enforced, although some improvements have been made.

Some of the big cattle ranches, especially in remote areas in the Amazon, are associated with forms of slave labour (officially described as working conditions akin to slavery). Some cattle ranches, and increasingly sugar-cane plantations (for ethanol production), keep workers in debt bondage and have armed guards to prevent them from leaving. The government fights this slave labour with a special task force, established in 1995, that raids large farms and businesses. Every year, several thousands are freed from slavery. Since 1995, 33,000 people have been thus freed. 2007 was a record year with almost 6,000 people being freed. In 2008, their number was 3,000. It is estimated that at least 25,000 Brazilians continue to toil in debt slavery conditions.

Over the last 10 years, another, relatively new and rapidly growing cause of deforestation (although much less important than cattle) has been the cultivation of soybeans. Since the late 1990s, soybean cultivation has grown rapidly, especially in the states of Mato Grosso and Pará, both in the Amazon region. Brazil now has become the largest soybean exporter of the world. Most of the crop is used as cattle food, with the USA, the Netherlands and China as the main destinations. Part of the soybeans imported into The Netherlands is exported further into Europe, but The Netherlands, with its intensive agriculture (cows, pigs, poultry) imports a quantity of soybeans that is grown on an area the size of half The Netherlands (Verweij *et al.* 2009).

In the Brazilian Amazon, deforestations for cattle and soybeans go hand-in-hand, for which reason some authors speak of the beef–soybean complex (Verweij *et al.* 2009). Deforestation for cattle and soybeans has only increased the already existing conflicts between forest exploiters and forest inhabitants. Cattle and soybeans have only added new reasons for deforestation and potential conflict, next to the longer existing causes of deforestation such as mining, logging, and the cultivation of sugar cane.

Conflicts and human rights violations against forest inhabitants are common, and various organisations have been set up to support them and publish reports about crimes. Greenpeace (2003), for example, published a well-documented report: *State of Conflict. An Investigation into the Landgrabbers, Loggers and Lawless Frontiers in Pará State, Amazon*. It describes in detail how, in the state of Pará, human rights are violated on a regular basis when areas are being deforested. It is not uncommon for locals to be driven away from forest communities by gunmen.

CIMI, the Indigenous Missionary Council, has addressed violence against indigenous peoples in Brazil for more than 20 years. It publishes annual reports with detailed reports of violence against indigenous property, territorial conflicts, environmental damage of indigenous areas, and violence against indigenous individuals, such as murders, murder threats and acts of racism (CIMI 2009). Every year, CIMI reports numerous cases, including the murders of several dozens of indigenous people, including minors, by loggers, miners or other land grabbers. CIMI also reports about the high suicide rate among Brazilians Indians of several tribes. This occurs especially in the state Mato Grosso do Sul, known for its deforestation for soybean and sugar-cane plantations, such as among the Guarani-Kaoiwá people. On 19 April 2009, the Day of the Indian, 500 indigenous leaders from all over Brazil met in the state Mato Grosso do Sul. They interpreted the day as 'a day of struggle', and declared: 'Our spirit of struggle and resistance is the only way to face the ranchers, gunmen and police, because the State does not protect the people' (www.cimi.org.br).

The Pastoral Land Commission (CPT) (Comissão Pastoral da Terra) is a Catholic Church organisation that deals with agrarian land reform and also reports on violence over land issues. It has many local branches and in the city of Santarém, in the state of Pará, also home of a large soybean export harbour (800 km from the Atlantic), CPT today has a special group that studies the soybean cultivation in the area. As international soybean prices were high the first years of this century, soybean cultivation grew rapidly around Santarém. In an interview (February 2009, Santarém), a CPT representative explained that conflicts have regularly occurred between forest inhabitants and soybean farmers who wish to clear the area. These 'new landowners' or 'land grabbers' are often accompanied by armed personnel or armed officials and sometimes show some kind of documents to the mostly illiterate inhabitants of forest communities.

Most of the deforestation in Brazil is illegal, as several studies show. Greenpeace Brazil (especially in Manaus, capital of state of Amazonas) has monitored it for years, using all available data and its own technical equipment, and has built up professional knowledge (as appeared from various interviews, April and May 2009). Greenpeace Brazil estimates that 60–80 per cent of the total deforestation in the Brazilian Amazon is illegal. Studies by Greenpeace, CIMI and CPT show that human rights are commonly violated in the process of deforestation in the Brazilian Amazon. The many case studies that are known over land use in the Amazon suggest that in conflicts over land use, forest inhabitants such as indigenous people are those who generally lose out and see their human rights abused. The case described at the beginning of this chapter, of protesting Amazonian tribes in Peru who successfully managed to get 'deforestation laws' be revoked by Congress, is therefore atypical.

Deforestation in equatorial Africa and Asia

The second and third largest rainforests of the planet, after the Amazon, are found further along the equator, in respectively central Africa, the Congo basin, and on the large tropical islands of Asia: Sumatra, Borneo and New Guinea. All these equatorial rainforests also suffer from large-scale deforestation.

What distinguishes these rainforests from the Amazon is that they grow on much more fertile soils and support much larger mammals. The Amazon basin, considering its extremely poor soils, does not seem capable of supporting large leaf-eaters (the only exception being the tapir), as the poor soils oblige plants to biochemically protect their leaves, necessary to catch energy in the form of sun (Roosmalen 2008: 136). For example, the Amazon 'only' has small monkeys of no more than 13 kg, whereas Africa and Asia have great apes, the animals genetically closest to humans, some with a (much) larger body weight than humans. All of the great apes are today threatened by deforestation and poaching. The orangutan in Borneo, and even more so in Sumatra, is seriously threatened, and the same is true for all great apes in Africa, not only the chimpanzee but particularly the gorilla (especially the eastern gorilla, with some 700 left) and the bonobo (maybe down to fewer than 5,000) in central Africa.

Equatorial Africa has known many armed conflicts, killing millions of people. In Rwanda, a large genocide took place in 1994, in which 800,000, mostly Tutsis, were killed. West of Rwanda, in the Democratic Republic of Congo (D.R. Congo), a conflict ended, or was reduced, in 2003. In Africa, it was referred to as the 'African World War', as nine African countries were involved in the war, in which some four million people died, the largest human loss since World War II.

The wars are obviously harmful to many people, but also to animals and the ecosystem. The abundant presence of natural resources in the Congo basin was the main reason for various countries to be involved in the Congo conflict. Control of natural resources was the key to income, and exploitation of the natural resources by government and rebel troops, kept the conflict alive. The African continent in general is rich in natural resources such as oil, gold, diamonds, and many other precious stones and minerals.

Less known than the diamond and gold mines are the tin, cobalt and coltan mines, which are especially found in D.R. Congo. Cobalt and coltan have been much in international demand over the last years for their use in electronic equipment such as mobile phones and laptops. D.R. Congo is the world's top producer of cobalt with 40 per cent of world production and one-third of world reserves. Of coltan, D.R. Congo has 60–80 per cent of the world's reserves. During the Congo war the coltan mines in the east of the D.R. Congo helped fund the conflict, and much of the coltan was smuggled out of the country to meet international demand. Increased coltan mining has destroyed the habitat of the mountain gorilla. As some gorillas live on 'coltan land', increasing use of mobile phones therefore is destructive to gorilla habitats. It has been suggested that avoiding multiple purchases of mobile phones may help to limit the destruction of forests via the opening of the new coltan mines in areas inhabited by gorillas in the DR Congo (Krief 2006).

Another important cause of deforestation in central Africa is logging. A problem particularly related to logging in Africa is that it further stimulates poaching and the trade in 'bushmeat'. A logging road means a major incursion into a forest, which is usually difficult to access. Logging roads enable hunters to go further into the forest, and make it easier to reach distant markets as well (Boekhout van Solinge 2008b).

Hunting wild animals is a common practice in many parts of Africa, the world's economically poorest continent. In Africa, logging leads to increased hunting and trade in so-called bushmeat. In cases of war, the practice of eating bushmeat increases due to less stable food markets and armed men roaming the country.

The illegal commercial hunting of African wildlife for sale as bushmeat has reached alarming levels, and immediate action is needed before it is too late (Bowen-Jones 2005: 133). The bushmeat varies from deer, gorillas and chimpanzees to crocodiles and elephants (Frank 2001). The bushmeat trade only further increases the endangerment of African wild animals such as great apes.

Not only in Africa, but also in Asia great apes are threatened with extinction. Asia's only great ape, the orangutan, lives on the islands of Sumatra and Borneo. When Alfred R. Wallace visited the islands in the mid-nineteenth century (as reported in *The Malay Archipelago: The Land of the Orangutan and Bird of Paradise*), these islands were still covered with rainforest. Many wild animals such as tigers, orangutans and birds of paradise lived in the forests. In the twentieth century, however, the Javanese and Balinese tiger became extinct and the number of orangutans declined by 90 per cent. The Sumatran tiger is today threatened by logging and poaching, just like the orangutans on Sumatra and Borneo, whose number are literally plummeting. If current trends continue, wild orangutan populations might be extinct in 20 years.

The deforestation rate in Indonesia, such as on Sumatra and Indonesian Borneo (Kalimantan), may even be higher than in the Amazon. Logging for timber, mostly illegal, and land conversion (especially for palm oil plantations) and, to some extent, paper (the world's two largest paper mills are found in Sumatra) are important causes of deforestation (Boekhout van Solinge 2008c). All national parks and protected forests in Indonesia suffer from illegal logging practices. Just as in the Amazon, conflicts over land use occur, as logging and mining often pollute (drinking and bathing) water and limit food sources.

Some of the illegal timber (e.g. logged in national parks) is being smuggled to neighbouring Malaysia, which exports surprisingly large quantities of tropical hardwood. Considering the timber-smuggling operations from Sumatra to peninsular Malaysia and from Indonesian Borneo (Kalimantan) to Malaysian Borneo (Sarawak and Saba), the Malaysian timber exports logically include illegal timber from Indonesia. In the Indonesian peninsula, deforestation has been moving from west to east. In the west, large parts of Indonesian Sumatra have already been logged. In Indonesian Borneo, much lowland has been logged and more is being logged. In recent years, the large eastern Indonesian province of Papua on the island of New Guinea has become the focus of large illegal logging operations, involving the Indonesian army and Malaysian timber traders (EIA and Telapak 2005). Their main target is the valuable merbau timber, which has flooded, sometimes via China, the Western timber and flooring markets.

The bird of paradise, almost exclusively found on the island of New Guinea, the world's largest tropical island and one of its most pristine natural places, was almost extinct a century ago. What threatened the bird of paradise was the women's fashion, especially in Europe, to use its feathers and sometimes complete birds as an ornament or jewellery of nature, to be worn as a hat or dress (Boekhout van Solinge 2008c). The famous and mythical bird of paradise did, however, not become extinct as a result of the growing consciousness that it could become extinct, leading to conservation measures, a ban trading it internationally, and collaboration between scientists and conservation movements.

Scientific arguments to preserve the bird of paradise for future generations eventually won over the commercial ones, although sentiment played a part as well. 'This combination of science and sentiment, as in contemporary environmental campaigns, put the economic arguments in favour of bird-of-paradise hunting at a great disadvantage' (Cribb 1997: 404). The analysis of the conservation history of the bird of paradise, saved almost a century ago, can serve as an example of how to conserve other species as well: 'The arguments for environmental protection have arisen primarily out of a modern, scientific understanding on the world. Thus the argument for conservation rests on an understanding that the extinction of a species is possible and that this can happen both by direct extermination and by destruction of its habitat' (Cribb 1997: 380–381).

Addressing and tackling tropical deforestation

This chapter discussed in a 'world tour' around the equator different problematic (harmful) aspects of tropical deforestation. Three types of, often illegal, activities characterise the deforestation of tropical rainforests today: logging, mining and land conversion for agriculture. Generally, more than half and sometimes most of the logging practices in tropical countries are illegal. Mining projects are another important cause of tropical deforestation. Land conversion, however, changing rainforest into agricultural land, is currently the main cause of tropical deforestation, especially in the Amazon.

The effects of deforesting the world's tropical rainforests are enormous. One can easily speak of an ecological disaster, something that could be labelled as ecologically harmful and an ecological crime. Forests disappear at such great speed that habitats for many forest inhabitants and wild animals as well are rapidly shrinking. Considering the rate of tropical deforestation, it is no surprise that forest inhabitants increasingly protest against the destruction and pollution of their environment, sometimes leading to violent conflicts.

Besides being problematic for those immediately affected by it, such as humans and animals living in and off those forests, tropical deforestation is now becoming an international political issue because it is responsible for 20 per cent of global greenhouse emissions. Indonesia and Brazil have now become respectively the third and fourth CO_2-emitting countries of the world, mainly as a result of clearing rainforest. Because of its influence on greenhouse emissions and climate change (see, for example, the Assessments Reports by the Intergovernmental Panel on Climate Change (IPCC)), tropical deforestation has truly become a global issue.

At the UN level, policies are being developed to reduce emissions by decreasing deforestation (REDD). Billions of dollars are available, but the big question is, who exactly is to pay for the preservation of rainforests? How can this money be spent in order to have the largest guarantee that the rainforests will indeed, in the general interest, be preserved? A question for the (near) future will be: how can the forest preservation be enforced and how can forest crime be prevented?

One way, today and in the future, that may help to preserve rainforests, limit forest crime and increase ecological justice is by pointing at the harm that is currently done to rainforests and their inhabitants, human and nonhuman. Growing awareness of the harm that is being done may stimulate citizens and governments to change their behaviour. For example, not many people are yet aware of the fact that the meat industry has been the driver of deforestation in the Amazon over the last 15 years. Addressing this deforestation problem therefore should include challenging high meat consumptions, the growing use of soybeans as cattle food, and the influence of the food industry (Pollan 2008).

Criminologists, lawyers, law enforcers and policymakers can also address tropical deforestation, an area of many criminal and otherwise harmful activities, while law enforcement is mostly absent. It can be argued that preservation of tropical rainforests is in the human interest (as a source of water, carbon, botanical knowledge and medicine, pleasure, etc.). If the latter argument is followed, we could argue that the (illegal) deforestation of tropical rainforests is harmful and thus deserves more attention from criminologists and other professionals. Maybe social scientists have a special role to play here. When we teach university students that hunter and gatherer societies are the oldest form of human society, we should maybe add in our lectures that these old societies still exist, but they are seriously threatened by tropical deforestation.

References

BBC (2006) 'Amazonian Tribe Protests at Oil Pollution', *BBC News*, Lima, Peru, 13 September 2006, by reporter Dan Collyns [online]. Available at: http://news.bbc.co.uk/2/hi/americas/5337802.stm (accessed July 2009).

BBC (2007) 'Peru's Amazon Oil Deals Denounced, *BBC News*, 3 February 2007, Lima, Peru, by reporter Dan Collyns [online]. Available at: http://news.bbc.co.uk/2/hi/americas/6326741.stm (accessed July 2009).

BBC (2008) 'Peruvian Tribes End Land Protests, *BBC News*, 21 August 2008 [online]. Available at: http://news.bbc.co.uk/2/hi/americas/7573887.stm (accessed July 2009).

BBC (2009) *BBC News* reports (17 May 2009 – 20 June 2009) on the conflicts in the Peruvian Amazon (nine articles), *BBC News* [online]. Available at: http://news.bbc.co.uk (accessed July 2009).

Beirne, P. and South, N. (eds) (2007) *Issues in Green Criminology. Confronting Harms Against Environments, Humanity and Other Animals*. Cullompton: Willan Publishing.

Boekhout van Solinge, T. (2008a) 'Eco-Crime: The Tropical Timber Trade', in D. Siegel and H. Nelen (eds), (2008) *Organized Crime. Culture, Markets and Policies*. New York: Springer, 97–111.

Boekhout van Solinge, T. (2008b) 'Crime, Conflicts and Ecology in Africa', in R. Sollund (ed.), *Global Harms. Ecological Crime and Speciesism*. New York: Nova Science 13–34.

Boekhout van Solinge, T. (2008c) 'The Land of the Orangutan and Bird of Paradise Under Threat', in R. Sollund (ed.), *Global Harms. Ecological Crime and Speciesism*. New York: Nova Science, 51–70.

Bowen-Jones, E. (2005) 'Bushmeat: Traditional Regulation or Adaptation to Market Forces', in S. Oldfield (ed.), *The Trade in Wildlife. Regulation for Conservation*. London: Earthscan, 132–145.

CIMI – Conselho Indigenista Missionário (2009) *Violência Contra os Povos Indígenas no Brasil*. Brasilia: CIMI.

Cribb, R. (1997) 'Birds of Paradise and Environmental Politics in Colonial Indonesia, 1890–1931', in P. Boomgaard, F. Colombijn and D. Henley (eds.), *Paper Landscapes. Explorations in the Environmental History of Indonesia*. Leiden: KITLV Press.

EIA (Environmental Investigation Agency) and Telapak (2004) *Profiting from Plunder: How Malaysia Smuggles Endangered Wood*. London: EIA.

EIA and Telapak (2005) *The Last Frontier. Illegal Logging in Papua and China's Massive Timber Theft*. London: EIA.

EIA and Telapak (2006) *Behind the Veneer: How Indonesia's Last Rainforests Are Being Felled for Flooring*. London: EIA.

Frank, A. (2001) ' "Bush Meat" Crisis Needs Urgent Action, Group Warns', *National Geographic News*, 22 May 2001.

Goulding, M., Barthem, R. and Ferreira, E. (2003) *The Smithsonian Atlas of the Amazon*. Washington, DC: Smithsonian, Institute.

Greenpeace International (2003) *State of Conflict. An Investigation into the Landgrabbers, Loggers and Lawless Frontiers in Pará State, Amazon*. Amsterdam: Greenpeace International.

Greenpeace Brazil (2008) *Desmatamento na Amazônia: O leão acordou. Uma análise do Plano de Ação para a Prevenção e Controle do Desmatamento na Amazônia Legal*. Manaus/São Paulo: Greenpeace Brazil.

Greenpeace Brazil (2009) *Amazon Cattle Footprint. Mato Grosso: State of Destruction*. Manaus/São Paulo: Greenpeace Brazil.

ISA — Instituto Socioambiental (2007) *Almanaque Brasil Socioambiental 2008*. São Paulo: ISA.

Krief, S. (2006) 'Are Humans Just Another Great Ape?' Interview by Mambaele Mankoto. *A World of Science*, 4: 13–15.

Malhi, Y., Roberts, J.T., Betts, R.A., (2008) 'Climate Change, Deforestation, and the Fate of the Amazon'. *Science*, 319 (5860): 169–192.

Pollan, M. (2008) *In Defence of Food. The Myth of Nutrition and the Pleasure of Eating*. London/New York: Penguin.

Roosmalen, M.G.M. van (2008) *Blootsvoets door de Amazone. De evolutie op het spoor*. Amsterdam: Bert Bakker.

Sollund, R. (ed.) (2008) *Global Harms. Ecological Crime and Speciesism*. New York: Nova Science.

Verweij, P., Schouten, M., van Beukering, P., *et al.* (2009) *Keeping the Amazon Forests Standing: A Matter of Values*. Zeist, The Netherlands: WWF Netherlands.

White, R. (2008) *Crimes Against Nature. Environmental Criminology and Ecological Justice*. Cullompton: Willan Publishing.

Wilson, E.O. (2003) *The Future of Life*. New York: Vintage Books.

Chapter 3

The global transference of toxic harms

Diane Heckenberg

Introduction

The advent of global warming and climate change has heightened awareness that our world is simultaneously borderless yet interconnected. Harm in one region of the world transfers to communities in other parts of the world, often taking on distinct forms in different locations (e.g. rising water in the deltas of Bangladesh, sinking atolls of the Pacific), but ultimately the repercussions are negative for human, non-human and environmental health. Similarly, the globalisation of trade has reshaped the world, by removing barriers and opening up borders to facilitate the global transference of goods, services and technologies. In some instances this involves the transference of harm from the environment in which we live to the environment of 'the body' (increased incidence of environmental toxins in breast milk; uptake of environmental toxins by animals), or from industrial activities to the environment of nature (CO_2 emissions, heavy metal pollution of water and soil), or it involves the transformation of something from one form to another (e.g. the recovery of lead from electronic waste to reprocess into jewellery). This chapter examines the movement of toxic harms across increasingly porous borders.

Environmental harm and the transference of harm

The way in which the environment is conceptualised determines the credence we give to certain environmental harms and crimes over others (White 2009). Environment here refers to the internal environment of 'the body', the external environment of the 'place' in which we live and move and have our being, and the environment of 'nature' or the natural world. No less important are the broader economic, social, political and cultural environments that shape identity and a sense of place in the world.

Harm refers to those acts or omissions that negatively impact people, animals, and nature. Perceptions of what constitutes harm, degrees of harm the severity of harm and the impact of harm are likely to differ among stakeholders and across geographic and 'cultural' (ethnic and commercial) domains. Shared understandings of harm may be filtered by power relationships, which in turn determine leverage for blame shifting and the capacity to 'spin' a particular message in the public domain.

Harm typically manifests itself as physical, economic or psychological (or emotional) or a combination of these and, according to Collins (1989), receives condemnation from the justice system in this order. Thus, 'harmful transactions that are intentional, visible, severe, repetitive, permanent and verifiable receive greater condemnation than those that are not (eg harms to humans vs harms to the ozone layer)' (Collins 1989: 5). For example,

> When the Hooker Electrochemical Company dumped chemical wastes in a landfill during the 1940s and early 1950s, the company was not condemned for its actions. However, thirty years later after homes had been built near the landfill and people were harmed by the chemicals, the company was highly condemned. (Collins 1989: 5)

Advancing technology, the dissolving of trade barriers, and the exponential increase in the international flow of goods, services and information mean that the potential for harm is increasingly global. At the same time, the production of goods is bordered by regional 'othering' that locates the production and delivery of specific goods, services and technologies in particular countries. In a world that promotes economic development as a panacea for poverty, tensions arise between the competing principles of development, subsistence, and the environment. At a macrolevel, corporations weigh production costs and demands for cheaper products against environment harms. Increasingly, the environment is losing out, and one of the solutions has been to transfer labour costs and environmental harms to off-shore 'supply chain cities' (Navarro 2007) where, at the microlevel, the priority to feed oneself and one's family understandably takes precedence over personal health and ecological well-being. Within these macro and micro environments, economic inequalities (e.g. unequal profit sharing) and social disparities (rich versus poor) create an uneven playing field, potentially conducive to opportunistic harms and crimes, particularly in political and commercial domains less open to regulatory and public scrutiny.

A theoretical approach that recognises this tension between ecology, the global, crime and justice is 'eco-global criminology' (White 2009). As the name suggests, ecoglobal criminology draws the links between ecology, justice, the 'global' and crime. It provides a theoretical and analytical tool for interrogating the legal/illegal divide, and the crime/harm and risk/harm dichotomies. It extends the criminological gaze beyond those harms traditionally defined as 'crimes', to a range of harms which in lay terms would be labelled 'criminal' in nature and impact. Informed by ecological considerations (White 2009), the analytical focus is on global crimes and harms that impact a part of, or the entire biosphere – that is, all living things that inhabit the whole of planet Earth, including the surface, atmosphere, sea and subterranean spaces.

Transference refers to the movement of something from one place or person to another. It is both a concept (a way of perceiving something) and a phenomenon (a fact that can be observed). Principle 14 of the Rio Declaration (1992) – originally adopted to address the risk that heavy materials and chemicals pose for people and environments – is a good starting point for thinking about the concept of transference.

> States [countries] should effectively co-operate to discourage or prevent the *relocation and transfer* to other states of any activities and substances that cause severe environmental degradation or are found to be harmful to human health.

Transferences of harm occur in a number of different ways. Examples include the movement of substances from one location to another (e.g. medical waste, hazardous waste), the relocation of specific activities from one region to another (e.g. shipbreaking, recycling of e-waste), the flow of toxins along global supply chains (e.g. lead, melamine, diethylene glycol (DEG)), the forced migration of communities of people (e.g. people trafficking, environmental refugees), the transformation of something from one form to another (via mislabelling, relabelling, recovery and reprocessing), the illegal movement of animals (e.g. wildlife trafficking), and so on. Transference, then, involves transactions, transmissions and exchanges within and across local, national, regional, transnational and global boundaries. Table 3.1 illustrates different forms of harm and modes of transference.

Toxic exposure

The above transferences of harm are all toxic and/or ecotoxic in nature and impact. Toxicity here refers to the degree to which something is 'poisonous' to somebody or something. Metaphorically, toxicity can also be used to describe toxic effects on larger and more complex groups such as the family unit or society at large. The toxicity of a substance can be affected by the exposure pathway (absorption, ingestion, inhalation, injection), the duration of the exposure (brief or long-term), the number of exposures (single, multiple or continuous), the physical form of the toxin (solid, liquid, gas), the timing of the exposure (early childhood), and the body weight (e.g. adult/child), genetic makeup, and overall health of potential victims.

Combined and cumulative exposure to toxins adds a further dimension to the concept of transference and was a recurring concern in the literature explored for this chapter.

- Available data indicate that combined exposure to melamine and cyanuric acid may be more toxic than exposure to each compound individually (WHO 2009).
- Lead and cadmium exposure from polyvinyl chloride (PVC) toys is in addition to exposure from phthalate esters (plasticisers used to make PVC soft and pliable) (Kumar and Pastore 2006).
- Even when regulated, the risks from chemical exposure are estimated for one chemical at a time, while children are exposed to many toxicants in complex mixtures throughout development (Schettler *et al.* 2000: 7).
- Multiple chemical exposures often interact to magnify damaging effects or cause new types of harm.
- The effects of lead are cumulative and the only way to prevent harm is to prevent exposure (Weidenhamer 2007a).

Table 3.1 Modes of transference

Form	Example	Conduit	Transference	Harm
Plants, animals, microbes	Northern Pacific seastar (a kind of starfish)	Ships ballast water	Northern Pacific to southern Australia	Reached plague proportions, threatening native marine ecosystems, feeding on shellfish, including commercially valuable scallop, oyster and clam species
Waste	Electronic waste	Recycling industry	Developed countries to developing countries	Exposure of workers to toxins such as lead, mercury, arsenic, cadmium and selenium, causing serious health problems and pollution of air, water and soil
Toxin	Pollution of Arctic food chain	Anthropocentric activities contributing to global warming	Toxic pollutants travel north from Central America to Europe and Asia	Arctic food chains and the Inuit people being poisoned by toxins created in other regions of the world
Global warming	Climate change	Burning of coal, oil and other fossil fuels	Rising sea temperatures	Polar bears cut off from their hunting grounds as ice bridges melt
Disease	SARS	Animal to human, then via international	Beijing, China to the world	SARS (severe acute respiratory syndrome), caused by a virus not previously seen in humans

Continued overleaf

Form	Example	Conduit	Transference	Harm
		travel routes		originated in Beijing, China in November 2002 and by June 2003 had spread across 29 countries, resulting in approximately 8,450 cases and 810 deaths
Information technology	40,000,000 credit cards compromised	Global credit card database	CardSystems, Phoenix, Arzona, to credit-card holders throughout the world	Hackers access names, account numbers and verification codes necessary to commit fraud/identity theft
Toxin	Blood thinner, heparin	Counterfeit industry	China to Australia, Canada, Denmark, France, Germany, Italy, Japan, The Netherlands, New Zealand and the USA	Found in drug supplies in at least 10 countries. The contaminant – oversulfated chondroitin sulfate (OSC) – known to function as a cheap filler – was linked to at least 100 deaths
Standards	Subprime mortgage crisis	Diluted lending standards led to high-risk mortgage contracts with clients who had little or no collateral, resulting in high foreclosure rates	USA to the world	Triggered the subprime crisis contributing to the current global financial crisis and the problem of 'toxic debt'

Continued on next page

Form	Example	Conduit	Transference	Harm
Technologies	Genetically modified organisms (GMO)	Corporate agricultural businesses	Traditional pastures to GMO croplands	Reduction of biodiversity, disease, unwanted transference from genetically modified crops to native species, compromising biodiversity, and leading to the potential development of 'super weeds'

- Infants are exposed to phthalates from multiple sources including the umbilical cord, breast milk, and dust in the air and also from sucking PVC plastic toys (Immig 2007).
- Since real-world exposures are to multiple chemicals, current regulatory standards based on single chemical exposures are inherently incapable of providing adequate margins of safety (Schettler *et al.* 2000: 7).

Analysis of transference necessarily takes account of wider social harms such as the victimisation of particular groups, reduced quality of life for surviving victims, exposure of foreign workers, and degradation of local and global environments. Using China as an example, Hawthorne (2007: 164) highlights the victimisation of women in toy factories, where 80 per cent of the world's toys are made, mostly for foreign-owned brands.

> In addition to the use of toxic substances, toy factories employ mostly young women between the ages of eighteen and thirty who live and work with restricted rights under an apartheid-like pass system. A typical work week includes ninety or more hours, and workers rarely get breaks during their twelve or more hour shifts. Pregnancy and lactation do not excuse these workers from toxic conditions. Pregnant workers are often forced to resign rather than being afforded protection under law. Workers who generally handle toxic chemical glues, paints and solvents, do not know the type of chemicals they are working with, nor are they educated on the health hazards of exposure. Chinese factories violate the Regulations for Toxic Substances to keep their production cheap.

Navarro (2007) says China is rapidly becoming one of the most polluted countries in the world, it is home to 16 of 20 of the world's most polluted cities, and 70 per cent of its major rivers are severely polluted, 80 per cent of which fail to meet standards for fishing. In 2007, the Chinese government attributed the artificially low price of Chinese exports to industry's failure to pay for the costs of pollution.

> The products are shipped abroad but the pollution is left in China. Export prices don't reflect the true costs, which is one of the reasons for our unreasonable trade surplus. (senior official in the Chinese Ministry of Commerce, cited in Spencer 2007)

Toxic harms victimise different groups in different ways – e.g. girls (chemicals associated with early onset of puberty); boys (chemicals associated with reproductive disorders and low sperm counts); the unborn child (toxins crossing the placenta, transferred in breast milk); people in poverty working or living in proximity to e-dumps (body burden of heavy metals and other toxins); foreign factory workers (exposed to toxins in the production process); people with lowered immune systems because of ill-health or older age; and infants and children around the world exposed to chemicals, heavy metals and toxic harms in their food, bibs, teething rings and toys, in addition to the toxins in the place in which they live and move and have their being (especially for the first few years, while crawling about inside and outside spaces at ground level).

Toxic distribution networks

Toxins have been found in human tissue, animal tissue and breast milk and in a range of products including food, cosmetics, medicines, computers and toys. Recently, diethylene glycol (DEG) and melamine killed hundreds of children around the world and lead re-emerged as a threat in infant products and children's toys and jewellery. A spate of toy recalls over the last three years has exposed the vulnerability of the supply chain as a conduit for toxic harms. In a recent publication reflecting on the global financial crisis, and titled *Is Risk Management Broken?*, Ernst and Young (2009: 10) describe the complex nature of today's supply chains as 'increasingly global, with business participants from developed and developing countries frequently separated by language, culture, geography, different time zones, physical distance and disparate systems using a variety of processes'. This understanding of supply chain dynamics is corroborated by the experience of those on the ground in China.

> The convoluted supply chain is probably one of the most underestimated and unrecognized risks in China. You really have to have experienced people on the ground who know what they're doing and know the language.
>
> (General Manager, Control Risks, cited in Barboza 2007)

In the toy supply chain, for instance, transference of harm was facilitated by the practice of repeated outsourcing. Suppliers outsourced to vendors who in turn outsourced to vendors, subvendors and sub-subvendors, 'creating a supply chain that was hard to follow let alone inspect' (Barboza 2007), compromising quality and reducing transparency and accountability.

Diethylene glycol (DEG)

A colourless, syrupy liquid, practically odourless, with a sharply sweetish taste (SCCP 2008: 6–7), DEG can cause severe kidney damage when ingested (Pierce 1998: 129), and over the years has been used as a cheap substitute for its more expensive chemical cousin glycerine, a common ingredient in medicine, food and household products (Bogdanich 2007).

The earliest recorded deaths from DEG occurred in the USA in 1937 when 71 adults and 34 children died after taking elixir sulfanilamide, containing 72 per cent DEG. In November 2008, DEG-contaminated teething mixture killed 34 infants in Nigeria. DEG poisoning is life-threatening, and its history of harm stretches across decades and around the world, as seen in Table 3.2.

The following case examples trace the transference of DEG in different supply chains, over time.

Case example 1: Haiti – 1995–96

Between November 1995 and July 1996, 88 children between the ages of 1 month and 13 years died of acute renal failure, after taking a locally manufactured antifever syrup. The majority of the children (85 per cent) were aged under 5 years (CDC 1996), with a median age of 29 months (O'Brien *et al.* 1998). In addition to renal failure, many children suffered 'severe vomiting, hepatitis, pancreatitis, neurological problems including respiratory failure, facial paralysis, encephalopathy and even coma' (Junod 1996: 81).

When US Food and Drug Administration investigators traced the glycerol to its source (see Figure 3.1), they discovered it had been shipped from The Netherlands, but invoiced through a German company, who revealed that it originated in China (Pierce 1998). The glycerol was manufactured in a 'fine chemical plant rather than a pharmaceutical plant' (Junod 1996). Two brands of medication, one a syrup in 4- ounce bottles and the other oral drops for neonates in 2-ounce bottles, contained 12–17 per cent and 3–5 per cent DEG respectively (Pierce 1998).

Pharval, the manufacturer of the product in Haiti, failed to test the glycerine, relying instead on the integrity of what they believed to be the country of origin.

> We bought the material from Germany – we did not test it, because everyone knows that materials made in Germany have good quality.
>
> (Pharval Managing Director, Haiti, cited in Toumi 2007: 20)

Table 3.2 Chain of harm – diethylene glycol: 1937 to 2008

Year	Country	Product	Approximate number of deaths
1937	USA	Sulfanilamide elixir	105 people 34 children, 71 adults
1969	South Africa	Sedative elixir	7 children
1985	Spain	Topical cream	5 people
1986	India	Medicinal glycerol	14 people
1990	Nigeria	Paracetamol syrup	47 children
1990–92	Bangladesh	Paracetamol syrup	236 children
1992	Argentina	Propolis syrup	15 people
1995–96	Haiti	Cough syrup	88 children
1995	Bangladesh	Paracetamol	51 children
1998	India	Cough syrup	33 children
2006	Panama	Cough syrup	78 people
2007	30 countries	Toothpaste	No known deaths
2008	Nigeria	Teething mixture	34 children
Total estimated number of victims			713 people
Estimated number of children who died			530 children (74.3%)

Source: *Time* (1937a), (1937b); Hanif *et al.* (1995); Hari *et al.* 2006; Toumi (2007); Rentz *et al.* (2008), SCCP (2008); Polgreen (2009); Bonati (2009); Sheehan (2009).

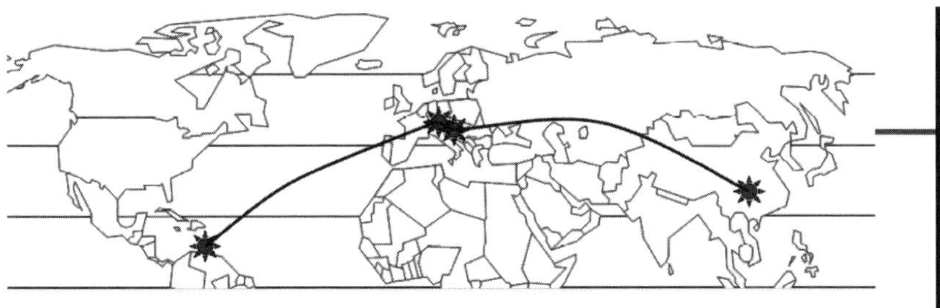

Product shipment	Invoice flow
Xiangang, China	Sinochem, Beijing, China *Manufacturer of contaminated glycerine*
Rotterdam, Netherlands	Metall-Chemie, Hamburg, Germany *Broker*
Port au Prince, Haiti	Vos, Alphem, Netherlands *Broker*
	CTC, Reinfeld, Germany *Distributor*
	Pharval, Port au Prince, Haiti *Manufacturer of antifever syrup*

Process of transference

- Metall-Chemie in Germany purchased glycerine from Chinese trader, Sinochem International.
- Metall-Chemie personnel photocopied Sinochem's Certificate of Analysis on to their own letterhead.
- Dutch Trader Vos BV. (subsidiary of German chemical conglomerate Helm AG), based in The Netherlands, acted as a broker, receiving the glycerine from Metall-Chemie.
- Chemical Trading and Consulting (CTC) received the glycerine from Vos BV, a subsidiary of Helm AG.
- Pharval purchased its raw ingredients from Haitian distributor, Chemical Trading and Consulting (CTC) headquartered in Reinfeld Germany, and mixed it into the final product.

Adapted from Junod (1996)

Figure 3.1 Movement of diethylene glycol from China to Haiti in 1996.
Source: Toumi 2007, World Health Organisation (italics added).

According to Toumi (2007: 21), excerpts from the UN Economic and Social Council's Commission on Human Rights (CN.4/199/46) reveal foreknowledge of the impurity of the glycerine.

> Vos BV, in Alpen [Netherlands] knew that the raw material for the medication was not pure, having had it examined before delivering it to the designated recipient. Although the test results showed that the glycerine was not suitable for medical use, it was sold, via a German company, with a 'pharmaceutical quality' certificate. (Toumi 2007: 21)

By the time investigators traced the glycerine to a Manchurain plant, the plant had closed and the records had been destroyed (Telzrow 2007).

Case example 2: Panama – 2006

In mid-September 2006, 78 people died after taking cough mixture contaminated with DEG. Lucia Cruz, a 74-year-old grandmother, who had not urinated for 2 days, was referred by her neighbourhood doctor to the local hospital, where her condition deteriorated (Lacey and Grady 2006).

> Wracked by nausea, vomiting and high fever, Lucia … watched as her limbs swelled to twice their normal size. Her painful journey came to an end just weeks after the onset of symptoms. Her doctors, fearful that she had succumbed to a deadly communicable disease, advised her family to cremate her body. (Telzrow 2007)

Some victims also exhibited symptoms of paralysis. Lucia was one of '119 official patients as at April 2007' (Rentz *et al.* 2008).

Government officials traced the movement of 46 barrels of syrup contaminated with DEG from the Panamanian port of Colón to its origins near the Yangtze Delta in a place local people call 'chemical country' (Bogdanich and Hooker 2007) (see Figure 3.2).

The full magnitude of this tragedy may never be known.

> In a small town in Sichuan Province a man named Zhou Lianghui said the authorities would not acknowledge that his wife had died from taking Amillarisan A. But Mr Zhou, 38, said he matched the identification number on the batch of medicine his wife received with a warning circular distributed by drug officials. (cited in Bogdanich and Hooker 2007)

Transference also takes into account survivors, the often forgotten victims in assessing the scope of harm. Bogdanich and Hooker (2007) describe what life is now like for Ernestio Osorio, a former high-school teacher in Panama city who was hospitalised for 2 months after taking the contaminated cough syrup.

> 'I'm not an eighth of what I used to be … I have trouble walking. Look at my face [partially paralysed], look at my tears.' The tears he said, apologetically, were not from emotion, but from nerve damage.

Case 3: Nigeria – 2008

In November 2008, over a 2-week period, 34 Nigerian children aged 4 months to 3 years died, and more than 50 others were hospitalised with severe kidney damage after taking 'My Pikin' ('my child' in pidgin), a teething mixture containing paracetamol (Bonati 2009). Typical symptoms included fever, vomiting, diarrhoea and inability to urinate.

> It all started that day when I got home and saw my baby having difficulty breathing. I raised alarm and asked my wife what she gave my baby. She said it was 'My Pikin' Teething Mixture. I instructed her to take her back to the hospital. The doctor told her that her kidney had been damaged. A drug that was supposed to heal my lovely daughter sent her to her untimely death.
>
> (father of baby Agnes, cited in Shokunbi and Jegede 2008)

The manufacturer of the teething mixture, Barewa Pharmaceuticals Pty Ltd, sourced the glycerol from an unlicensed chemical dealer in Lagos. At the time the first child was treated in November 2008, 5,000 bottles of the mixture were taken off the market. Polgreen (2009), in an article in *The New York Times*, noted that the DEG was in such high concentrations that three-quarters of the children who fell sick, subsequently died. The gravity of the situation was captured by Nigeria's Minister of Health:

> The poison has caused many deaths in children between the ages of 2 months and 7 years old … the death of any Nigerian child is a great loss to the nation.
>
> (Nigerian Minister of Health, cited in Polgreen 2009)

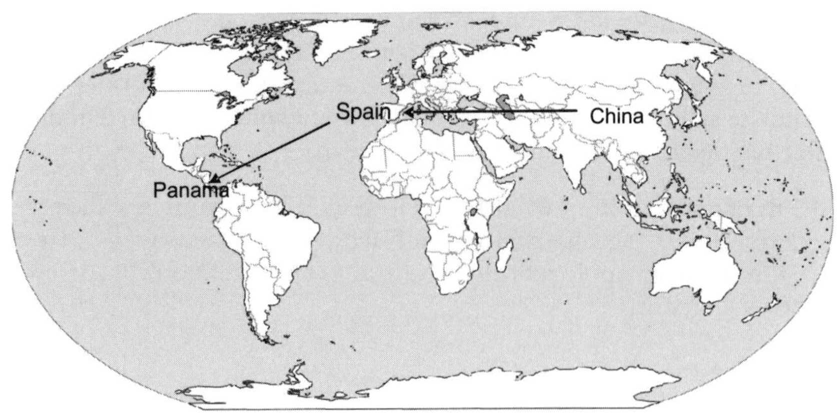

Product shipment	Traders	Process of transference
Hengxiang China	Taixing Glycerine Factory	Manufacturer of the syrup, Taixing Glycerine Factory, provided a Certificate of Analysis showing the glycerine to be 99.5 per cent pure
Beijing, China	CNSC Fortune Way, broker	CNSC Fortune Way translated Taixing's Certificate of Analysis into English, putting its logo at the top of the document, before shipping the barrels to a second trading company in Barcelona
Barcelona, Spain	Rasfer Inter-national, trader	Spanish Company, Rasfer, received the barrels in September 2003, but did not test the contents. They copied the chemical analysis provided by Fortune Way onto their letterhead and shipped the barrels to Panama
Port of Colón Panama		46 barrels of syrup arrived from Barcelona on the container ship *Tobias Maersk*. Shipping records confirmed the content as 99.5% pure glycerine

Continued on next page

Continued from previous page

Panama	Medicom, business group	In Panama the barrels sat unused for more than 2 years, during which time Medicom never tested the product, although according to Panamanian officials they did improperly change the expiration date on the syrup
Panama	Government laboratory	The Panamanian government purchased the 46 barrels of contaminated syrup, incorporating it into 260,000 bottles of cough mixture without testing of the raw material or final product

Process of Transference

- Taixing Glycerine Factory was not certified to manufacture pharmaceutical grade glycerine. They have never publicly disclosed whether or not they tested the glycerine.
- In the course of its journey, the toxin passed through three trading companies on three continents.
- Not one of the companies tested the syrup to confirm what was on the label.
- Along the way, a certificate falsely attesting to the purity of the shipment was repeatedly altered, eliminating the name of the manufacturer and the previous owner. As a result, traders bought the syrup without knowing where it came from or who made it.
- During storage, the expiration date of the syrup was improperly changed.
- Over 60,000 bottles of the prescription cough syrup were distributed to consumers.

Figure 3.2 Movement of diethylene glycol from China to Panama in 2006. Adapted from Bogdanich and Hooker (2007)

According to a media report from Lagos, 'Barewa Pharmaceuticals Limited attempted to debunk the allegation of NAFDAC that the teething mixture "My Pikin" … was responsible for the death of the innocent children across the country. The company not only denied a link but described the allegation as baseless' (Shokunbi and Jegede 2008). On 26 November 2008, the Nigerian National Agency for Food and Drug Administration shut down Barewa Pharmaceuticals.

Complexities of transference

Toxic harms flow along both licit and illicit supply chains and distribution networks. The following examples illustrate some of the complexities of transference including the role of repeated outsourcing, unscrupulous operators, circuitous routes, and free-trade zones in facilitating the transference of harm.

Toxins in the illicit supply chain

Free-trade zones were originally set up to facilitate trade, by providing off-shore tax incentives to legitimate businesses as well as the fast-tracking of goods, often within an environment of relaxed bureaucracy. Instead they have become a haven for unscrupulous operators to hide 'suspect goods' and move them along 'suspicious routes'. In a similar vein as airline passengers, goods 'transit' rather than officially 'enter' the country. In something resembling a huge 'logistics transit lounge', unscrupulous operators can take advantage of fast-track processes to load, unload, warehouse, move and reroute containers, with minimal scrutiny.

On 26 May 2006, customs officials at Heathrow Airport (London) intercepted a container of counterfeit pharmaceuticals, bound for the Bahamas, including well-known brands such as Merck, Novartis, AstraZeneca, Pfizer and Proctor & Gamble (Bogdanich 2007) (see Figure 3.3).

Prescriptions followed a different, but similarly circuitous route, designed to hide the origin of the medicine and 'piggy back' on the credibility of countries like Canada and the UK with high quality and safety standards. The victims of this harm were 'uninsured and underinsured Americans, many elderly' (Bogdanich 2007), deceived into believing their drugs came from a trustworthy source (see table).

In January 2008, RxNorth transferred its customer base to Canadadrugs.com (Canadadrugs.com 2008), a PharmacyChecker.com-

Prescription route	
Bahamas	Individual prescriptions were filled, put into packets and sent to the UK
UK	In the UK, UK postage was affixed and the packages were mailed to the USA
USA	Consumers received their medication in packages identified as originating in the UK, rather than the real source, which was Bahamas

Source: Bogdanich (2007).

verified drug seller. PharmacyChecker is a verification programme designed to give validity to Internet drug sellers, although, according to Liang and Mackey (2009), 'the verification program allows for foreign and suspect online sellers to advertise on primary search engines with virtual impunity.'

Toxins in the licit supply chain

Further examples of transference that deserve closer scrutiny include melamine in the human and animal food chain, and heavy metals such as lead in the toy supply chain. Unlike the previous example, in this case toxins were introduced into licit supply networks engaged in legitimate manufacture of branded products for large foreign corporations.

Melamine to infants and pets

In 2007, melamine, an industrial chemical, was found in milk, candy, infant formula, body paint, wheat gluten exports, pet food and livestock feed. In China, melamine-contaminated infant formula and related dairy products resulted in '6 deaths and 294,000 affected infants, more than 50,000 of whom were hospitalised with urinary problems, possible renal tube blockages and possible kidney stones' (WHO 2009: 1). Rich in nitrogen, melamine is relatively cheap and adding it to substandard or watered-down milk increases the nitrogen concentration, making the milk's protein level appear higher (Reuters India 2009), fooling standard quality tests, which estimate protein levels by measuring nitrogen content. Overall, 22 companies were implicated with most contaminated brands containing levels of melamine between 40 and 120 times the total daily intake (TDI) of 0.2 mg/kg body weight.

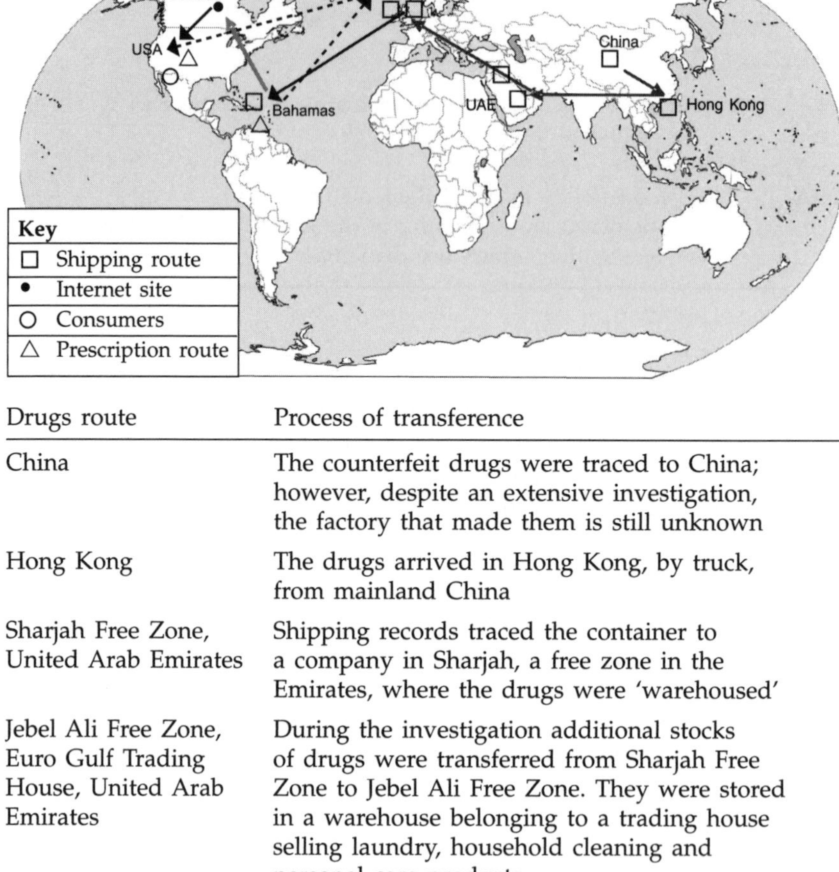

Drugs route	Process of transference
China	The counterfeit drugs were traced to China; however, despite an extensive investigation, the factory that made them is still unknown
Hong Kong	The drugs arrived in Hong Kong, by truck, from mainland China
Sharjah Free Zone, United Arab Emirates	Shipping records traced the container to a company in Sharjah, a free zone in the Emirates, where the drugs were 'warehoused'
Jebel Ali Free Zone, Euro Gulf Trading House, United Arab Emirates	During the investigation additional stocks of drugs were transferred from Sharjah Free Zone to Jebel Ali Free Zone. They were stored in a warehouse belonging to a trading house selling laundry, household cleaning and personal care products
Heathrow Airport, London	Container of counterfeit pharmaceuticals bound for the Bahamas intercepted at Heathrow Airport, triggering an extensive investigation
Personal Touch Pharmacy, Freeport Bahamas	Intended recipient of the containers, Personal Touch Pharmacy in the Bahamas, was found to have computers linked to a server hosting a Canadian Internet site
RxNorth, Internet Pharmacy, Canada	The Internet site belonged to RxNorth, one of Canada's largest Internet pharmacies
USA	Consumers in the USA thought they were buying low-cost drugs from Canada

Figure 3.3 Movement of counterfeit pharmaceuticals from China to the Bahamas in 2006. Adapted from Bogdanich (2007).

Animals too were the victims of melamine when wheat gluten contaminated with melamine scrap was added to over 60 million containers of pet food in the USA, causing approximately 8,000 animal deaths (Pelzrow 2007). In a second incident, melamine in pet food resulted in the recall of 1,154 different products and the deaths of more than 1,000 cats and dogs as a result of kidney failure.

Lead, toys, jewellery and e-waste

Over the last three years, lead has re-emerged as a threat in the toy supply chain. Excessive levels of lead have been found in the painted surfaces of a range of children's wooden and plastic toys, in baby bibs, on lunch boxes, in face-painting kits, and in promotional toys given away with footwear and fast-food meals. Along with barium and cadmium, lead was also found in the contents of 'show bags' in Australia, which included fake teeth, masks, jewellery and painted wooden blocks; in vending-machine candy in the USA; and on the surface of PVC toys in India.

PVC toys represent a case of double exposure for children, sometimes containing lead as a stabiliser as well as phthalates (chemicals which make the toys soft). Both of these substances can leach out of toys subject to the normal mouthing behaviour of children (e.g. biting, licking, chewing) and/or through normal wear and tear that results in damage to the surface of the product (e.g. cracked or broken). Described as 'foul smelling' like shower curtains, in poor countries like India, Kumar and Pastore (2006) say, these soft plastic toys are targeted at the urban poor and often passed down to successive generations of children. This is a significant market, as Argarwal (2007: 4) estimates that of the nearly 130 million children below 6 years of age in India, 6 million live in urban slums, and 1 in 6 children aged 0-6 years is a slum dweller.

Weidenhamer and Clement (2007) propose a link between lead-contaminated jewellery and electronic waste, specifically the recycling of solder. The recovered lead is sold to metal traders and alloy makers, who mix it with other materials to make children's jewellery, sometimes containing toxic levels of lead. Heavy metals subsequently end up in local environments, locked in soil and water. A Greenpeace study (cited in Liu 2009) describes how in Guiyu, China, the site of one of the world's largest e-dumps, 'the river runs black' and diseases of the skin, stomach, respiratory tract and other organs are common among the men and women who work there. In China and India, pollution of local environments is exacerbated by unsafe recycling practices that include the burning of PVC in the open, releasing dioxins into the atmosphere.

Conclusion

I have argued that transference is a useful concept for studying the movement of something from one person or place to another, through the lens of ecoglobal criminology. Analysis of these case examples reveals that, to varying degrees, transference was facilitated by both actions (e.g. substitution, mislabelling, counterfeiting, falsification of documents) and omissions (failure to test raw materials, inadequate quality control and poor risk management). Activities such as wrongdoing, misconduct, lawbreaking, corruption, forgery and differential victimisation are at the heart of criminology, but such transgressions are subject to less scrutiny when they involve licit networks and occur in a white-collar context. A key question for criminologists is why some transgressions continue to be defined as 'harms' when in lay terms they are 'criminal' in nature and impact.

The process of transference in each of these cases is disturbingly similar. In a series of transactions, unlicensed, unauthorised and unscrupulous individuals or companies manufactured and supplied contaminated or counterfeit products, to one or more brokers/traders. They in turn shipped products to interim destinations, variously falsifying critical documents en route to disguise the origin, composition, toxicity and expiry date of products. Unverified and untested raw materials were incorporated into final products and/or distributed to unsuspecting consumers. Transference was facilitated by transiting multiple ports, moving products between free-trade zones, lack or absence of testing, and the closure or relocation of suspect companies to avoid detection and prosecution. Convoluted supply chains and circuitous shipping and distribution networks made the origins and transference of harm more difficult to trace.

Emerging themes in these case studies include entrenched practices (substitutions, dilutions, forgery), a foreknowledge of similar or identical past harms, corruption and organised crime, forgery of critical documents, and the absence of a 'corporate memory' of harm (as also seen in the recent global financial crisis). Responsibility for harm was usually initially denied, then acknowledged, and finally accepted, but was frequently minimised by whitewashing (covering up or hiding unpleasant facts). Apportioning blame was complicated by convoluted supply chains, circuitous routes and transiting multiple ports and countries with differing cultures, language and regulatory spaces. The practice of locating different stages of production and distribution at widely dispersed locations across the world also provides a vehicle for shifting blame, rather than apportioning blame. A key question is how the practice of transferring or rerouting products through countries with high standards (e.g. The Netherlands, Germany, Canada, the UK) legitimises substandard products and what harm nation states sustain as a result. These and many other questions remain to be answered.

Toxic harms are especially heinous because they are preventable. These case examples illustrate the victimisation of vulnerable groups within the community of consumers, including the poor in developing and developed countries, the elderly, surviving victims of toxic harms, and those with existing medical conditions. Children (born and unborn) stand out most starkly as being over-represented, exposed to toxins in breast milk, infant formula, teething mixture, medicine, bibs, toys and jewellery. For instance, of the 713 people who died from DEG poisoning, at least 530 or 74.3 per cent were children. For child survivors of toxic harms, there are questions surrounding developmental difficulties, special tuition, health-care costs, and the capacity to reach their full potential. Similarly, adult survivors of toxic harms face reduced income and quality of life, mental health issues, and ongoing medical costs.

What can we learn from detailed case studies of the transference of harm? It is hoped that by analysing and reflecting on different examples, we will better understand and be able to respond to the whole range of issues surrounding the global movement of toxic harms and develop methods of intervention that go to the heart of transference.

References

Agarwal, R. (2006) *Toying with Toxins: An Investigation of Lead and Cadmium in Soft Plastic Toys in Three Cities in India.* PowerPoint presentation, IFCS Forum V, 2006. Toxicslink, India [online]. Available at: http://www.who.int/ifcs/documents/forums/forum5/toying_agarwal.pdf (accessed 4 September 2009).

Barboza, D. (2007). 'Why Lead in Toy Paint? It's Cheaper', *New York Times,* 11 September [online]. Avaialble at: http://www.nytimes.com/2007/09/11/business/worldbusiness/11iht-11lead.7458568.html (accessed October 2007).

Barboza, D. and Barrionuevo, A. (2007) 'Filler in Animal Feed is Open Secret in China'. *New York Times,* 30 April. [online]. Available at: http://www.nytimes.com/2007/04/30/business/worldbusiness/30food.html?_i=1&pagewanted=print (accessed 17 September 2009).

Bogdanich, W. (2007) 'Counterfeit Drugs' Path Eased by Free Trade Zones', *New York Times*, 17 December [online]. Available at: http://www.drfarrell.net/COUNTERFEIT%20DRUGS%20FROM%20NY%20...doc (accessed February 2008).

Bogdanich, W. and Hooker, J. (2007) 'From China to Panama, a Trail of Poisoned Medicine', *New York Times*, 6 May [online]. Available at: http://www.nytimes.com/2007/05/06/world/americas/06poison.html?_r=1&pagewanted=print (accessed August 2007).

Bonati, M. (2009) 'One Again, Children are the Main Victims of Fake Drugs', *Archives of Disease in Childhood*, 94 (6) 468–469 [online]. Available at: adc.bumj.com (accessed 16 August 2009).

Canadadrugs.com (2008) 'Canada Drugs.com is Proud to Serve RxNorth Customers' [online]. Available at: http://www.canadadrugs.com/rxnorth/index.php?REF=Redirect (accessed October 2009).

Centers for Disease Control (CDC) (1996) 'Fatalities Associated with Ingestion of Diethylene Glycol-Contaminated Glycerin Used to Manufacture Acetaminophen Syrup – Haiti – November 1995–June 1996. *Morbidity and Mortality Weekly Report*, 45 (30): 649–50.

Centers for Disease Control and Prevention (CDC) (2004) 'Brief Report – Lead Poisoning from a Toy Necklace', *Morbidity and Mortality Weekly Report*. 53(23): 509–511 (18 June) [online]. Available at: http://www.cdc.gov/mmwr/preview/mmwrhtml/mm5323a5.htm (accessed September 2009).

Centers for Disease Control and Prevention (CDC) (2006) 'Death of a Child After Ingestion of a Metallic Charm – Minnesota 2006', *Morbidity and Mortality Weekly Report*, 55: 1–2 [online]. Available at: http://www.cdc.gov/mmwr/preview/mmwrhtml/mm55d323a1.htm (accessed 25 September 2009).

Centers for Disease Control (CDC) (2007) 'Interpreting and Managing Blood Lead Levels <10 µg/dl in Children and Reducing Childhood Exposures to Lead', *Morbidity and Mortality Weekly Report*, 56(RR08): 1–14;16 (2 November) [online]. Available at: http://www.cdc.gov/mmwr/preview/mmwrhtml/rr5608a1.htm (accessed September 2009).

Chan, E.Y., Griffiths, S.M. and Chan, C.W. (2008) 'Public-Health Risks of Melamine in Milk Products', *Lancet*, 372 (9648): 1444–1445.

Collins, D. (1989) 'Organisational Harm, Legal Condemnation and Stakeholder Retaliation. A Typology, Research Agenda and Application', *Journal of Business Ethics*, 8(1): 1–13.

Ernst & Young (2009) 'Is Risk Management Broken? – an Australian and New Zealand Perspective on the Current and Future State of Risk Management'. At the Helm [online]. Available at: http://www.ey.com/Publication/vwLUAssets/Is_risk_management_broken/$FILE/Is%20risk%20management%20broken.pdf (accessed 7 September 2009).

Hanif, M., Mobarak, M.R., Ronan, A., *et al.* (1995) 'Fatal Renal Failure Caused by Diethylene Glycol in Paracetamol Elixir: The Bangladesh Epidemic',

British Medical Journal, 311: 88–91 [online]. Available at: http://www.bmj.com/cgi/content/abstract/311/6997/88 (accessed September 2009).

Hari, P., Jain, Y. and Kabra, S.K. (2006) 'Case Report: Fatal Encephalopathy and Renal Failure Caused by Diethylene Glycol Poisoning', *Journal of Tropical Pediatrics*, 56 (2): 442–44.

Hawthorne, M.L. (2007) 'Confronting Toxic Work Exposure in China: The Precautionary Principle and Burden Shifting', *Environmental Law*, 37 (1): 151–174.

Hitchock, L. and Mierzwinski, E. (2008) *Trouble in Toyland.* The 23rd Annual Survey of Toy Safety. Vermont Public Interest Research and Education Fund (PIRG). November 2008.

Immig, J. (2007) 'Toy Story: The Tale of How Plastics and Toxins are Endangering Children's Health', *Kindred Magazine*, 29–32.

Junod, S.W. (2000) 'Diethylene Glycol Deaths in Haiti', *Public Health Reports*, 115 (1): 78–86 [online]. Available at: http://www.jstor.org/stable/4598485 (accessed 19 September 2009).

Kumar, A. and Pastore, P. (2006) *Toying with Toxics: An Investigation of Lead and Cadmium in Soft Toys in Three Cities in India*. New Delhi, India: Toxics Link.

Lacey, M. and Grady, D. (2006) 'Behind Deaths in Panama, a Culprit: Cough Medicine', *International Herald Tribune*, 16 October [online]. Available at: http://www.iht.com/articles/2006/10/16/news/panama.php (accessed November 2007).

Liang, B.A. and Mackey, T. (2009) 'Searching for Safety: Addressing Search Engine, Website, and Provider Accountability for Illicit Online Drug Sales', *American Journal of Law and Medicine*, 35: 125–184 [online]. Available at: http://www.safemedicines.org/resources/LiangMackeyAJLM.pdf (accessed September 2009).

Lipton, B. (2007) 'Some Baby Bibs Said to Contain Levels of Lead', *New York Times*, 15 August [online]. Available at: http:/www.nytimes.com/2007/08/15/business/15lead.html?pagewanted=print (accessed 12 September 2008).

Liu, Y. (2008) *Recycling and Waste Management – Case Study of China E-Waste Recycling Industry.* Worldwatch Institute [online]. Available at: http://www.ilo.org/public/english/region/asro/bangkok/events/greenjobs/download/paper25.pdf (accessed September 2009).

Mihm, S. (2007). 'A Tragic Lesson', *Boston Globe*, 26 August 2007 [online]. Available at: http://www.boston.com/news/globe/ideas/articles/2007/08/26/a_tragic_lesson?mode=PF (accessed 23 August 2009).

Navarro, D. (2007) *Report of the China Price Project*. Merage School of Business, University of California-Irvine [online]. Available at: http://works.bepress.com/cgi/viewcontent.cgi?article=1001&context=peter_navarro (accessed July 2007).

O'Brien, K.L., Selanikio, J.D., Hecdivert, C., *et al.* (1998) 'Epidemic of Pediatric Deaths from Acute Rental Failure Caused by Diethylene Glycol Poisoning',

Journal of the American Medical Association, 279 (15): 1175–80. [online]. Available at: http://origin.cdc.gov/nceh/dls/pdf/JAMAHaitiAntifreeze.pdf (accessed 10 September 2009).

Pellow, D.N. (2006) 'Social Inequalities and Environmental Conflict', *Horizontes Anthropologicos*, 12: 15–29.

Pierce, G. (1998) 'Glycerol Contaminated with Diethylene Glycol', *World Health Drug Information*, 12 (3): 129–130.

Polgreen, L. (2009) '84 Children Are Killed by Medicine in Nigeria', *New York Times*, 6 February.

Rentz, E.D., Lewis, L., Mujica, O., *et al.* (2008) 'Outbreak of Acute Renal Failure in Panama in 2006: A Case-Control Study', *World Health Organisation Bulletin*, 86 (10): 749–756 [online]. Available at: http://www.who.int/bulletin/volumes/86/10/07-049965/en/print.html (accessed 4 September 2009).

Reuters India (2009) FACTBOX: What is Melamine and Why Add It to Milk? *Reuters India*, 22 January [online]. Available at: http://in.reuters.com/article/domesticNews/idINT12657320080925?sp=true (accessed: 21 September 2009).

Schettler, T. Stein, J., Reich, F., *et al.* (2000) *In Harm's Way: Toxic Threats to Child Development.* Report by Greater Boston Physicians for Social Responsibility, prepared for a joint project with Clean Water Fund [online]. Available at: http://www.igc.org/psr/ (accessed August 2007).

Scientific Committee on Consumer Products (SCCP) (2008) *Opinion on Diethylene Glycol.* Health and Consumer Protection Directorate-General. European Commission. Opinion adopted at the SCCP's 16th plenary on 24 June 2008 [online]. Available at: http://ec.europa.eu/health/ph_risk/risk_en.htm (accessed September 2009).

Sheehan, C. (2009) *DEG/EG Contamination Overview.* Propylene Glycol and Sorbitol Solution Open Microphone Web Meetings. 16 and 17 March, 2009. PowerPoint presentation [online]. Available at: 16%20PGSSWebMeetingsMasterPres.pdf (accessed 20 September 2009).

Shokunbi, Y. and Jegede, M. (2008) 'My Pikin – Tragedy of a Killer Mixture', *Daily Independent* (Lagos), 6 December [online]. Available at: http://allafrica.com/stories/200812080547.html (accessed 8 September 2009).

Shtargot, S. (2007) '43,000 Toys Pulled Over Lead Paint Concern', *The Age*, 3 August.

Sing, J., Dutta, A.K., Khare, S., (2001) 'Diethylene Glycol Poisoning in Gurgaon, India, 1998', *Bulletin of the World Health Organisation*, 2001, 79(2): 88–95 [online]. Available at: http://www.scielosp.org/pdf/bwho/v79n2/v79n2a01.pdf (accessed 4 September 2009).

Spencer, R. (2007) 'Human Story Behind China's Toxic Toy Scandal', *The Age* [online]. Available at: http://www.theage.com.au/news/world/human-story-behind-chinas-toxic-toy-scandal/2007/08 (accessed 31 March, 2008).

Sustainability Purchasing Network Newsletter (SPN) (2007) 'Toxins in the Supply Chain', October, Issue 8, November, Vancouver, [online]. Available at: http://www.buysmartbc.com/index.php?option=com_ydm_phplist&Itemid=36&message=106 (accessed September 2009).

Telzrow, M. (2007) 'The New Chinese Take-Out', *The New American*, [online]. Available at: http://www.thenewamerican.com/node/5001/print (accessed 7 November 2007).

Time Magazine (1937a) 'Medicine: Fatal Remedy', No. 18 (1 November) [online]. Available at: http://www.time.com/time/printout/0,8816,882914,00.html# (accessed 23 August 2009).

Time Magazine (1937b) 'Medicine: Post-Mortem', 20 December [online]. Available at: http://www.time.com/time/printout/0,8816,758704,00.html (accessed 23 August 2009).

Tomlinson, K. (2006) 'Ex-Worker Blows Whistle on Popular Web Pharmacy', *CTV News*, 25 May, Canada [online]. Available at: http://www.ctv.ca/servlet/ArticleNews/story/CTVNews/20060510/whistleblower_internetdrugs_060525/20060525/ (accessed September 2009).

Toumi, A. (2007) *Counterfeit Drugs Kill!* International Medical Products Anti-Counterfeiting Taskforce. Tunisia: World Health Organisation.

Weidenhamer, J.D. and Clement, M.L. (2007a) 'Leaded Electronic Waste is a Possible Source Material for Lead-Contaminated Jewelry', *Chemosphere*, 69(7): 111–115.

Weidenhamer, J.D. and Clement, M.L. (2007b) 'Evidence of Recycling of Lead Battery Waste into Highly Leaded Jewelry', *Chemosphere*, 69(10: 1670–1672.

White, R. (ed.) (2009) *Environmental Crime: A Reader.* Cullompton: Willan Publishing.

World Health Organisation (WHO 2007a) *Diethylene Glycol – Draft Poisons Information Monograph for Peer Review*, October. International Programme on Chemical Safety [online]. Available at: http://www.who.int/ipcs/poisons/pim_diethyleneglcol.pdf (accessed 10 September 2009).

World Health Organisation (WHO 2007b) *Lead Exposure in Children.* Information Note, 6 August [online]. Available at: http://www.who.int/phe/news/Lead_in_Toys_note_060807.pdf (accessed 4 September 2009).

World Health Organisation (2008) *Melamine and Cyanuric Acid: Toxicity, Preliminary Risk Assessment and Guidance on Levels in Food.* Updated 30 October 2008 [online]. Available at: http://www.who.int/foodsafety/fs_management/Melamine.pdf (accessed 4 September 2009).

World Health Organisation (2009) *Toxicological and Health Aspects of Melamine and Cyanuric Acid.* Report of a WHO Expert Meeting in collaboration with FAO, Supported by Health Canada, 1–4 December 2008. World Health Organisation, Geneva [online]. Available at: http://whqlibdoc.who.int/publications/2009/9789241597951_eng.pdf (accessed September 2009).

Xinhua News Agency (2008) 'Official Sacked, Former Sanlu Chairwoman Detained in Milk Scandal', *China org.Cn.* 17 September [online]. Available at: http://www.china.org.cn/china/national/2008-09/17/content_16494420.htm (accessed October 2009).

Chapter 4

Global warming, global crime: a green criminological perspective

Michael J. Lynch and Paul B. Stretesky

Introduction

Criminologists have been slow to consider climate change as a relevant issue. This chapter addresses that shortcoming by drawing on climate change research to illustrate the intersection of criminology with the science of global warming. Our goal is to explore the *variety* of harms associated with climate change, examine how these harms impinge on humans (as individuals, populations, cultures, and societies), non-human species, and the natural environment, and to describe how climate change may impact crime, its definition, and crime policy.

To begin, we examine climate change as a public issue, review the scientific foundation of global warming, establish human responsibility for global warming, and explore the consequences of global warming for both human and non-human species. Next, we examine global warming as a crime enhanced by the complicity between state and corporate actors, and influenced by state-supported cultures of consumption and production as opposed to sustainable cultures. We then examine the implications of climate change on the redesign of criminal justice processes, explore how global warming mitigation can be related to criminal justice policy, and argue that it is necessary for criminal justice policymakers to evaluate how their policies impact the environment in order to address ecological justice as well as criminal justice.

Before beginning, note that the terms 'climate change' and 'global warming' are often used interchangeably. We use the term 'global warming' throughout this chapter to focus on problems that result from the long-term pattern of increasing global temperatures (Office of Air Radiation 2009: 3).

Global warming as a global issue

Global warming stands out from other contemporary social problems because it is a *global* problem. While many social and economic problems *appear* to be global (e.g. terrorism), this has more to do with their definitions than their scope. To be sure, there are social and economic problems of *global importance* such as economic inequality, poverty, famine and hunger, or health-care delivery. These problems are global because all nations face them. The severity of many social problems, however, is dependent on national policy (e.g. Korpi and Palme 1998). A good example is national health-care delivery, which, while a global concern, is country-dependent and related to national-level politics and priorities (Evans *et al.* 2001).

As a social problem, global warming is similar to health-care access because people in different parts of the world are impacted differentially by each. In both cases, the wealthy can buffer themselves against the negative effects of these social problems (e.g. Harlan *et al.* 2006 in the case of heat islands). These social problems differ to the extent that no nation can escape the effects of rising temperatures. The fact that some people can 'make themselves comfortable' in an era of global warming does not erase its global impacts. In addition, part of the global nature of climate change includes its far-reaching consequences for non-human species as well as ecosystem segments (e.g. waterways, ice caps, land masses, weather, air). Thus, in contrast to other 'global' social problems *that impact only humans*, global warming is unique because it affects all species and the ecosystem itself.[1]

The science of global warming

Global warming, though an intensely modern concern, has been of interest to scientists since James Fourier discovered that gases in the earth's atmosphere could cause a 'greenhouse' effect by absorbing radiant heat (Cowie 2007; Weart 2008). Later, Tyndall (1861, 1863, 1873) identified carbon dioxide and water vapour as central to this process. In 1896, these observations allowed the Swedish chemist, Savante Arrhenius, to demonstrate how increased levels of atmospheric carbon dioxide could alter the earth's atmospheric temperature (Arrhenius 1908). Arrhenius' study was widely criticised (Humphries 1920; for rebuttal see Hulburt 1931) until Callendar (1938) provided empirical evidence of a positive association between levels of carbon dioxide and the earth's temperature.

In the 1950s and 1960s, computer modelling (Plass 1956a, 1956b, 1959) and advanced measurements of atmospheric carbon dioxide concentrations by Charles Keeling (which yielded the Keeling Curve) became the foundation for widespread concern with global warming in later decades (see Lovelock 2006; Santer *et al.* 1996). Studies began to focus on explaining the origins of global warming. Today, most scientists agree with Mann *et al.*'s (1998) conclusion that human sources of carbon dioxide emissions overrode the natural causes of warming during the twentieth century (Tett *et al.* 1999; Crowley 2000).

Who is responsible for global warming?

Scientific consensus suggests that contemporary global warming has anthropogenic causes (IPCC 2007; Weart 2008). What the scientific community does not emphasise is that there is a large amount of variation in the production of global warming gases and that everyone is not equally responsible for current warming trends. The more an individual or culture consumes, the more that person or culture contributes to climate change. One way to illustrate this point is to assess the 'ecological footprint' of a nation, a measure of how much land and water are used to produce the commodities each country's population consumes (Wackernagel *et al.* 1999). Only 17 nations live on ecologically sustainable footprints or consume less than what nature provides (Wackernagel *et al.* 1999: 385). Despite its wealth of natural resources, the nation with the largest ecological footprint is the USA (Wackernagel *et al.* 1999: 286–387), making it the largest contributor to the problem of global warming.

To illustrate this point, Table 4.1 displays the distribution of global warming gases in carbon dioxide equivalents (non-carbon dioxide sources are converted to carbon dioxide units for purposes of comparison) for the top 20 contributing nations, and the total for each region in the world (e.g. South America). In Table 4.1, the columns display the following information: column 1, carbon dioxide equivalents in 1000s of tonnes; column 2, the percentage of global warming gas equivalents produced by each nation; column 3, the percentage of the world population living within a nation; column

4, the ratio of global warming gases to world population (column 2/column 3); column 5, carbon dioxide tonnes per capita; column 6, gross domestic product (GDP) for each nation in US dollars as an indicator of economic output.

Table 4.1 suggests that the problem of global warming is driven by economically 'advanced' nations or nations with high GDP. The nine nations with per capita GDP in excess of US $38,000 produce 33.5 per cent of all global warming gases but contain only 11.9 per cent of the world's population. A major share of this pollution is produced by the USA, which contains 4.5 per cent of the world's population but produces 18.7 per cent of all global warming gases.

Nations with large populations also contribute significantly to global warming, though some of these nations contribute little to this problem in a relative (ecological footprint) sense. The most populace nations, China, India and the USA, represent 41.5 per cent of the world's population, and 45 per cent of global warming gas production. Though highly populated, both India's and China's contributions to global warming are relatively small – China produces 1.35 tonnes of global warming gas per capita, while India contributes 0.37 tonnes per capita. The USA is by far the largest offender, contributing 5.12 tonnes of global warming gases per capita – 3.8 times more than China and nearly 14 times more than India on a per capita basis. To be sure, in an absolute sense, China and India make significant contributions to the total production of global warming gases (slightly more than 26 per cent). Yet, relatively, these nations contribute little to the problem of global warming because they run a relatively small ecological deficit. The per capita ecological deficit can be thought of as the amount of land (in hectares) that a particular country needs per capita beyond what the average person uses to produce the carbon-based goods and services they consume. While the ecological deficits of China (–0.04 hectares or 0.988 acres per person) and India (–0.03 hectares or 0.741 acres per person) are rather small, the US carbon-based ecological deficit is very large (–3.6 hectares or 8.892 acres per person (see Wackernagel *et al.* 1999: 286–387). This means that the USA must import carbon-based products from other countries (and therefore increase their ecological deficit) or draw down the natural resources within its own borders in a non-sustainable way to meet current consumption patterns. If the USA tried to reduce its ecological deficit by eliminating trade, it would completely deplete its natural resources (e.g. vegetation, coal and other energy sources) in a relatively short time.

Table 4.1 Top 20 carbon dioxide equivalent-producing nations, with regional totals (2007)*

	CO_2 tonnes (1000s)	% World CO_2	% World population	CO_2 population ratio	CO_2 tonnes per capita	Per capita GDP $US
USA	1,586,213	18.7	4.52	4.14	5.12	47,103
Canada	144,738	1.7	0.5	3.4	4.36	47,090
Mexico	121,452	1.4	1.63	0.86	1.11	10,395
Total North America	1,852,401					
Brazil	96,102	1.1	2.81	0.39	0.5	8,480
Total South America	290,836					
France	98,343	1.2	0.97	1.24	1.51	46,489
Germany	209,624	2.5	1.22	2.05	2.55	46,352
Italy	121,081	1.4	0.89	1.57	2.01	41,259
Poland	85,742	1	0.57	1.75	2.25	14,737
Russian Federation	432,486	5.1	2.11	2.42	3.05	12,487
Spain	95,356	1.1	0.68	1.61	2.08	41,565
Ukraine	87,737	1	0.69	1.45	1.9	4,305
UK	144,726	1.7	0.92	1.85	2.35	45,731
Total Europe/Eurasia	1,842,357					
Iran	129,855	1.5	1.05	1.43	1.82	5,803
Total Middle East	413,386					
South Africa	118,367	1.4	0.71	1.97	2.41	6,158
Total Africa	317,246					

Australia	102,763	1.2	0.32	3.75	4.73	50,887
China	1,801,932	21.2	19.87	1.07	1.35	3,174
India	429,601	5.1	17.16	0.3	0.37	1,078
Indonesia	113,567	1.3	3.42	0.38	0.49	2,151
Japan	337,364	4	1.9	2.11	2.64	38,055
Taiwan	71,753	0.8	0.34	2.35	3.12	17,521
Total for Asian Pacific	3,320,003					
20 Nation totals	6,328,802	74.4	62.29			
20 Nation means	316,440	3.7	3.11	1.81	2.21	24,541

*Tonnes measure global warming gas production in thousand tonnes of carbon dioxide-equivalent units. CO_2 tonnes measure global warming gas production in thousand tonne-equivalent units; % world CO_2 is the percentage of the total global CO_2 equivalent tonnes produced within a nation; % world population is the percentage of the world population residing within a nation; CO_2/population ratio measures a country's contribution to CO_2 production as standardised by that country's population size (e.g. a ratio of 1 would indicate equivalence between a country's CO_2 production and its population. Countries below 1.0 produce less CO_2 relative to their population while countries with ratios above 1.0 produce more CO_2 relative to their population; CO_2 tonnes per capita is the number of CO_2-equivalent tonnes divided by population size; GDP per capita in $US measures the GDP per capita in US dollars reported in the *CIA Factbook* (nearest year to 2007). The total world tonnes of CO_2 is 8,470,855.

Sources:
1. Carbon dioxide measures: (US) Carbon Dioxide Information Analysis Center, *Preliminary 2006–2007 Global and National Estimates*.
2. Population estimates employed in this table were derived from United Nations *Population Estimates* and Euro-Stats *Population Estimates*. The time estimates calculated vary between November 2006 and December, 2008.

From a relative tonnes per capita standpoint, the largest contributors to global warming include 12 nations: the USA (5.12), Australia (4.73), Canada (4.36), Taiwan (3.12), Russia (3.05), Japan (2.64), Germany (2.55), South Africa (2.41), the UK (2.35), Poland (2.25), Spain (2.08), and Italy (2.01), which together produce 40.6 per cent of global warming gas emissions, but represent only 14.7 per cent of the world's population. These data indicate the level of inequality that exists in terms of the contribution nations make to the problem of global warming, with economically 'advanced' nations with high standards of living and elevated rates of consumption contributing disproportionately to the problem.

For many, China and India, with their large populations, stand out as central concerns because of their efforts to industrialise and enhance living standards for their citizens. For this reason, advanced nations often accuse China and India of being environmentally destructive to distract attention from their own global footprint effects. If China and India reach their economic productivity and consumption goals in the near future (e.g. an ecological footprint deficit of –3.6 hectares per person), there would be an incredible increase in global warming gas production. For example, if China produced as much per capita global warming gas as the USA, it would contribute 3.79 times as much global warming gas as it produces now – 6,829,322,000 tonnes, or 80 per cent of the global warming gases the world now produces. Such an extensive release of global warming gas would create an environmental catastrophe. Thus, China and India are 'problems' to the extent that current levels of global warming gas production by economically advanced nations are accepted as an appropriate benchmark for development.

There must be different solutions to the problem of global warming in different cultural contexts. In economically advanced nations, the problems are overconsumption and excessive energy use, meaning that alternative energy sources are needed there (Dovi *et al.* 2009). While many advanced nations are developing energy alternatives, some (the USA, Canada, Australia) lag behind, and until these nations take greater responsibility for their contributions to global warming pollution, there is little hope of controlling global warming. In the USA, in particular, the development of alternative energy sources, the promotion of mass transit, the shift to non-coal-based electrical production, and the promotion of efficient and smaller vehicles are all necessary steps to reduce global warming.

For some nations, the problem is not overconsumption but rather population growth. The contributions of China and India to global warming, for example, are driven by population expansion combined with accelerating standards of living, and programmes that address population control in these nations are needed to reduce global warming (for criticisms of this approach, see White 1994). Yet, at the same time, population expansion in these nations would be less of a concern if economically advanced nations consumed less. For example, recent evidence suggests that US consumption patterns are strongly related to the expansion and contraction of carbon dioxide levels in countries around the world (Stretesky and Lynch 2009). In other nations, the problem is that they supply raw materials, especially wood, to advanced economies (Stretesky and Lynch 2009). Large swathes of Asia and South America, for example, have been deforested to feed consumption-driven economies (Dudley *et al.* 1995). Measures protecting forest land are a step in the right direction, but these protections will be less successful until advanced economies change consumption patterns and consume less.

Living with less and developing an environmental ethos in high-consumption nations must become part of the policy response to global warming. In the end, it is necessary to bear in mind that global warming is a global problem with divergent and different regional impacts that necessitates a global response that may exhibit regionally specific and targeted policies. Thus, while some nations bear more responsibility than others for driving global warming, it is a mistake to focus solely on responsibility where this issue undermines positive action.

Global warming and criminology

Global warming appears, at first glance, to be far removed from the study of crime, law and justice, especially if one adopts the traditional, orthodox focus of criminology on street crimes and offenders (e.g. murder/murderers, robbery/robbers) and the social control of these offences and offenders. If, however, one thinks broadly about criminological matters, the connection between criminology and global warming becomes clear.

Criminologically relevant subject matter

Global warming is a subject of concern for green criminology. There is no singular definition of green criminology, which is still expanding as a result of the diverse subjects criminologists include under this heading (Lynch and Stretesky 2003; South and Beirne 2006, 2007; Lynch 2007a; White 2008). Nevertheless, it is useful to provide some idea of what this term means. In our view, green criminology integrates the study of the following: (1) harms that directly damage the ecosystem or its parts (direct victimisation of the environment), or victimise species through ecosystem damage (indirect victimisation); (2) the types, extent, and consequences of environmental harms that may or may not be defined as crimes under current forms of law; (3) processes for controlling green crimes; and (4) perspectives, hypotheses, and theories that promote analysis of environmental harms and law, crime, and justice concerns (South 1997; Beirne and South 2007; Lynch *et al.* 2008; White 2008). Put another way, green criminology examines forms of victimisation, harms, crime, law and justice that relate to and stem from damaging the natural environment. In such a view, it becomes relevant to examine a diverse array of issues related to global warming. In the short compass of this chapter, we cannot address all of the criminological issues associated with global warming, which include a 'laundry list' of possible subjects.[2] Below we address several relevant issues in greater detail.

The expansion of environmental harms due to global warming

Scientists such as Ziska *et al.* (2009) are concerned that the public fails to appreciate the integral connection between the environment and the various species that live within those environments, leading the public to ignore how increased CO_2 levels produce prominent 'background' effects that are a central concern of the scientific community. For example, a significant scientific concern is the effect of global warming on the chemical structure and toxicology of the natural world. It is well known that temperature changes how species respond to chemicals, and elevated temperatures can increase chemical toxicity or diminish toxicity thresholds (Mayer *et al.* 1991; Richards and Beitinger 1995; Patra *et al.* 2007; Noyes *et al.* 2009; Ziska *et al.* 2009). This aspect of global warming has been examined with respect to the spread and geography of disease and disease-carrying insects (Brownstein *et al.* 2005), the distribution of naturally occurring heavy metals (Bargagli 2000), the acceleration of endocrine-disrupting chemical effects (Jennsen 2006), and other human health issues (Michael *et al.* 2003).

Serious concerns about the effect of global warming were raised by Noyes *et al.*'s (2009) review of scientific literature on the interaction of toxicants (e.g. persistent organic pollutants (POPs), organochlorine pesticides), temperature, precipitation, and salinity. This review indicated that elevated temperature amplifies pollutant toxicity (though it can also accelerate chemical degradation). Based on this review, global warming is likely to adversely impact human health in urban areas, where it intensifies toxic exposure by concentrating environmental toxins, accelerating toxin uptake, and altering biological responses to toxins (e.g. metabolism and excretion). Global warming also appears to impact the food chain by expanding POP concentrations in water, soil, and biota. Areas impacted by increased precipitation forced by global warming may experience expanded exposure to environmental toxicants through storm run-offs, while areas with reduced precipitation may encounter accelerated exposure to toxic air pollutants. Likewise, altered salinity stresses aquatic environments and may increase the toxicity of environmental pollution. It is unknown whether these impacts will be accelerated by global warming tipping points (Pearce 2008).

Scientists are continually discovering new ways in which global warming produces harm. It is important for green criminologists to stay abreast of this literature in order to address the varieties of victimisation and emerging crimes and harms science identifies. In doing so, it is important to remember that our human attitude toward the environment impacts how we treat and interpret the environmental harms we produce. As Bill McKibben wrote in *The End of Nature*, 'In the past, we spoiled and polluted parts of … nature … we never thought we had wrecked nature. Deep down, we never thought we really could: it was too big and too old; its forces – the wind, the rain, the sun – were too strong, too elemental' (1988: 41). Essentially, this lie we told ourselves allowed us to continually plunder nature, to take from it without offering it any protection. Global warming, as James Lovelock (2006) writes, is Gaia's (the living system of the Earth) revenge for our past crimes against it.

State crimes and global warming

Another important area that requires criminological attention is the intersection of global warming, governmental action – or inaction – and corporate behaviour in ways that produce state-corporate crimes of global warming. Here, researchers can address state policies that undermine state and corporate responsibilities to address global warming. The first hurdle in this research is convincing other criminologists that the behaviours under examination amount to crimes, since these behaviours are legal and do not directly violate the law. But the fact that a behaviour has been 'normalized' (Moynihan 1993) does not mean that it should be acceptable, especially when what is at stake is a significant degree of harm. It is possible, for example, to equate state-corporate crimes of global warming to state crimes such as genocide. Within the nation engaged in such activities, genocide is not viewed as criminal (Chambliss 1989). It is, however, the definition of outsiders that may be more important in determining the criminal nature of the behaviours in question. Thus, definitions of crime and harm external to the state may be more useful in these cases.

Studies of state and state-corporate crime have gained wider acceptance, and researchers have examined a variety of issues under this heading (Michalowski and Kramer 2006). Not all studies of state-corporate crime have been performed by criminologists. For example, studies similar to those criminologists would label as state-corporate crime research have been undertaken with respect to environmental policies (Markowitz and Rosner 2003), or with respect to specific state officials and offices. An example is Robert Kennedy, Jr.'s book, *Crimes Against Nature*, which details how the administration of George W. Bush undermined environmental regulations, and how it was often influenced in these decisions by powerful corporate leaders. This research would address processes such as lobbying, and how lobbyists use their power and influence to impact and direct governmental policies related to global warming.

Global warming and criminal justice policy

Green criminology also directs attention to the intersection of global warming and criminal justice policy. Criminologists and criminal justice policymakers tend to consider crime responses in isolation from other important social considerations, and view crime policy only in relation to theories and philosophies of justice and legal principles and practice. In the contemporary era, however, existing definitions of justice designed around fairness and protection issues related solely to criminal suspects and crimes are no longer broad enough to address the needs of modern societies. If doing justice through criminal justice produces external harms, it may be necessary to reconsider the philosophical basis of those approaches.

One example of an external harm involves the effect of criminal justice energy consumption on global warming. That is, when we consider the connection between criminal justice and environmental justice in its broadest sense, it becomes clear that criminal justice policy ought to address its own harms, such as the harm it causes to the environment. This approach produces a new basis for doing justice that is more encompassing and capable of fulfilling the need for criminal and environmental justice simultaneously.

In addition to its limited understanding and definition of justice, criminal justice policy is often based on *an assumption* that expanding policing, corrections and the courts or expanding the scope of surveillance and punishment is the most appropriate way to control crime. We call this an assumption because much research demonstrates that there is little empirical support for expansionist hypotheses (Lynch 2007b). Yet, despite contrary empirical research, criminal justice functions are continually expanded to reduce crime. There is a clear parallel here between criminal justice assumptions about expansion and general economic assumptions about expansion; both assume that growth is beneficial. Indeed, growth assumptions are pervasive in nations with advanced economies. For example, the USA has the world's largest correctional, court and policing systems. From an environmental perspective, these systems are energy intensive and inefficient. When it comes to doing justice under expansionist assumptions, no consideration is given to the negative environmental effects of expanding justice processes. The overriding concern is the assumption that expansion improves crime control.

Illustrating this point, policing in the USA is typically based on a 'one-size fits all' approach, in which patrol officers are issued the largest, most powerful vehicles regardless of the type of work they perform or where they perform it. There is some evidence that this dominant ideology may be changing, as a few police departments in major US cities have experimented with smaller, more efficient, alternatively fuelled vehicles (e.g. New York City has experimented with about three dozen hybrid Nissan Altmas, while other departments have used Toyota or Ford hybrids). Nevertheless, these experiments are rather insignificant with respect to the number of large police cruisers employed by US police departments. In contrast, in many European cities, smaller police vehicles have predominated for decades. Yet, in the USA, the common choice for a police vehicle is a large, eight-cylinder cruiser, often staffed by one officer. The choice of these vehicles is based on the exception – the need for high-speed pursuit of criminal suspects, and the need to create roadblocks

– rather than the more typical, mundane and daily uses to which these vehicles are put.

Imagine, for the moment, a police department with 200 vehicles, all eight-cylinder cruisers that each travel 50,000 miles a year and average 10 miles per gallon (mpg). These vehicles produce 8,890,000 kg of CO_2 pollution. If this fleet were replaced with appropriate vehicles, (one might arrive at a fleet of 50 cruisers 100 hybrid cars and 50 electric cars), which would produce a reduction of 5,216,000 kg of CO_2 (assuming that hybrids average 30 mpg and no reduction in miles driven, as could be achieved by increasing foot patrol, reorganising police precincts, and expanding the use of electronic traffic monitoring, thus lowering carbon emissions even further). Now, imagine the CO_2 saving if the 100 largest police forces in the USA were all this size, and each reconfigured its vehicle force. The savings would amount to 521,600,000 kg (575,000 tonnes) of CO_2 emissions, or about a 5 per cent reduction in greenhouse gas emissions in the USA – just from reorganising the use of police vehicles in large cities.

One might imagine other transformations of US policing that would reduce environmental stress such as the use of smaller, decentralised police stations with more limited need for gasoline-powered vehicle patrols. These station houses would be fitted with solar and wind collectors and geothermal energy, reducing the police drain on the electrical grid, and providing the fuel needed for alternative energy police cars, and the ability to channel any excess energy back to communities, which could be used for street lights, lowering public consumption of electricity and the municipal electricity bill. At the same time, police would become more visible in communities, enhancing police–community relations. And, more importantly, policing would become greener and less environmentally destructive.

To be sure, we could extend our vision to green prisons and jails, all of which could be solar equipped or fitted for geothermal heating and cooling. Large, remote prisons, common in the USA, could feature electrical wind farms, producing green energy for prison use, which could also be stored for emergency use or channelled back to the electrical grid. Inmates could be taught relevant job skills for a new green economy such as installing and maintaining solar, geothermal, and wind equipment. For example, in Arizona, the Department of Corrections uses solar panels to produce energy at one facility (May *et al.* 2000). In the few short months the panels were in operation, the energy savings were substantial – nearly 1 tonne of carbon dioxide, sulfur dioxide, and nitrogen oxide emissions. And, clearly, if this could be done with prisons and jails, one could imagine a green courthouse, or the proliferation of community courts that would be less energy intensive than the current centralised model preferred in the USA. These changes, which we imagine here, are within the realm of possibility, and constitute some of the issues criminologists can examine from a green perspective. These possibilities demonstrate how environmental concerns can influence the practice of criminal justice.

Moreover, since a bigger criminal justice system is not necessarily better – better in the sense that it reduces crime, or generates more justice, or that criminal justice expenditures are efficient (e.g. in terms of a ratio of expenditures to crime reduction savings) – attention ought also to be directed toward reducing the criminal justice system. Is it necessary for the USA to operate the world's largest prison system, one that incarcerates 1.6 million inmates at substantial costs? To make this determination, it is necessary to consider the definition of the term 'costs'. In traditional criminal justice policy analysis, costs that are typically system-related expenditures (e.g. the bill for hiring correctional personnel, building prisons, inmate upkeep, and financing). Costs, in this view, become a ratio of the cost of reducing one crime through the expenditures associated with expanding imprisonment.

From a green perspective, there are environmental costs to consider when assessing the overall costs of criminal justice policies such as expanding the prison system. These environmental costs include not only additional energy costs and consequently the costs of global warming, but also the environmental costs related to building, maintaining and expanding the prison system. This array of costs includes placing a value on numerous outcomes that ordinarily escape criminal justice policy examinations, including the costs of the loss of land designated for use as the prison grounds (e.g. conversion of natural space to concrete); the use of energy-intensive building materials for concrete walls and cells as well as razor-wire security perimeters; waste-water streams related to cleaning clothes, cells, dinner ware, and so forth; the loss of natural habitat that promotes the life cycle of specific species; and the global warming impact of each of these processes. While it could be argued that expanding the criminal justice system and punishing a larger number of offenders provides more 'criminal justice', this is being done at a cost to other forms of justice – in this case, environmental justice – the rights of the natural world to thrive, the rights of species that depend on natural spaces, and even the rights of humans to have natural spaces needed for human survival. What we are suggesting is that, at some point, not only do these environmental rights and issues need to be considered, but also that they outweigh the human desire for criminal justice.

The unequal distribution of global warming harms

As noted above, global warming is a global phenomenon with divergent outcomes. While some locations warm faster than others, or experience longer cold spells, or more or less precipitation, droughts, floods, or ice melts, globally temperatures rise, though in some locations they may fall in either the long or short term (Weart 2008), and some geographic locations experience these changes sooner than others or in more dramatic fashion.

In November 2001, planning began for the evacuation of more than 11,000 residents on the Tuvalu Islands due to rising sea level. The rising sea not only encroached on residences, but also seeped into the water supply (Brown 2001). A similar situation emerged in the Carteret Islands where the inhabitants of the village of Shishmaref in Alaska, faced evacuation as waves, normally buffered by sea ice, eroded the coast and invaded their village (NOAA 2007). Global warming has also impacted poor and native residents in other locations. In Bangladesh, for example, it has been estimated that 19,000 acres a year are lost to rising sea levels and river erosion associated with global warming. This estimate suggests that 1 million of the area's residents are affected (Gain 2002). Ironically, these examples illustrate that the first human settlements affected by global warming are those that contribute least to this problem. More importantly, these examples are just that – examples of what will happen more often as the Earth's temperature rises.

Poorer nations are most adversely impacted by global warming. In some locations, climate change produces conditions for the spread of insect-borne diseases and increases the likelihood of climate-related deaths, as warmer weather extends insect-breeding seasons (Epstein and Mills 2006). In effect, there is extensive inequality in the distribution of the harms caused by global warming. These inequalities, however, are not confined to less developed nations. In their study of heat-related mortality in six cities (Boston, Budapest, Dallas, Lisbon, London and Sydney), Gosling *et al.* (2007) indicated that summer heatwaves induced by global warming will increase heat-related mortality (see also Casimiro *et al.* 2006; on mortality during the 2003 heatwave in France, see Fouillet *et al.* 2006). Even in such situations, the poor are more likely to be victims of heat-related fatalities, as they lack resources for air-conditioning or necessary medical care, a problem evident in locations where such heatwaves have already occurred.

There are other inequalities related to global warming that must be addressed because they are central to taking up a green position such as the harms imposed upon non-human species. In what sense are these harms also inequalities? They are so because, it could be argued, non-human species harms are inflicted by humans in violation of the state of nature and its equilibrium. Moreover, one could argue that the following additional factors contribute to human–non-human inequality, including the extent to which non-human species: (1) cannot alter their situation because they lack the ability and power to do so; (2) do not produce the circumstances to which they are subjected; (3) are held captive in this process by human actions that abuse the environment and human inactions that fail to correct these imbalances. In effect, the harms that result from unequal power relations between human and non-human species could be defined as acts of domination (e.g. see Beirne 1999 for discussion).

International laws, regulations and treaties

One of the important areas to which criminologists might contribute is in the analysis and discussion of international laws, regulations and treaties related to climate change. On some level, international agreements such as the Kyoto Protocol will be required to help alleviate global warming. If nothing else, such agreements signal the kind of concerted, worldwide action needed to tackle global warming. Moreover, it strikes us that such agreements are necessary in order to fundamentally alter the worldwide free-market economic relationships and forces currently in place that facilitate global warming (Stretesky and Lynch 2009).

At the same time, international regulations are likely to be ineffective in social and economic contexts that continue to be oriented toward measuring human development solely in terms of economic outputs and levels of consumption (e.g. GDP; import/export balances). Altering the tendency to define human development solely in economic terms is a significantly large endeavour, one that requires more than regulation, and rather depends on the development of a new ethos that redefines concepts such as human development, success and achievement. This latter form of change requires that societies adopt 'new' philosophical orientations emphasising the sanctity of the environment, and devoted to concepts including sustainable development (Daly 1997). Doing so may require international agreements devoted to developing educational strategies that socialise new and existing generations of humans to accept the idea of sustainability and an environmentally sensitive existence based on constraining human appetites for continuous expansion. These agreements, if reached, cannot simply be imposed by developed nations on developing nations: they must include developed nations as more than target populations and allow them to contribute to building these programmes within the cultural context of each nation.

The future of crime?

The final topical area we touch upon is the future of crime in a world beset by global warming. We recognise that anything we say here is speculative and subject to future developments and investigation. As noted earlier, the impacts of global warming will be unequally distributed. One could imagine that the hardships caused by global warming will, in some locations, generate crime. At the same time, any changes that these impacts initiate in crime will also be distributed unequally and reflect the unequal development of global warming.

With respect to crime one might expect increases in forms of crime that, at first, emerge as accommodations to the consequences of global warming. In poorer nations and even in wealthier nations among the poor, these hardships may produce new forms of crime (food and water crimes), or black markets that develop around items people desire or need in a world impacted by global warming. Since a warming climate will produce 'ordinary' economic hardships such as recessions, declining food production and rising prices, one may also expect a rise in ordinary forms of property crime or even violence that results from frustration as responses to climate change.

In a more advanced scenario, additional violence might be expected as the victims of global warming react to their circumstances (e.g. unrelenting heatwaves, floods, droughts). In these cases, violence may result from frustration or as an outgrowth of the development of consciousness concerning the causes of these social problems. Again, one can only guess what might happen, but large-scale riots are not hard to imagine if conditions become severe (Carballo 2008).

In response to suppositions about the future of crime in a world impacted by global warming, an orthodox criminologist might respond that these predictions indicate a need to further expand social control in the form of emergency responses, policing and the correctional system. This type of response, of course, is misguided because it is oriented toward controlling the outcome rather than addressing the causes of the problem. In addition, the idea that an expanding criminal justice system can control crime produced by global warming is based on a traditional notion of doing justice in a criminal justice context, a context that ignores notions of environmental justice. Thus, addressing the future of crime in an era of global warming requires thinking about policies that alleviate the problem of global warming, not social control policies that address potential crime-related outcomes.

Conclusion

This chapter examined the criminological implications of global warming. There is little we can offer here in terms of a conclusion except to note that there is much work for criminologists to perform on this subject. And it is criminologists who must perform much of the work discussed above, applying the knowledge natural scientists have produced to an understanding of the criminological implications of global warming. Even if the nations of the world respond appropriately to global warming, a number of the issues discussed above will remain relevant for criminology in the decades ahead.

Notes

1 An exception is toxic crimes which have broad global effects that span nations, species and environmental medium effects (Lynch and Stretesky 2001; Lynch *et al.* 2006, 2008).

2 This list includes: (1) mountain top mining (Stretesky *et al.* 2008); (2) state-corporate crimes that facilitate global warming; (3) oil and coal exploration in ecologically sensitive regions; (4) automobile fuel economy regulations (Burns and Lynch 2002); (5) deforestation (Frank and Lynch 1992); (6) global warming pollution regulations and treaties including carbon trading markets; (7) green manufacturing processes and regulations (Lynch and Stretesky 2001, 2003); (8) logging and forestry regulations and management (Frank and Lynch 1992); (9) the intersection of environmental justice and global warming issues; (10) the differential impact of global warming on the poor within and across nations; (11) regulation of wetlands, rivers, lakes and streams as these relate to global warming; (12) alternative energy regulation and subsidies; (13) potential changes in the nature and distribution of crime in an age of global warming and potential policy responses; (14) the effects of global warming on species

(including plants, animals, microbes, and humans); (15) the relationship between international trade and the production of global warming gases (Stretesky and Lynch 2009); (16) the disruption of indigenous-based subsistence economies; (17) mass transportation plans, grants and other forms of funding; (18) the impact of global warming on the concentration and uptake of toxic pollutants.

References

Arrhenius, S. (1896) 'On the Influence of Carbonic Acid Upon the Temperature of the Ground', *Philosophical Magazine*, 41: 237–6.

Arrhenius, S. (1908) *Worlds in the Making*. New York: Harper & Brothers.

Bargagli, R. (2000) 'Trace Metals in Antarctica Related to Climate Change and Increasing Human Impact', *Reviews of Environmental Contamination and Toxicology*, 166: 129–73.

Beirne, P. (1999) 'For a Nonspeciesist Criminology: Animal Abuse as an Object of Study', *Criminology*, 37: 117–47.

Beirne, P. and South, N. (eds) (2006) *Green Criminology*. Aldershot: Ashgate.

Beirne, P. and South, N. (eds) (2007) *Issues in Green Criminology: Confronting Harms Against Environments, Other Animals and Humanity*. Cullompton: Willan Publishing.

Brown, L. (2001) 'Rising Sea Level Forces Evacuation of Island Country', Earth Policy Institute [online]. Available at: www.earth-policy.org/Updates/Update2.htm (accessed 3 December 2009).

Brownstein, J.S., Holford, T.R. and Fish, D. (2005) 'Effect of Climate Change on Lyme Disease Risk in North America', *EcoHealth*, 2(1): 38–46.

Burns, R.G. and Lynch, M.J. (2004) *Environmental Crime: A Sourcebook*. New York: LFB Scholarly.

Burns, R.G. and Lynch, M.J. (2002) 'Another Fine Mess ... a Preliminary Examination of the Use of Fines by the National Highway Traffic Safety Administration', *Criminal Justice Review*, 27 (1): 1–25.

Callendar, G.S. (1938) 'The Artificial Production of Carbon Dioxide and Its Influence on Temperature', *Quarterly Journal of the Royal Meteorological Society*, 64: 223–240.

Carballo, M. (2008) 'Climate Change, Migration and Health', *World Hospitals and Health Services*, 44: 47–48.

Casimiro, E., Calheiros, J., Santos, F.D. and Kovats, S. (2006) 'National Assessment of Human Health Effects of Climate Change in Portugal: Approach and Key Findings', *Environmental Health Perspectives*, 114: 1950–1956.

Chambliss, W.J. (1989) 'State-Organized Crime', *Criminology*, 27: 183–208.

Cowie, J. (2007) *Climate Change: Biological and Human Aspects*. Cambridge: Cambridge University Press.

Crowley, T.J. (2000) 'Causes of Climate Change over the Past 1000 Years', *Science*, 289: 270–276.

Daly, H. (1997) *Beyond Growth: The Economics of Sustainable Development*. Boston: Beacon Press.

Dovì, V.G., Friedler, F., Huisingh, D. and Klemes, J.J. (2009) 'Cleaner Energy for Sustainable Future', *Journal of Cleaner Production*, 17: 889–95.

Dudley, N., Jeanrenaud, J.P. and Sullivan, E. (1995). *Bad Harvest? The Timber Trade and the Degradation of the World's Forests*. London: Earthscan.

Epstein, P.R. and Mills, R. (eds) (2006) *Climate Change Futures: Health, Ecological and Economic Dimensions*. Boston, MA: Harvard Medical School Center for Health and the Global Environment [online]. Available at: http://chge.med.harvard.edu/programs/ccf/documents/ccf_report_oct_06.pdf (accessed 3 December 2009).

Evans, D.B., Tandon, A., Murray, C.J.L. and Lauer, J.A. (2001) 'Comparative Efficiency of National Health Systems: Cross National Econometric Analysis', *British Medical Journal*, 323: 307–10.

Fouillet, A., Rey, G., Laurent, F. *et al.* (2006) 'Excess Mortality Related to the August 2003 Heat Wave in France', *International Archives of Occupational Environmental Health*, 80 (1): 16–24.

Frank, N. and Lynch, M.J. (1992) *Corporate Crime, Corporate Violence*. Albany, NY: Harrow and Heston.

Gain, P. (ed.) (2002) *Bangladesh Environment: Facing the 21st Century*. Dhaka: Society for Environment and Human Development.

Gosling, S.N., McGregor, G.R. and Páldy, A. (2007) 'Climate Change and Heat-Related Mortality in Six Cities. Part 1: Model Construction and Validation', *International Journal of Biometeorology*, 51 (6): 525–40.

Gosling, S.N., McGregor, G.R. and Lowe, J.A. (2008) 'Climate Change and Heat-Related Mortality in Six Cities. Part 2: Climate Model Evaluation and Projected Impacts from Changes in the Mean and Variability of Temperature with Climate Change', *International Journal of Biometeorology*, 53 (1): 31–51.

Harlan, S.L., Brazel, A.J., Prashad, L. *et al.* (2006) 'Neighborhood Microclimates and Vulnerability to Heat Stress', *Social Science and Medicine*, 63: 2847–63.

Hulburt, E.O. (1931) 'The Temperature of the Lower Atmosphere of the Earth', *Physical Review*, (38): 1876–1890.

Humphreys, W.J. (1920) *Physics of the Air*. Philadelphia: J.B. Lippincott.

IPCC (Intergovernmental Panel on Climate Change) (2007) *Climate Change 2007: Synthesis Report*. Contribution of Working Groups I, II and III to the Fourth Assessment Report of the Intergovernmental Panel on Climate Change [Core Writing Team, R.K. Pachauri and A. Reisinger (eds)]. Geneva: IPCC, 104 pp.

Jennsen, B. (2006) 'Endocrine-Disrupting Chemical and Climate Change: A Worst Case Combination for Arctic Marine Mammals and Seabirds?', *Environmental Health Perspectives*, 114: 76–80.

Korpi, W. and Palme, J. (1998) 'The Paradox of Redistribution and Strategies of Equality: Welfare State Institutions, Inequality, and Poverty in the Western Countries', *American Sociological Review*, 63: 661–87.

Lovelock, J. (2006) *The Revenge of Gaia: Earth's Climate Crisis and the Fate of Humanity.* New York: Basic Books.

Lynch, M.J. (2007a) [1990] 'The Greening of Criminology: A Perspective for the 1990s', in P. Beirne and N. South (eds), *Green Criminology*. Aldershot: Ashgate [originally published in *The Critical Criminologist*, 1990, 2 (3): 3–4,11–12].

Lynch, M.J. (2007b) *Big Prisons, Big Dreams: Crime and the Failure of the US Prison System.* New Brunswick, NJ: Rutgers University Press.

Lynch, M.J. and Stretesky, P.B. (2001) 'Toxic Crimes: Examining Corporate Victimization of the General Public Employing Medical and Epidemiological Evidence', *Critical Criminology*, 10 (3): 153–72.

Lynch, M.J. and Stretesky, P.B. (2003) 'The Meaning of Green: Contrasting Criminological Perspectives', *Theoretical Criminology*, 7 (2): 217–38.

Lynch, M.J., Schwendinger, H. and Schwendinger, J. (2006) 'The Status of Empirical Research in Radical Criminology', in F.T. Cullen, J.P. Wright and K.R. Blevins (eds), *Taking Stock: The Status of Criminological Theory.* Advances in Criminological Theory, vol. 15. New Brunswick, NJ: Transaction.

Lynch, M.J., Burns, R.G. and Stretesky, P.B. (2008) *Environmental Crime, Law and Justice: An Introduction.* New York: LFB Scholarly.

Mann, M.E., Bradley, R.S. and Hughes, M.K. (1998) 'Global-Scale Temperature Patterns and Climate Forcing over the Past Six Centuries', *Nature*, 392: 779–787.

Markowitz, G. and Rosner, D. (2003) *Deceit and Denial: The Deadly Politics of Industrial Pollution.* Berkeley, CA: University of California Press.

May, K.G. Barker, G., Hancock, E. *et al.* (2000) 'Performance of a Large Parabolic Trough Solar Water Heating System at Phoenix Federal Correctional Institution', *Journal of Solar Energy Engineering*, 122: 165–69.

Mayer, F.L., Marking, G.E., Brecken, J.A. *et al.* (1991). 'Physico-chemical Factors Affecting Toxicity: pH, Salinity, and Temperature. Part 1: Literature Review.' EPA 600/X-89/033. Gulf Breeze, FL: US Environmental Protection Agency.

McKibben, B. (1989) *The End of Nature*. New York: Random House.

Michael, A.J., Campbell-Lendrum, D.H., Corvalan, C.F. *et al.* (2003) *Climate Change and Human Health: Risks and Responses.* Geneva: World Health Organisation.

Michalowski, R.J. and Kramer, R. (eds) (2006) *State-Corporate Crime: Wrongdoing at the Intersection of Business and Government.* New Brunswick, NJ: Rutgers University Press.

Moynihan, D.P. (1993) 'What Is Normal? Defining Deviancy Down', *American Scholar*, 62: 10–18.

NOAA (National Oceanic and Atmospheric Administration) (2007) 'Human and Economic Indicators – Shishmmaref'. Arctic Change: A Near-Realtime

Arctic Change Indicator Website [online]. Available at: www.arctic.noaa.gov/detect/human-shishmaref.shtml (accessed 3 December 2009).

Noyes, P.D., McElwee, M.K., Miller, H.D. *et al.* (2009) 'The Toxicology of Climate Change: Environmental Contaminants in a Warming World', *Environment International*, 35: 971–986.

Office of Air and Radiation (US) (2009) 'Frequenctly Asked Questions About Global Warming and Climate Change: Back to Basics', United States Environmental Protection Agency, Washington, DC.

Patra, R.W., Chapman, J.C., Lim, R.P. and Gehrke, P.C. (2007) 'The Effects of Three Organic Chemicals on the Upper Thermal Tolerances of Four Freshwater Fishes', *Environmental Toxicology and Chemistry*, 26 (7): 1454–59.

Pearce, F. (2008) *With Speed and Violence: Why Scientists Fear Tipping Points in Climate Change*. Boston, MA: Beacon Press.

Plass, G.N. (1956a) 'Infrared Radiation in the Atmosphere', *American Journal of Physics*, 24: 303–21.

Plass, G.N. (1959b) 'Carbon Dioxide and the Climate', *American Scientist*, 44: 302–16.

Plass, G.N. (1959) 'Carbon Dioxide and Climate', *Scientific American*, 201(1): 41–47.

Richards, V.L. and Beitinger, T.L. (1995) 'Reciprocal Influences of Temperature and Copper on Survival of Fathead Minnows, *Pimephales promelas*', *Bulletin of Environmental Contamination and Toxicology*, 55: 230–36.

Santer, B.D., Taylor, K.E., Wigley, T.M.L. *et al.* (1996) 'A Search for Human Influences on the Thermal Structure of the Atmosphere', *Nature*, 382: 39–46.

South, N. (1997) 'A Green Field for Criminology? A Proposal for a Perspective', *Theoretical Criminology*, 2 (2): 211–33.

Stretesky, P.B. and Lynch, M.J. (2009) 'A Cross-National Study of the Association Between Per Capita Carbon Dioxide Emissions and Exports to the United States', *Social Science Research*, 38: 239–50.

Tett, S.F.B., Stott, P.A., Allen, M.R. *et al.* (1999) 'Causes of Twentieth-Century Temperature Change Near the Earth's Surface', *Nature*, 399: 569–72.

Tyndall, J. (1861) 'On the Absorption and Radiation of Heat by Gases and Vapours', *Philosophical Magazine*, 4 (22): 169–94, 273–85.

Tyndall, J. (1863) 'On Radiation Through the Earth's Atmosphere', *Philosophical Magazine*, 4 (24): 200–06.

Tyndall, J. (1873) *Contributions to Molecular Physics in the Domain of Radiant Heat*. New York: Appleton.

Wackernagel, M., Onisto, L., Bello, P. *et al.* (1999) 'National Natural Capital Accounting with the Ecological Footprint Concept', *Ecological Economics*, 29: 375–90.

Wearth, S. 2008. *The Discovery of Global Warming*. Cambridge, MA: Harvard University Press.

White, R. (1994) 'Green Politics and the Question of Population', *Journal of Australian Studies*, 40: 27–43.
White, R. (2008) *Crimes Against Nature: Environmental Criminology and Ecological Justice.* Cullompton: Willan Publishing.
Ziska, L.H., Epstein, P.R. and Schlesinger, W.H. (2009) 'Rising CO_2, Climate Change, and Public Health: Exploring the Links to Plant Biology', *Environmental Health Perspectives*, 117 (2): 155–58.

Part II

Specific issues

Chapter 5

The Canadian-Alberta tar sands: a case study of state-corporate environmental crime

Russell Smandych and Rodney Kueneman

Introduction

This chapter offers a critical criminological analysis of the environmental degradation being wrought by the Alberta tar sands project in Canada. There are opposing views in Canada (between corporate and governmental greenwashers, and their critics) over the use of the term 'tar sands', rather than the less-dirty-sounding term 'oil sands'. The term 'tar sands' best describes the immense, multinational state–corporate project that is currently under way in the northern part of the province of Alberta, since the task is to extract and refine naturally created, tar-bearing sand into exportable and consumable oil. What is undeniable is that the tar sands project, as we have chosen to call it, is having profound effects on Canada's economy and ecology, its diplomatic and trade relations with the USA, and its ability to create Canadian energy security. It is also, concomitantly, affecting Canada's capacity as a sovereign nation to sign and follow up on international treaties and protocols aimed at reducing forms of global environmental degradation, including global warming, carbon dioxide emissions, environmental pollution, and water depletion. Among its recent critics, the Alberta tar sands project has been described as 'the world's biggest energy project' and 'one of the world's most fantastic concentrations of toxic waste' (Nikiforuk 2008: 78), as 'Canada's number one global warming machine' (Clarke 2008: 149), and as a key cause of the 'environmental Armageddon' now confronting Canadians (Marsden 2008).

In this chapter, we provide a description of the enormity of the environmental carnage being caused by the Alberta tar sands project along with an analysis of the factors driving the tar sands development boom in Canada since the 1980s. In addition, we offer an assessment of the harm to the ecosystem, humans, and other animal species it has caused to date, and which is projected to worsen in the future if the predicted growth of operations materialises over the next decade. While the ecological issues raised by the current and future-projected development of Alberta's 'oil sands' have been discussed widely in Canada and the USA by politicians, environmental activists, and an array of other interest groups with a stake in Alberta's oil patch, to our knowledge this chapter represents the first attempt to apply a green criminological perspective to examining the nature, growth, and potential outcomes of this glaring case of human-caused global environmental harm. In line with White's (2008: 274) prescriptions for doing 'critical environmental criminology', our primary concern in this chapter is to provide an account of 'social forces and actors involved in portraying, causing' and 'responding to' the environmental issues raised by the Alberta tar sands project.

With regard to the most prominent social forces and actors we argue, first and foremost, that since the late 1980s Canada has in effect surrendered sovereignty over its energy resources to the USA. Achieved by way of the myopic decisions made by various federal and Alberta provincial governments, this has contributed to a more secure supply of energy to the USA for its domestic and military purposes, at the expense of energy independence for Canada, which, unlike most other developed countries, does not have a national energy plan aimed at guaranteeing long-term energy security. Specifically, we show that this disturbing state of affairs is the deliberate result of the efforts by the Conservative government of the Province of Alberta – and, more recently, the closely allied Conservative federal government of Canada – working hand-in-hand with the oil industry – that is, mainly US-based multinational energy corporations. Together they have discouraged open public scrutiny and potential opposition to the development of the Alberta tar sands, thereby significantly reducing the likelihood of successful interventions by environmental regulatory agencies, and smothering the public awareness needed to begin labelling the environmental destruction, and the animal and human suffering caused by tar sands development as 'criminal' activity (Ermann and Clements 1987). Drawing on the insights of a global environmental criminology, we discuss the implications of the findings of this case study for taking action against multinational energy corporations and their political backers in the Alberta tar sands development, as well as for understanding and responding to similar cases of state–corporate crime and the politics of the denial of environmental harm occurring elsewhere in the world.

Conventional and contested 'facts' about Alberta's tar sands

It is important to describe at the outset some of the conventional (relatively widely agreed upon) and other contested 'facts' claimed about Alberta's tar sands development by proponents and critics of the project. While on some matters, there are only small differences of opinion between the two groups, on other issues tar sands backers and their opponents are fundamentally divided in their interpretation of the nature and consequences of tar sands development. Particular attention is given here to variously claimed 'facts' about the ecological importance of the geographical area in which it is located, the major government and energy industry players in the tar sands, the techniques used for extracting crude oil, and the amount of 'recoverable' oil and likely degree of future growth in tar sands production in Alberta and the neighbouring province of Saskatchewan. Although governments and the oil industry knew of the existence and potential profitability of the tar sands as a source of crude oil for much of the twentieth century, the aggressive state–corporate development of the tar sands did not take off until the 1990s.

The location of the tar sands: what is there to lose?

The promoters of tar sands expansion would like us to believe that northern Alberta is an empty desolate place waiting to be 'developed'. However, it is significant that of the 13 World Heritage Sites that exist in Canada, five can be found in the province of Alberta. One of these World Heritage Sites, the Wood Buffalo National Park, which is the second largest national park in the world, lies not far to the north and downstream from the current major tar sands development. The park is quaintly described in online tourist travel information produced by the government of Alberta as a 'vast chunk of lonely boreal forest and shallow lakes … home to the world's largest free-roaming herd of wood bison' and 'the last natural nesting habitat of the rare whooping crane' (Travel Alberta Canada: Scenic Road Trips, UNESCO Trail; accessed 6 February 2009). While ecologically important in itself, this World Heritage Site is only part of the picture. Prior to the arrival of the oil companies and tar sands development, much of northern Alberta was covered by pristine boreal forest stands, which were also home to many other animals including bears, wolves, caribou, and lynx, and which even today continue to provide a breeding ground for up to '30 percent of North America's songbirds and 40 percent of [North America's] waterfowl' (Juhasz 2008: 291). Although until recently the human population of the region was small relative to the existing land mass and waterways, northern Alberta has long been part of the traditional territory of 'several native or First Nations communities, including the Mikisew Cree, Athabasca Chipewyan, Dehcho, Akaitcho Dene, and Woodland Cree' (Juhasz 2008: 291; Marsden 2008).

The current major tar sands operations are located in three primary districts – the Peace, Athabasca, and Cold Lake districts – surrounding the booming hub city of Fort McMurray (Clarke 2008: 20). Fort McMurray is located within the large amalgamated municipality of Wood Buffalo, which, at 68,450 km^2, is 'twice the size of Belgium, equal to Ireland and only slightly smaller than Austria' (Marsden 2008: 137), or also roughly the size of Tasmania (Nikiforuk 2008: 39). This region is also located within the much larger 'Mackenzie River Basin', which encompasses a vast territory of lands (including boreal forest and tundra) and waterways (including the massive Athabasca and Mackenzie rivers) that flow northward from central Alberta and British Columbia to the Arctic Beaufort Sea (Nikiforuk 2008: 60). Environmental scientists point out that the boreal forest that still covers much of this territory is crucial for the health of the world's ecosystem. Specifically, scientists have referred to Canada's boreal forest as 'the northern lungs of the planet', comparing them to the planet's 'southern lungs' including the tropical rainforests of Africa and South America (Nikiforuk 2008: 149). The main reason for this designation is that boreal ecosystems have 'the potential to recapture more carbon from greenhouse gas emissions than any other ecosystem in the world', while 'boreal peat lands, soils and trees are a natural storehouse for carbon' (Nikiforuk 2008: 149). This region provides ecological services which are priceless to humans and other animal and plant species. However, according to the logic of the industry and government supporters of tar sands development, all of these important uses of the biosphere are worthless to capital since it cannot invest in them in order to gather a return on an investment. For capital, the only thing of value in this landscape is the tar sand deposits. As such, it is hardly surprising that all of the activity sponsored by the oil companies is directed at extracting this resource, a process that, if not strictly controlled, will continue to destroy the ecosphere and assail the interests of indigenous peoples and harm the other life forms in the region.

Fort McMurray, which is at the centre of tar sands development activity, has grown from a small town 'of a few thousands trappers and salt miners' in the 1960s, to a population of 34,000 in 1996, and 65,400 in 2007, and until recently (that is, before the global recession took hold in Canada in the last quarter of 2008), it was predicted that the population would grow to 100,000 sometime between 2010 and 2012 (Marsden 2008: 137; Fort McMurray 2009; Krugel 2009). Although the global economic meltdown of 2008 put a temporary hold on investment in the tar sands, oil companies have once again ramped up production goals (Healing 2009).

Major government and energy industry players

Following on the heels of the early tar sands 'pioneers' Syncrude and Suncor, numerous well-known multinationals and a host of smaller Canadian-based companies have collectively invested billions of dollars in the tar sands. The largest of these include the 'international conglomerate', Shell Oil; 'the third largest US petroleum company', ConocoPhillips; 'the world's largest oil giant', ExxonMobil; the growing Canadian-based players Canadian Natural Resources Ltd., and Petro-Canada; and the other foreign-controlled corporations, Husky Energy (private, '70 per cent owned by Li Ka-shing'), Sinopec ('China's largest refiner and marketer of petroleum products'), and Total SA (of France) (Clarke 2008: 83-85). These energy companies are very large, powerful and skilled in negotiating favourable terms with governments.

It would be easy to simply blame the 'Big Oil' multinationals for the 'ecological nightmare' (Clarke 2008: 148) that is unfolding in northern Alberta and coming to haunt other parts of North America. On a global scale, they are the major players who are driving the development of this energy resource as conventional oil supplies have peaked and overall consumption levels continue to grow worldwide. However, the tar sands picture would also look very different today if it were not for decisions made in the past by both federal Canadian and provincial Alberta governments concerning 'free trade' with the USA and the effective 'deregulation' of the Alberta oil industry, including tar sands development. There is also evidence that the government of Alberta has actively pursued a 'greenwashing' campaign aimed at countering scientific data and arguments regarding the ecological and human harms linked to the development of the tar sands.

The cementing of Canada's position as a major energy supplier to the USA occurred in 1989 with the signing of the Canada–USA Free Trade Agreement (FTA), which contained a 'proportional sharing clause' (in Article 904) that 'obligated Canada to provide continuous exports of energy resources to the US'. Under this rule, which Brian Mulroney's Conservative federal government agreed to as one of the 'bargaining chips' to get US negotiators to sign the deal, 'Canada was prohibited from placing a ban or even a quota on its exports of oil and natural gas to the US, even in times of critical domestic shortages, unless Canadian consumption were cut back by a proportional amount' (Clarke 2008: 45–46; Marsden 2008: 73). To assert that the FTA made Canada's oil and natural gas a 'continental resource to be shared with the US' is not meant to cynically imply that there was somehow a dark, hidden agenda underlying the agreement, since at the time it was signed, Prime Minister Mulroney himself publicly stated that 'the practice of preserving portions of Canada's oil reserves for Canadians was "odious" and had to be abandoned in order to finalize a free-trade deal with the US that had many other distinct advantages for Canada' (Clarke 2008: 45). In 1994, Canada signed an additional North American Free Trade Agreement (NAFTA) with the USA and Mexico, which continues to obligate Canada to share its energy resources with the USA, under the 'proportionality clause' contained in Article 605. While Canada's NAFTA negotiators caved in to 'U.S. insistence' on this clause, Mexico did not agree to it because 'Mexican negotiators realized the clause could severely limit the country's sovereignty over its own vital energy resources' (Marsden 2008: 74).

Canadian critics of the FTA and NAFTA widely agree that 'Canada has effectively surrendered its sovereignty over the country's energy resources through the new free trade regime' and that in doing so it has become the USA's leading 'energy satellite' (Clarke 2008: 110–111). While Canada's more recent Conservative prime minister, Stephen Harper, has described Canada as an 'energy superpower', it is more accurate to recognise that it is an 'energy pussycat' (Clarke 2008: 79). Whichever term one might choose to use, there is no doubt that the signing of the FTA and the NAFTA has helped transform the Canadian economy into one that is even more dependent than ever on the extraction and exporting of natural resources, and particularly oil.

However, it is quite disconcerting to find that few Canadians and even fewer Americas know how important Canada has become to the USA as a relatively politically stable and secure energy provider.

As Andrew Nikiforuk (2008: 30) points out, thanks to NAFTA and the Alberta tar sands boom, by 1999 Canada 'had become the largest foreign supplier of oil to the United States', and by 2002, it 'had officially replaced Saudi Arabia and Mexico as America's number-one oil source'. Currently, Canada supplies 18 per cent of US oil imports (equal to 12 per cent of US consumption), and the continuing development of the tar sands is expected to double or triple these figures. Describing it differently, Antonia Juhasz (2008: 296) points out that currently 'Three-fourths of Canada's oil exports go to the United States', and that 'while Canada's domestic demand for oil has stabilized, its exports to the United States continue to climb. Thus, while Canadians get the land, air, and water pollution of tar sands production, the United States gets most of the oil.' In the absence of a west–east pipeline in Canada and the absence of a Canadian energy policy, oil is shipped south to the USA while Ontario, Quebec, and the Maritime Provinces in Canada import oil from unstable Middle East sources. In keeping with the NAFTA proportionality clause, the only way that Canada could ship oil to eastern provinces would be to increase the overall rate of oil extraction to keep the US imports proportional.

Techniques used for extracting crude oil: why is it so damaging?

While it is known that the first users of tar sands were local, indigenous peoples, who even before contact with Europeans used the sticky tar to seal their canoes, it was not until the early twentieth century that scientists working for the Canadian government, and later the Alberta government, took an interest in the tar sands, recognising it for its potential value as a source of crude oil. The tar sands in the Fort McMurray region consists of a mixture of 85 per cent sand, clay, and silt; 5 per cent water, and 10 per cent crude bitumen (Juhasz 2008: 292). By the middle of 2008, there were 69 tar sands projects under way and many more being planned for start-up over the next decade (Clarke 2008: 82). While a range of methods of mining bitumen were proposed and experimented with over the years (Marsden 2008), two methods are in use today: the surface 'strip-mining method' and the underground '*in situ* method' of bitumen extraction, both of which are environmentally disastrous. While strip mining destroys boreal forest and creates millions of gallons of toxic waste, underground '*in situ*' mining uses pressurised steam, created with large quantities of water heated by natural gas, to soften tar so it can be pumped to the surface.

While the damaging ecological and human health effects of these mining techniques could be described at length, the ones that have attracted greatest attention, both from environmental groups in Canada and, more recently, internationally (Macdonald 2009; Mouawad 2009), include the devastation of the boreal forest, the pollution of the Athabasca watershed, and the depletion of Canada's natural-gas reserves. For example, Syncrude Canada Ltd operates 'the largest open-pit mining operation in the world' close to Fort McMurray, currently consisting of two mines, the larger one (the North Mine) having a triangular shape measuring 22 by 21 by 21 km, and the smaller one (the Aurora mine) having a rectangular shape measuring 12 by 6 km. However, 'these mines represent only about a quarter of Syncrude's eight oil sands leases, which total approximately 250,000 acres.' Overall, the current open-pit mining leases held by multinational and Canadian-based companies in northern Alberta cover 'an area equivalent in size to the state of Florida' (Marsden 2008: 145-146). There is also growing evidence that massive tailing ponds, which are supposed to permanently contain the toxic waste and polluted water created from the open-pit mining process, are allowing toxins to leach into the Athabasca watershed and enter the animal and human food chain.

With regard to *in situ* mining, a major concern is that it uses enormous amounts of both fresh water and cleaner-burning, expensive natural gas. While it is hard to disentangle the amount of natural gas and water consumed through strip-mining as opposed to the even more 'energy-intensive process' of *in situ* extraction (Juhasz 2008: 293), the overall combined estimates are staggering. In 2005, Canada produced 6.2 trillion (US measure) cubic feet (TCF) of natural gas, 3.7 TCF of which was shipped to the USA, and of the remaining roughly 2.5 TCF (or 40 per cent) left for Canadians, tar sands production is annually consuming an increasing proportion. In 2006, the tar sands demand rose to about 300 million cubic feet per day, and the Alberta government predicted (in mid-2008) that by 2015, natural-gas consumption in the tar sands would triple. If this prediction holds true, by 2015 tar sands production will use the equivalent of about one-third of Canada's current annual domestic natural gas consumption (Marsden 2008: 120). With respect to water consumption, annually since 2005, 'water withdrawals from the Athabasca River system' for both mining and *in situ* operations have 'amounted to more than twice the volume of water used annually by the entire population of Calgary (population 1.2 million)' (Clarke 2008: 162), and, unlike many other types of industrial water use, very little of the water used in tar sands oil production can be reintroduced to the environment because of the high concentrations of toxins.

Estimates of 'recoverable' crude oil and the future of the tar sands

A further appreciation of reasons behind the expansion of the Alberta tar sands over the last decade can be gained by looking at estimates of 'recoverable' crude oil. Oil industry analysts and critics make a distinction between estimates based on the use of 'available technology' and yet-to-be developed technology. For example, Juhasz (2008: 292) notes: 'Using available technology, an estimated 175 billion barrels of oil are believed to be lurking in Alberta's tar', and that this figure 'is second only to Saudi Arabia's 260 billion barrels of conventional oil reserves'. However, she also highlights that '[t]ar sands-boosters claim that as much as 1.7 *trillion* barrels of crude will be found, if and when the right technology becomes available.' Similarly, Clarke (2008: 18–19) notes that '[e]stimates put the total amount of potential crude oil' in the Alberta tar sands 'at a whopping 2.5 trillion barrels'; however, 'only a portion' (between 175 and 200 billion barrels) 'is recoverable' given 'current technologies'. At the same time, he cites the more optimistic estimate, based on different assumptions and a different notion of 'recoverability', offered by the Canadian Association of Petroleum Producers, which predicts 'that there are some 315 billion barrels of recoverable crude oil in the [Alberta] tar sands, a greater reserve than that of Saudi Arabia', and an additional 1.1 billion barrels in the smaller tar sands of Saskatchewan.

Given these estimates, regardless of which one you choose, combined with the geopolitical military concerns of the USA since 11 September 2001, it is not hard to understand why multinational energy corporations have invested heavily in the tar sands in recent years. Indeed, the last 15 years have seen spectacular growth in tar sands investment. Juhasz (2008: 295) also notes: 'Plans for an overall fivefold expansion in production across the tar sands have been facilitated in part by streamlined environmental regulations for new projects', a point that we will take up in a later section of this chapter. From a global environmental criminology perspective, the question we must turn to now is, to what extent should the actors involved in portraying, causing and profiting from (White 2008: 274) the development and continued growth of the Alberta tar sands industry be viewed as engaging in a form of state–corporate environmental crime?

State–corporate environmental crime

The concept of state–corporate environmental crime used in this study is developed as an extension of the definition of state–corporate crime introduced and refined mainly in the work of Ronald Kramer and Raymond Michalowski (Aulette and Michalowski 1993; Kramer and Michalowski 1993; Kramer *et al.* 2002). Although it must be acknowledged that the concept owes much to Richard Quinney's earlier work of the 1970s on 'the construction of political power in a capitalist society', the more immediate inspiration of the development of the concept was Kramer's attempt to develop a criminological perspective on the Challenger space-shuttle 'disaster' that occurred in 1986 (Kramer *et al.* 2002: 268).

In working with Michalowski and others, the concept was refined to take the following form: 'State–corporate crimes are illegal or socially injurious actions that result from a mutually reinforcing interaction between (1) policies and/or practices in pursuit of the goals of one or more institutions of political governance and (2) policies and/or practices in pursuit of the goals of one or more institutions of economic production and distribution' (Aulette and Michalowski 1993: 175). This concept is useful for the study of environmental crime for several reasons. First, it allows for the study of state–corporate activities 'where government omissions [such as lax environmental regulations] permit corporations to pursue illegal and potentially harmful courses of action that, in a general way, facilitate the fulfillment of certain state policies' (Kramer *et al.* 2002: 271).

Secondly, it allows for a deeper probing of the causes of state–corporate crime by recognising that it can take two different forms: 'state-initiated corporate crime' (such as the Challenger explosion), which occurs 'when corporations, employed by the government' engage 'in organizational deviance at the direction of, or with the tacit approval of, the government', and 'state-facilitated corporate crime' (such as the Imperial Food Products fire in Hamlet, North Carolina) (Aulette and Michalowski 1993), which occurs 'when government regulatory institutions' fail 'to restrain deviant business activities, either because of direct collusion between business and government or because they adhere to shared goals whose attainment would be hampered by aggressive regulation' (Kramer *et al.* 2002: 272).

In addition, the concept importantly recognises that, given the nature of the construction of political power in a capitalist society (see Quinney), any definition of 'environmental crime' also needs to allow for the study of 'socially injurious' and 'deviant' actions that are not necessary defined currently as 'illegal' or 'criminal' by the state. In our view, this definition of state–corporate crime is ideally suited to study the acts of commission and omission carried out by various levels of government in collusion with energy corporations in the Alberta tar sands that are responsible for causing a range of different types of harm to the ecosystem and animals, including humans. In the following discussion, we illustrate the suitability of this concept for examining government and corporate greenwashing, the manipulation of environmental regulations, ecological destruction, and the health effects of Alberta tar sands development on humans and other animal species.

Government and corporate greenwashing

In part, the Alberta tar sands development stands out as a case of state–corporate environmental crime because of the extent to which it involves consciously planned and executed campaigns aimed at deceiving the public about the actual harms and risks posed by the aggressive expansion of the tar sands. In 1999, the *Oxford English Dictionary* added the word 'greenwash', which it defined as 'disinformation disseminated by an organization so as to present an environmentally responsible public image' (cited in Holcomb 2008: 203). Holcomb (2008: 205) points out that the Internet is beginning to play 'a significant role in greenwashing, as corporate websites and environmental websites often offer quite different pictures'. Holcomb claims that, overall, corporate greenwashing campaigns often appear to have the upper hand, mainly because 'when conflicting information regarding environmental practices is so readily available' people may 'become discouraged by inconsistent reports' (Holcomb 2008: 205). Holcomb (2008: 210) concludes that '[c]orporate offenders seem to be beyond the reach of the law and its justice system' and '[g]reenwashing helps them achieve and maintain this status because it misleads consumers and leaves "reality" in doubt'.

Other recent research lends support to the view that the greenwashing efforts of governments and corporations can have serious environmental and social impacts (MacDonald 2008; Vos 2009). With respect to environmental impacts, Vos (2009: 685) argues that 'many of the world's biggest greenwashers are the world's biggest polluters' and that 'greenwashing often leads to more egregious offenses from corporations that already cause large shares of the problems.' In a similar vein, in her recent comprehensive study of the cooptation of conservation groups by corporations, Macdonald (2008: 177) offers the example of how giant home-building and retailing companies in the USA (like Centex, Home Depot, and Walmart), whose enterprises have contributed significantly to deforestation and urban sprawl, have proved able to respond quickly and effectively to 'the wrath' of 'militant environmental groups' through greenwashing strategies that entail improving their public image by purchasing 'reputational insurance' from more moderate and high-profile conservation groups; this, in turn, enables them to avoid taking more genuine steps to reduce their environmental footprint. Regarding the possible social impacts of greenwashing, Vos (2009: 686–687) notes that there is a risk to their legitimacy when 'greenwashing corporations attempt to hide their moral wrongs' by 'obfuscating the damage they do to ecosystems'. The uncovering of such subterfuge can also increase public disillusionment when corporations are exposed for 'misleading customers and destroying ecosystems'. While both militant and more moderate environmental and conservation groups are now focusing attention on the Alberta tar sands, it is also apparent that the greenwashing efforts of the state–corporate backers of Alberta tar sands expansion are continuing to have their intended environmental and social effects.

While the state and corporate players know that the tar sands extraction process is very toxic and ecologically harmful, they have deliberately sought to suppress this information and to provide misinformation in its stead. One clear example of deception on the part of the government of Alberta, and in particular Ralph Klein, dates from the late 1980s, when he was the province's environment minister. In 1988, the Energy Efficiency Branch of the provincial Department of Energy produced a discussion paper on the link between carbon dioxide emissions and global warming and outlined the steps that could taken to reduce Alberta's greenhouse gas emissions by 20 per cent below 1988 levels by 2005. While the former premier, Ralph Klein, was environment minister, the report was hidden away in the government's archives, and after he became premier 'he terminated the Energy Efficiency Branch and promptly slashed budgets related to renewable energy and environmental protection.' In addition, throughout the 1990s, 'Klein and his ministers openly campaigned against the Kyoto Accord' and 'members of Klein's Conservative Party and the former Reform and Alliance Parties', in collaboration with oil industry representatives, 'were instrumental in forming an organization called Friends of Science, which steadfastly denied that global warming is caused by human activities and campaigned vigorously against Kyoto' (Clarke 2008: 150). By cultivating the notion that there was a lack of consensus in the scientific community between climate change and human economic activity, it provided the public with the psychologically attractive option of accepting the doubt rather than face the hard and increasingly frightening prospect that radical change in human activity is necessary to save our species from extinction.

Government and those businesses which stand to profit from such technologies have also been collectively responsible for popularising another psychologically attractive greenwashing proposal that the solution to greenhouse gas emissions from the tar sands resides in newly developed 'undertaker' technologies such as carbon capture and storage (CCS). As Andrew Nikiforuk (2008: 124) rather cynically notes regarding the most recent Canadian federal government CCS greenwashing initiative, 'With great fanfare and lots of adjectives – *tough* was the favourite – the Canadian government announced in March 2008 that it would create an innovative class of carbon undertakers subsidized by taxpayers. It was proposed that all new coal-fired plants and tar sands projects will capture their carbon dioxide, tidily compress the elusive climate changers (kind of like stuffing a body into a suitcase), and then inject the waste deep under the prairie by 2018. Following that, alert federal or provincial civil servants will monitor the carbon for thousands of years.'

Regarding the more recent involvement of the provincial government of Alberta in similar greenwashing efforts, Nikiforuk (2008: 160) argues that, like other 'petrostates' that 'know how to control the conversation of ordinary people', the Alberta government has explicitly attempted to shape public thinking on the tar sands by establishing a propaganda department called the provincial 'Public Affairs Bureau'. According to this critic, 'The Alberta government currently spends $14 million [CA$] a year and employs 117 full-time staff in its Public Affairs Bureau to tell Albertans what to think. It has devoted another CA$25 million to convincing both Alberta's citizens and the US oil consumers that the tar sands are greener than Kermit the Frog.' It needs to be noted that the Alberta government's propaganda bureau is not an isolated enterprise, but rather is in keeping with the global greenwashing efforts of the oil industry, which in recent years have included 'expensive media campaigns designed to convince the public that Big Oil's money is being put to good use – namely, that the companies are investing their vast wealth in clean, green, sustainable energy solutions' (Juhasz 2008: 276). Juhasz (2008: 281) argues that this is in fact one of Big Oil's biggest lies, and that, instead 'among the oil industry's primary "emerging energy technologies" are investments in "frontier hydrocarbons" – tar sands, oil shale, and gas-to-liquids – methods of oil extraction that are even more environmentally harmful and risky than traditional methods.' These are only a few examples of government and corporate greenwashing about the Alberta tar sands, but they should be sufficient to make the point, similar to the one made by Holcomb (2008), that greenwashing can be used to help multinational energy corporations remain beyond the reach of the law and the justice system.

Manipulation of environmental regulations

Perhaps an even better way to help corporations remain beyond the reach of the law is to make the law itself disappear (Snider 2000), and there is ample evidence that both Canadian federal and Alberta provincial governments have been party to the manipulation of environmental regulations to benefit those now exploiting the tar sands. It was noted earlier that when Ralph Klein became the premier of Alberta one of his first moves was to slash budgets related to energy renewal and environmental protection (Clarke 2008). However, there are many other such examples that can be documented to substantiate the argument that both the Alberta and Canadian governments have been complicit with multinational energy corporations in underfunding research on alternative energy sources (such as solar and wind power), and in gutting government environmental regulations that could have been used to reduce the ecological and human harms linked to unfettered tar sands development.

Environmental 'watchdog' or tar sands industry 'enabler'?

In a recent study of the ecological and human health costs of the tar sands and emerging opposition to tar sands development, Andres Hayden (2009: 10–11) points out that the corporate forces that would profit from such output expansion have consistently applied considerable political and economic power to protect tar sands growth from carbon constraints, while promoting 'business as usual' thinking that significantly undermined Canada's capacity to develop strong climate policies. This business-as-usual thinking, we argue, is also reflected in the way governments and oil companies have worked together to undermine previously mandated environmental protection policies and practices.

There is quite clear evidence that when the Harper Conservative government came to power in 2006, it undertook a well-planned attempt to create a 'firewall' around Alberta that would allow the tar sands industry to develop without federal government interference. Prior to being elected to Parliament, in 2001, Harper resided in Calgary where he 'was president of the right-wing National Citizens Coalition' and actively promoted "a stronger and more autonomous Alberta" '. Early in 2001, Harper's 'firewall' agenda for Alberta gained national attention when he 'outlined a set of proposals labelled an "Alberta Agenda"', and had the text published as an 'Open Letter to Ralph Klein' in the nationally circulated conservative newspaper, the *National Post*. In it, Harper said, 'It was imperative to take the initiative, to build a firewall around Alberta, to limit the extent to which an aggressive and hostile federal government can encroach upon legitimate provincial jurisdiction.' Not surprisingly, soon after they came to power in Ottawa, 'the Harper team' began 'quietly building a "firewall" around the tar sands, in collaboration with the oil companies and the Alberta government' (Clarke 2008: 104–106). A critical patch in this firewall was the Harper government's environmental regulations passed in 2007 and 2008 that introduced a schedule for the reduction of greenhouse gas emissions, and the government's CCS legislation. Although the 2007 regulations required that 'all other industries in Canada must comply immediately', the tar sands industry was not required to begin reducing greenhouse gas emissions until 2011, while the 2008 legislation stated that the tar sand industry had until 2018 to fully comply with the CCS initiative (Clarke 2008).

In effect, the Alberta government has been left to decide on its own how to put into place and enforce environmental regulations in the tar sands. In his aptly titled book, *Stupid to the Last Drop*, William Marsden notes that 'since 1993 the Alberta and federal environment departments have greatly reduced their monitoring of river flows and snow pack cover' for toxic pollutants downstream from the tar sands. In addition, he points out that since the early 1990s, when Klein became premier, 'the Alberta government has basically imposed a moratorium on serious environmental regulations until the sands have been fully exploited.' This was no doubt helped by the fact that the province also 'gutted its environment department' by reducing its staff by one-third and by closing its chemistry laboratory, to the point that it 'now has neither the manpower nor the tools to monitor climate change, or even to enforce environmental laws' (Marsden 2008: 73, 110–111). According to the Toronto-based environmental interest group Environmental Defence, in its report on *Canada's Toxic Tar Sands* (2008: 5), while '[g]overnment is responsible for ensuring that development does not harm the environment or human health ... instead of properly managing the Tar Sands, [the Alberta] government has "outsourced" monitoring to the industry itself, creating a classic situation of the fox guarding the henhouse.' It notes in its report that currently the tar sands

> industry funds and chairs stakeholder groups that monitor environmental impacts. For water pollution, industry runs the Regional Aquatics Monitoring Program (RAMP). But as with air pollution and cumulative environmental impacts, the studies on aquatic pollution could not be better designed to ensure that no solid conclusions can be reached. The most important testing programs, such as sediment (where the toxic chemicals settle) in the Athabasca Delta, are erratic. In the most recent year of monitoring, the RAMP simply did not test in these areas at all.

The Environmental Defence group also notes that independent university-based environmental scientists are highly sceptical of the methodology and results of RAMP's testing, and that the First Nations communities downstream from the tar sands are even more blunt in their criticisms; as one spokesperson for the Mikisew Cree community stated, '[RAMP is like] a parking lot where everything, all the major issues are placed. Meanwhile, approvals [for new Tar Sands projects] are approved.' Although, until recently, downstream First Nations community representatives nominally belonged to RAMP, they have now 'pulled out of the industry-driven process' (Environmental Defence 2008: 5). Meanwhile, as Marsden (2008: 163–165) documents, air quality in the tar sands region is monitored by the Wood Buffalo Environmental Association (WBEA), while another organisation, the Cumulative Environmental Management Association (CEMA), also 'created by the Alberta government and the oil sands industry', has the official mandate of developing recommendations 'on how to best manage cumulative impacts of oil sands development and protect the environment', '... [t]he effect has been to absolve the Alberta environment department and therefore the government of practically any responsibility for the environment in Wood Buffalo.' The Mikisew Cree band also withdrew from participating in CEMA in 2006, because, as one of the community elders explained, 'Guess who puts the money in it? Industry. So who controls the whole group? It's like saying to the Alberta government, "We control you."

It's controlled by one group that wants development to occur and yet they are given the responsibility to look after the environment. It's crazy.'

Assessing the ecological and human costs

There is now emerging a vast array of alternative sources of information on the Alberta tar sands that collectively documents the horrific ecological and human costs of the tar sands operation (in addition to the already cited sources, see Laxer 2006; Bouchard 2009; Cryderman 2009; Russell 2009a, 2009b). Together they provide an indictment of the practices that governments and the oil industry have undertaken in this regard. These can be summarily outlined as follows below.

Count 1: ecological destruction

- *Global warming.* 'Tar sands oil production generates almost three times more global warming than does conventional oil production ... Tar sands oil production is already the single largest contributor to the increase of global warming pollution in Canada and is responsible for a regional increase in air pollution from nitrogen oxides, sulphur dioxide, volatile organic compounds, and particulate matter' (Juhasz 2008: 292–3).
- *The destruction of the boreal forest.* 'Canada's boreal forest holds 186 billion tons of carbon, and the Mackenzie River Basin protects about 28 percent of that. Planting giant bitumen mines and factories in the forest is like opening a bank vault to a gang of thieves' (Nikiforuk 2008: 119). 'In order to deliver adequate supplies of natural gas to the region, a vast network of new pipelines has been proposed, including a 758-mile series of pipelines and gas fields through First Nation land and the pristine boreal wilderness of the Mackenzie Valley in the Northwest Territories, one of the last large, intact portions of the forest' (Juhasz 2008: 293).
- *Natural gas depletion and air pollution.* '[T]hree of Canada's top five industrial polluters are now from the tar sands industry' (Clarke 2008: 152). A significant amount of this pollution comes from the intensive use of natural gas in the tar sands extraction and refining process. The ecological damage caused from sacrificing large reserves of cleaner-burning natural gas to produce synthetic crude

from bitumen may be considered a sadly ironic act of 'ecocide' (Broswimmer 2002).

- *Water depletion and groundwater pollution.* 'Tar sands oil production uses enormous amounts of both water and energy – from mining and drilling the tar sands to processing the bitumen that is eventually converted to oil' (Juhasz 2008: 293). '[I]t takes between two to five barrels of water to produce one barrel of crude oil from the tar sands' and consequently the tar sands is 'rapidly depleting and contaminating the rivers, streams and aquifers of northern Alberta and the North West Territories, thereby contributing further to the unfolding ecological nightmare' (Clarke 2008: 161).

Count 2: the assault on humans and other animal species

- *Waterfowl populations.* 'Although Canada's Migratory Birds Convention Act says it's against the law to kill birds by sliming them with bitumen or other toxic waste ... the toxic ponds [of the Alberta tar sands] lie under a major migratory flyway for birds travelling to the Peace-Athabasca Delta, which Environment Canada calls 'one of the most important waterfowl nesting and staging areas in North America' (Nikiforuk 2008: 81).
- *Effects on aquatic life and animals.* Due to 'notorious carcinogens', in sediments and waterways, fish and other wildlife animals in the region have been found 'covered with tumours and mutations', and downstream pickerel fish in Lake Athabasca are caught that are severely deformed and smell of burning plastic when they are cooked. In addition, arsenic levels in moose meat, a staple part of the diet of local Aboriginal peoples, have been estimated to be 'as much as 453 times the acceptable levels', although this estimate has been disputed by the Alberta government (Clarke 2008: 169; Environmental Defence 2008: 3).
- *Human health effects on local residents and 'downstream' First Nations communities.* The tar sands region is also becoming an increasingly dangerous place for humans to live. 'The residents of Fort Chipewyan, a community of about twelve hundred people three hundred kilometres downstream from Fort McMurray, have already been diagnosed with a high number of illnesses, including leukemia, lymphomas, lupus, and other autoimmune diseases' (Juhasz 2008: 294), which have been directly linked to water contamination from the tar sands. In Fort McKay, an Aboriginal community 45 miles north of Fort McMurray, '[t]he stench of hydrocarbons from

the surrounding mines often hangs heavily in the air ... and an ammonia release from a Syncrude facility in 2006 hospitalized more than twenty children' (Nikiforuk 2008: 87). The tar sands 'tailing ponds' contain numerous 'proven human carcinogens', two of the 'really nasty' types being polycyclic aromatic hydrocarbons (PAH) and naphthenic acids. The testing of 25 PAHS by the US Environmental Protection Agency found that many 'produce skin cancers in "practically all animal species tested" '. These carcinogens are as much, and perhaps even more of, a danger to tar sands workers than local residents and Aboriginal peoples, as 'Even the Canadian Association of Petroleum Producers' has recognised 'that a "significant increase in processing of heavy oil and tar sands in Western Canada in recent years has led to the rising concerns on worker exposure to polycyclic aromatic hydrocarbons" ' (Nikiforuk 2008: 82).

- *The assault on the worker (tar sands workers and their families).* Tar sands workers are also victimised in other ways. 'The gruelling pace of bitumen's development has also made Alberta a dangerous place to work. In 2007, the boom killed 154 people on the job (a 24 per cent increase over 2006) and injured 34,000. Prosecutions for workplace health and safety violations are as rare as environmental investigations' (Nikiforuk 2008). Tar sands workers and their families are also victimised by more traditional forms of crime. In recent years the crime rate in Fort McMurray has soared: assaults 'are reportedly 89 percent higher than in the rest of Alberta' and 'arrests for drug-related offences are 215 percent higher', while it is estimated that every week 6.5 million [Canadian] dollars' worth of crack cocaine makes its way into the city (Clarke 2008: 185–186).
- *The assault on democracy and the decline of citizen engagement.* 'Citizen engagement is largely a spent force in Alberta.' One sign of this is that only 40 per cent of the Alberta electorate voted in the province's 2008 provincial election, 'the lowest voter turnout in the history of Canada', while, even worse, 'only 21 percent of the people in the Fort McMurray area voted in the 2008 provincial election.' Despite this, '[p]olls show that Albertans overwhelmingly favour real reductions in carbon emissions' and that '[m]ost people want a slow down in the tar sands, but the government will hear nothing of it.' Some critics place much of the blame for the democratic deficit in Alberta squarely on the shoulders of former Premier Ralph Klein, along with Prime Minister Stephen Harper, who has for long had close ties to friends and family in the oil industry,

like his father, who once worked for Imperial Oil (Nikiforuk 2008: 157, 162).

Conclusion: where do we go from here?

The case study of state–corporate crime of the Alberta tar sands project as presented in this chapter has implications for the development of strategies aimed at taking action against multinational energy corporations and their political backers in the Alberta tar sands, as well as for understanding and responding to similar cases of state–corporate crime and the politics of the denial of environmental harm that are also occurring elsewhere in the world. First, we need to acknowledge and recognise that criminology for most of its history has itself been complicit in 'ecocide' (Broswimmer 2002; Smandych and Kueneman 2009) and that any strategy we adopt to attempt to stop state–corporate environmental crime must take into account the extent to which environmental crime is a global problem that demands both – ideally, coordinated – local and global responses (Aas 2007; Larsen and Smandych 2008; White 2008; Muncie *et al.* 2009). The question remains, where do we go from here?

Can stricter criminal and environmental laws be useful ingredients of an approach aimed at preventing or reducing harms to the environment caused by corporations? Proponents of the concept of 'state–corporate crime' (Kramer *et al.* 2002) have warned against this approach, noting that while tougher laws may perhaps be part of a perceived-successful 'local solution', laws enacted at a state (or national) level ignore the global dimensions and effects of state–corporate environmental crime. At the same time, however, it would be a mistake not to continue to try to prosecute state–corporate criminals in domestic national and state courts, for, as we have seen in the current case study, the actions of major corporate and governmental backers of tar sands expansion have been clearly premeditated and deliberate. It is evident that those masterminding this development have either been clearly knowledgeable about, or wilfully blind to, the harmful consequences of their actions. While national and state courts have so far largely declined to prosecute these types of ecological harms as criminal acts, we need to persist in this line of reasoning and provide a critical analysis of why such remedies are warranted.

Yet it is also obvious that political action is needed at both local and global levels to force the state and corporations to take more rapid steps to reduce our ecological footprint and undoing the serious ecological harms already caused by the largely unfettered corporate global exploitation of the ecosystem. In the Canadian context, it is clear that the Canadian government has been remiss in its duties to provide energy security and a long-term sustainable Canadian energy policy for future generations, while the Alberta government has also failed future generations of Canadians by not extracting appropriate levels of compensation from oil companies through negotiating adequate royalty fees. Norway, which mandates that 94 per cent of its oil royalties go in to a national heritage fund (Nikoforuk 2008: 151), demonstrates just how poorly the Canadian government has performed in this context.

In our view, an important starting point in making the Canadian government more environmentally responsible would be to support political action aimed at forcing it to regain national energy sovereignty by withdrawing from the free-trade agreement and the proportionality clause. Given the nature of current global geopolitics, however, it remains questionable whether the USA would respect Canadian sovereignty and allow Canada to leave the tar sands buried under the 'lungs of the Northern Hemisphere', or whether it would retaliate with punitive trade barriers to Canadian manufactured goods, or simply mobilise to access this energy deposit in the name of US national defence. Until the Canadian government can be pressured to actively promote the interests of Canadian citizens and the Canadian ecosystem, we have no way of knowing how free it really is to act on its citizens' behalf and afford the country protection from avoidable harm.

References

Aas, K.F. (2007) *Globalization and Crime*. London: Sage.

Aulette, J.R. and Michalowski, R. (1993) 'Fire in Hamlet: A Case Study of a State–Corporate Crime', in K. Tunnell (ed.), *Political Crime in Contemporary America: A Critical Approach*. New York: Garland, 171–206.

Bouchard, L. (2009) 'A Pastoral Letter on the Integrity of Creation and the Athabasca Oil Sands by Luc Bouchard, Bishop of St. Paul in Alberta', 25 January [online]. Available at: http://www.dioceseofstpaul.ca/index.php?option=com content&task=view&id=135 (accessed 24 November 2009).

Broswimmer, F. (2002) *Ecocide: A Short History of the Mass Extinction of the Species*. London: Pluto Press.

Clarke, T. (2008). *Tar Sands Showdown: Canada and the New Politics of Oil in an Age of Climate Change*. Toronto: James Lorimer.

Cryderman, K. (2009) 'Alberta Bishop Calls for Halt on Oilsands Growth', *Calgary Herald*, 27 January [online]. Available at: http://www.canada.com/calgaryherald/news/story.html?id=106898cf-af89-431f-8aa9-094dedf0236c (accessed 24 November 2009).

Environmental Defence (2008) *Canada's Toxic Tar Sands: The Most Destructive Project on Earth*. Toronto: Environmental Defence [online]. Available at: http://www.environmentaldefence.ca/reports/tarsands.htm (accessed 11 February 2008).

Ermann, D.M. and William H. Clement II. (1987) 'The Campaign Against Marketing of Infant Formula in the Third World', in D. Ermann and R. Lundman (eds), *Corporate and Governmental Deviance: Problems of Organizational Behavior in Contemporary Society* (3rd edn). Oxford: Oxford University Press.

Fort McMurray (2009) *A Guide to Fort McMurray and the Regional Municipality of Wood Buffalo*. http://www.fortmcmurraytourism.com/ (accessed 12 February 2009).

Hayden, A. (2009) 'Alberta's Tar Sands' (unpublished manuscript) [We would like to thank the author for sharing this work in progress.]

Healing, D. (2009) 'Imperial Proceeds with Oilsands Mine', *Winnipeg Free Press*, 26 May, B7.

Holcomb, J. (2008) 'Environmentalism and the Internet: Corporate Greenwashers and Environmental Groups', *Contemporary Justice Review*, 11: 203–11.

Juhasz, A. (2008). *The Tyranny of Oil: The World's Most Powerful Industry – and What We Must Do to Stop It*. New York: HarperCollins.

Kramer, R. and Michalowski, R. (1993) *State–Corporate Crime: Case Studies in Organizational Deviance*. Unpublished manuscript.

Kramer, R., Michalowski, R. and Kauzlarich, D. (2002) 'The Origins and Development of the Concept of State–Corporate Crime', *Crime and Delinquency*, 48: 263–82.

Krugel, L. (2009) 'Oil Rush to Become "Oil Slumber": Think-Tank Warns of Alberta Slump', *Winnipeg Free Press*, 6 February, BII.

Larsen, N. and Smandych, R. (eds.) (2008) *Global Criminology and Criminal Justice: Current Issues and Perspectives*. Peterborough: Broadview Press.

Laxer, G. (2006). 'Missing But Badly Needed: A Canada-First Energy Policy', *Canadian Centre for Policy Alternatives Monitor*, November.

Macdonald, C. (2008) *Green, Inc. An Environmental Insider Reveals How a Good Cause Has Gone Bad*. Guilford, CT: Lyons Press.

Macdonald, N. (2009) 'Euros Protest Investing in Our Oil Sands', *MacLean's*, 15 June, 25.

Marsden, W. (2008) *Stupid to the Last Drop: How Alberta is Bringing Environmental Armageddon to Canada (and Doesn't Seem to Care)*. Toronto: Alfred A. Knopf.

Mouawad, J. (2009) 'Report Weighs Fallout of Canada's Oil Sands', *New York Times*, 18 May [online]. Available at: http://www.nytimes.com/2009/05/18/business/energy-environment/18oilsands.html (accessed 24 November 2009).

Muncie, J., Talbot, D. and Walters, R. (eds) (2009) *Crime: Local and Global*. Cullompton: Willan Publishing.

Nikiforuk, A. (2008) *Tar Sands: Dirty Oil and the Future of the Continent*. Vancouver: Greystone Books.

Russell, F. (2009a) 'Oil's Not Well in Canada', *Winnipeg Free Press*, 25 February, A13.

Russell, F. (2009b) 'Canada: Gas Jockey to the United States', *Winnipeg Free Press*, 11 March, A11.

Smandych, R. and Kueneman, R. (2009) 'Ecocidal Criminology? Recasting the Role of Criminology in Responding to Humanly Created Ecological Harm'. Invited paper presented at the Institute of Criminology, School of Social and Cultural Studies, Victoria University of Wellington, Wellington, New Zealand.

Snider, L. (2000) 'The Sociology of Corporate Crime: An Obituary (Or: Whose Knowledge Claims have Legs?)', *Theoretical Criminology*, 4: 169–206.

Travel Alberta Canada: Scenic Road Trips, UNESCO Trail [online]. Available at: http://www.travelalberta.com/en/Pages/default.aspx (accessed 24 November).

Vos, J. (2009) 'Actions Speak Louder Than Words: Greenwashing in Corporate America', *Notre Dame Journal of Law, Ethics, and Public Policy*, 23: 673–95.

White, R. (2008). *Crimes Against Nature: Environmental Criminology and Ecological Justice*. Cullompton: Willan Publishing.

Chapter 6

The illegal reptile trade as a form of conservation crime: a South African criminological investigation

Joe Herbig

Introduction

Natural resource and environmental degradation through illegal exploitation in its various forms has for many years now been of critical concern to those interested in biodiversity conservation and sustainable utilisation issues. Frequently, intervention programmes have, due to public outcry and censure, been implemented to check and control environmental perturbation. Sadly, most have been directed almost exclusively at protecting those species perceived to possess a higher intrinsic value or profile in the public arena, as in rhino and elephant poaching, cycad smuggling and even abalone and rock lobster plundering along certain of South Africa's seaboards.

Reptiles, including species such as snakes, lizards, turtles, tortoises, alligators and crocodiles, are, in terms of public opinion, and often because of the negative stereotypes attached to them, unfortunately considered less desirable creatures and consequently afforded less attention. So what if a few lizards, snakes or other creepy-crawlies are poached, smuggled or destroyed? – less of them to harm my family or me. Reptiles are, furthermore, often dealt with illegally in a very surreptitious and criminally professional manner within extremely exclusive circles, making the illegal trade therein appear almost inconsequential. The damage caused is, however, very profound and if permitted to continue unabated will, in all probability, lead to many valuable, rare, indigenous and endemic species vanishing from South Africa's shores, compromising its rich natural heritage and negatively impacting on biotic diversity.

Reptiles exemplify an important part of a country's natural heritage. If these organisms find themselves jeopardised, then we as humans can expect serious repercussions, since reptiles can be considered the sentinels of humankind's environmental health. What happens to herpetofauna is a sign of what could happen to other wildlife and ultimately even humankind. Diversity has become an indicator of strength, health and well-being in biological communities as well as in societies and organisations, and disturbance in this domain will not bode well for the future of humanity. It is no secret that millions of animals suffer and die in the illegal reptile trade every year. Wild populations of reptiles in South Africa and abroad, including some of the rarest species on Earth, are threatened by injudicious and illegal exploitation. Given South Africa's high level of herpetological endemism, the illegal trade of highly sought after and valuable species has grown in the past few years and is believed to contribute significantly to bolstering Eastern, American and even global illegal trade statistics.

This chapter explores the nature and complexity of the illegal national and international trade in protected South African reptile and amphibian species insofar as it transcends national and international borders, transgresses the laws of foreign states, fuels international participation, and causes negative impacts in other countries. The criminological relationship embedded in this illegal trade dynamic is, furthermore, interrogated by broadening conservation crime precincts and revealing strategic underlying issues.

The threat to reptiles

Reptiles, although essentially lacking the charismatic appeal of their more anthropomorphic cousins, have long been associated with humans, either in legends, as a source of victuals, as ornaments, as pets, and/or as medicine/curative ingredients. Generally lacking defence mechanisms, they have also been overexploited to such an extent that it has become problematical, if not impossible, for some populations to remain viable. What is even more disconcerting is that reptiles have lived for almost 200 million years and have survived the major natural catastrophes, which eliminated the dinosaurs, but are now being extirpated by humans through unregulated trade, habitat loss and other criminally related threats.

Throughout the world, reptiles are endangered by a plethora of problems to which they are succumbing. Populations are shrinking and species everywhere are threatened and vulnerable. Many are critically endangered, others hover on the very brink of extinction, and some already have reached the point of no return. Survivors of countless millennia, the planet's reptile heritage is being systematically squandered, and is facing imminent demise at the hands of humankind. Compounding this situation in the South African context is the general lack of understanding, and awareness of issues such as conservation crime, and an ostensibly generic Third World attitude among South Africans towards such deviance, which in many other countries would be regarded as morally wrong. In this regard, Kidd (1998) suggests that the outlook of many South Africans has to a large extent been anaesthetised by the widespread concern over rampant 'ordinary' criminal activity, which most people regard as more serious than natural resource/conservation offences. Echoing these sentiments, I submit that there exists in South Africa a widely manifested indifference to conservation crime issues, a general environmental myopia, and an unsophisticated lack of appreciation and knowledge of the extent and gravity of, particularly, the illegal reptile trade problem (Herbig 2003). Due to misperceptions about the sustainability of the reptile resource, policy disparity within conservation agencies, and even, in many cases, the total absence of identifiable provincial and/or national strategy regarding herpetological resources, as well as derisory conservation/scientific policing/regulatory interest, a low general concern about reptiles has resulted in these organisms lacking a strong advocacy in wildlife protection, scientific research and conservation from within the South African community.

Reptiles as crime targets

According to Bruwer (1997), reptiles are habitually traded and illegally exploited in a surreptitious and criminally professional manner within very exclusive circles, making the illegal trade therein appear almost fictional and the prosecution of offenders a task of virtual impossibility. The damage caused by these acts is, however, exceedingly negative and if allowed to burgeon uninhibited will, in all probability, lead to many valuable species vanishing from South Africa's shores. As with most animal and plant species, there are usually certain characteristics common to a number of them, but seldom one characteristic that is ubiquitous in relation to all, or most, of the various species. In the case of reptiles, however, there seems to be one rather atypical central element that applies equally to them all, namely that they are, for the most part, albeit stereotypically, abhorred by the majority of society. Just the mention of the word 'reptile' usually conjures up visions of cold, emotionless and malicious organisms that one would rather, according to Bruwer (1997), avoid; in fact, the average person would prefer to see them dead rather than alive. This fact is generally shrugged off as irrelevant, but it is nonetheless pivotal with regard to deviance in this sphere, with miscreant individuals (originating from both the national and international arena) making full use of this sentiment, and the opportunities created thereby, to promote and pursue their trade (Herbig 2003).

Reptiles, independently and as a group, possess distinct and unique biological inimitability and have a specific ecology in terms of habitat requirements, behaviour, distribution, and associations with other species, as well as with the inorganic environment. Most of these factors, apart from determining the particular species' niche in the natural environment, also have a significant bearing on and are inextricably linked to their criminal exploitation. They dictate, for example, how vulnerable the organism/s will be to criminal exploitation, and by whom, where, and by which method they stand to be exploited as well as the economic or commercial value of the various organisms – in essence, therefore, these factors delimit the resource's attractiveness, accessibility and the degree of guardianship it enjoys or should enjoy.

South Africa is a land of many contrasts and habitat extremes. Even within provinces, climatic conditions and vegetation types can vary greatly, resulting in the formation of diverse habitats, a fact that is reflected and corroborated by the country's rich natural faunal and floral multiplicity. There are in fact more reptile species in southern Africa than there are mammal as well as more endemic species than of any other vertebrate (Branch 1998). Of the 339 reptile species found in South Africa, 145 occur in the Western Cape Province (Baard 2002). Due to the abundance and diversity of habitats found specifically in the Western Cape, more endemic, rare and endangered species are located here than in any other province in the country, resulting in its being labelled 'the centre of endemism' (Baard 2002). Owing to these reasons, South Africa and this province in particular are also understandably among the most attractive for herpetologists, naturalists, and, of course, criminals (Baard 2002; Gildenhuys 2002 2009; Van der Westhuizen 2002).

Since reptiles do not generate heat internally by metabolising food, as do mammals and birds, they possess a distinct advantage in terms of fuel efficiency, as no fuel needs to be converted to heat.

This intrinsic activity, apart from being highly functional, also brings many reptiles out into the open, making them more noticeable and, coupled with the fact that many of them are restricted to specific locales/habitats, therefore more susceptible to injudicious harvesting and disturbance.

The following summary serves as a biological *aide-memoire* with regard to the significance and criminal allure of certain South African reptile species. According to Baard (1994), there are 40 species of land tortoise in the world, of which southern Africa has 12, plus five species of marine turtle and eight species of freshwater terrapin. Baard (1994) states that in the Western Cape Province alone there are nine species of land tortoise (of which two are divided into five subspecies), including the world's rarest and smallest, and one freshwater terrapin, making the Western Cape Province richer in land tortoise species than any other region in the world. According to Baard (2002), South Africa boasts 105 indigenous snake species, of which 41 are found in the Western Cape. Indigenous and endemic Western Cape snakes are highly sought after by collectors for the pet trade, and it would appear that tremendous pressure is being placed on natural populations to satisfy both local and international demand (Baard 2002; Gildenhuys 2002; Hignett 2002; Van der Westhuizen 2002). South Africa also has 213 lizard species, of which 92 occur in the Western Cape. Nineteen of these species are endemic to this province, including three which are listed as vulnerable and four which are listed as near-threatened (Baard 2002).

Specifically attractive individual reptile examples would include the geometric tortoise, which is endemic to the south-western part of the Western Cape, and undoubtedly one of the most endangered and threatened tortoise species in the world, with only 2,000–3,000 individuals remaining (Baard 1994; Branch 2000), making it, for obvious reasons, a most desirable and valuable commodity to trade. Furthermore, the southern speckled padloper is the world's smallest tortoise, never weighing more than 100 g (Branch 2000), and can easily fit into the breast pocket of a jacket (O'Hagan 1989). Although it only occurs in isolated places, which should ordinarily enhance a species' conservation, this also in the absence of effective guardianship, unfortunately and somewhat ironically, facilitates the illegal exploitation thereof. The tent tortoise is another endemic tortoise that presents in a bewildering range of shapes and colours and is greatly sought by pet traders, resulting in the loss of large numbers from their natural habitat (O'Hagan 1989). The endemic angulate or bowsprit tortoise is fairly common in the Western Cape, but despite their abundant status, these tortoises remain a highly sought-after commodity, especially for the pet trade, both locally and abroad (Baard 2002; Gildenhuys 2002; Van der Westhuizen 2002). The endemic armadillo girdled lizard characteristically bites into its tail and rolls into an impregnable little hoop when caught in the open and is the only lizard in the world to display this behaviour (O'Hagan 1989; Branch 1998). This small, harmless lizard is listed as 'vulnerable' in the South African Red Data Book of threatened reptiles and amphibians and is all too often collected illegally for the pet trade (Branch 2000; Baard 2002).

Although by no means an exhaustive exposition of all the valuable and scarce reptiles in South Africa, the foregoing overview aims to sensitise and orientate in relation to the significance and exquisiteness of some of the more high-profile reptile species in South Africa and in particular the Western Cape Province as well as to place the illegal exploitation of this often neglected and definitely underestimated natural resource into criminological perspective.

Modus operandi and crime scenes

Modus operandi and crime scenes, although often quite diverse, dynamic and regularly incongruent in nature, are integrally linked not only to one or more of the characteristics or incentives discussed in the preceding section, but also to each other, and can thus be regarded as fundamental pieces of the enigma that is the illegal reptile trade. *Modi operandi* can be divided into three broad categories. These categories can be identified in ascending order of complexity, injurious conservation impact and premeditation as the following: *incidental exploitation*, *subsistence exploitation* and *intentional exploitation* (Gildenhuys 2002, 2009).

Incidental exploitation

This refers to *ad hoc*, and even accidental, illegal capture or removal of reptiles from their natural environment, whether fortuitously or intentionally, and their subsequent illegal transport and/or possession. While perhaps not 'illegal trade' in the true sense of the word, this form of illegal exploitation is considered an integral part of the larger illegal trade dynamic (Herbig 2003). Involvement at this level could well be the catalyst that triggers the further, and more resolute, participation in the illegal exploitation of these natural resources and should subsequently not be trivialised. Incidental exploitation occurs out of ignorance, good Samaritanism, curiosity, pity, amusement and/or novelty (Van der Westhuizen 2002); therefore, it has a distinct bearing on the methods employed to acquire organisms, and naturally also the crime scenes.

Target reptiles are usually those that are less shy by nature and often venture out into the open where they are easily noticed. Due to insufficient conservation policing capacity and resources, these organisms are simply collected with impunity by hand from a particular location, transported to a residence, and more often than not retained as pets or curiosities. The novelty of having such a 'rescued' animal as a 'pet' usually wears off rapidly, and the organism is then returned back to the wild. Placing such captive animals into unfamiliar habitats will, however, apart from the unauthorised transport and release thereof being illegal, typically result in the animal's demise, as it will in all probability be highly traumatised and not suitably adapted to the new habitat (Baard 2002; Gildenhuys 2002; Van der Westhuizen 2002). Arbitrary rehabilitation by the uninitiated could, furthermore, cause diseases to be spread indiscriminately (Van Dijk 2000; Baard 2002).

Although these activities appear to be of low impact and, therefore, insignificant in conservation terms, they can, in fact, due to their frequency and regular nature, cause large negative conservation impacts. Incidental exploitation is due to its very nature, an exploitation mechanism that is extremely difficult to quantify, but is undoubtedly a matter that has to be factored into the illegal reptile trade equation.

Subsistence exploitation

Subsistence exploitation essentially involves the intentional removal/harvesting of reptiles by unemployed or poverty-stricken individuals from the natural environment for subsistence reasons. Reptiles (seen as a 'free' resource) are either harvested as victuals or for the purposes of resale, the proceeds of which are then used to purchase rations and miscellaneous provisions (Van Wyk 2002). Harvesting for victuals mainly occurs where people have fallen on hard times and need to supplement their diet with natural resources in order to survive. Reptiles, especially tortoises, are a readily available source of protein in the more rural and peri-urban locales, which can, due to their predominantly reptant nature and somewhat leisurely gait, be effortlessly exploited by even the youngest participant.

Productive areas are basically entered on foot by itinerants and indigent community members, driven by hunger and survival instincts, and surreptitiously and systematically stripped of their edible herpetofauna, until all but the best-hidden and inedible species remain. Sustained onslaughts will rapidly serve to generate sterile environments and severely disturbed ecosystems, yielding a multitude of related crime problems when the resource harvest begins to wane (Herbig 2003). Scenarios such as these are not conducive to urban and peri-urban conservation initiatives, which have for some time now been in vogue, or even crime prevention efforts for that matter, and will, in the final analysis, reduce the quality of life for all. Conservation endeavours will therefore have to recognise these socio-economic community issues as a fundamental aspect of the illegal reptile trade, and hence address them when it comes to developing suitable intervention programmes.

Harvesting for resale purposes, on the other hand, often involves the collection of high-value reptile species found within restricted habitats by destitute indigenous individuals in order to service orders placed by criminally oriented collectors, traders and dealers – a classic example of the greedy exploiting the needy. In this way, criminally orientated traders reduce their exposure to miscreant activities and therefore also the risk of being apprehended. Middlemen, agents or runners are also often engaged as the contact between the illegal harvesters and the collector, dealer or trader, who is thus seldom physically involved in the actual reptile acquisition process, making their detection and prosecution virtually impossible (Gildenhuys 2002). These individuals only really become involved in benefactor form, promoting, as it were, the secretiveness that is so synonymous with the illegal reptile trade (Bruwer 1997).

Such actions not only rape the natural environment, but serve to instil criminal tendencies and antisocial behaviour among the youth that are exposed to these actions and who look to their parents and other community role models for guidance, readily emulating and normalising deviant behaviour perceived to be the norm (Herbig 2003). This state of affairs, essentially social learning, undoubtedly serves to weaken social controls and results in the manifestation of poor self-control mechanisms, in essence predisposing the youth to crime (Van der Hoven and Joubert 1997), and in this manner escalating the illegal reptile exploitation dilemma. In a more candid criminological context, social learning, as suggested above, typically entails the imitation of observed (criminal) behaviour performed by venerated role models (as well as the (enriching) consequences of the behaviour), which has been reinforced and defined as desirable (Brown *et al.* 2007), facilitating, as it were, the transition to criminal behaviour.

Intentional exploitation

This category not only contains the largest miscellany of exploiters, and is the most enduring, but also, concomitantly, is the most complex and varied in terms of *modus operandi*. Intentional exploiters can be divided into two groups, namely traders, collectors, and dealers, essentially the poachers and rustlers of the reptile fraternity, and miscellaneous exploiters who basically undermine, misuse and abuse opportunities created by the legal conservation mandates and authorisations they obtain for personal benefit (for example, scientific research exemptions, errant snake collection, reptile rehabilitation authority, and captive breeding immunity). The premeditated and malicious intent of this group distinguishes it from those already mentioned. According to Bruwer (1997), a number of independent, but interlinked international syndicates at present operate in South Africa. This author goes on to state that most of them keep fairly much to themselves, but as a result of the South African herpetological community being so close-knit, they are obliged to interact. Furthermore, the various traders deal almost exclusively by means of facsimile messages and electronic mail, making it exceedingly difficult to intercept consignments (Bruwer 1997). Damm (2002) maintains in this regard that while there is evidence that organised crime is becoming increasingly involved in the lucrative wildlife trade, much of this illegal trade starts at the individual collector/enthusiast level.

Reptile laundering

As with money laundering, the laundering of reptiles involves the disposal of illegal proceeds through ostensibly legal means. This form of deviance is rife in South Africa, especially with regard to reptiles and certain species of avifauna (Hignett 2002). Hignett (2002) states that deviance in this sector is compounded by a lack of conservation policing and monitoring capacity, antagonism between the (permit-issuing) conservation staff of the various provinces, and disparate legislation between provinces. Launderers make full use of these inadequacies to pursue their dishonest goals. Launderers also make use of poor policing capacity to move species lookalikes. Often species are similar in appearance to the untrained eye. Highly sought-after species are exported under the guise of these less important species due to identification ignorance and lack of expertise in this field.

Bruwer (1997) and Hignett (2002) are of the opinion that the large number of indigenous snakes, tortoises, girdled lizards and invertebrates offered for sale on the World Wide Web by foreign Internet users were in all probability exported by unethical traders with dubious documents. Bruwer (1997) holds the view that reptiles illegally exported from South Africa are often exchanged by the recipients for specimens favoured by the trade in South Africa such as iguanas or boa species listed in the Convention on the International Trade in Endangered Species (CITES) Appendix I, which are then illegally imported (smuggled) into South Africa. These reptiles are then presumably traded or exchanged in South Africa, and the process starts all over again. Franke and Telecky (2001) state that just as counterfeit money is laundered through commercial interests into the legitimate currency trade, illegally wild-caught reptiles are laundered through dealers as supposedly captive-bred reptiles because captive-bred reptiles generally command higher prices than their wild-caught counterparts. Reptile laundering would certainly appear, therefore, to be somewhat of a worldwide trend and certainly not a tactic that is only restricted to South Africa. According to Franke and Telecky (2001), the pet trade affords dealers a perfect opportunity to 'launder' shipments of tortoises and turtles; for example, Indian star tortoises are smuggled in their thousands through the United Arab Emirates (UAE), from where they are re-exported as 'captive-bred' specimens with UAE official CITES documentation.

Collection from the wild

Criminally deviant traders, dealers and collectors are more often than not experts in the field of herpetology and can effortlessly identify areas where naturally occurring populations of reptile species occur. Due to their knowledge of reptile ecology and characteristics, they can easily locate the desired reptiles in their natural habitats, given the fact that many have severely restricted ranges and specialised habitat requirements, and remove them (Baard 2002; Gildenhuys 2002; Malherbe 2002; Van der Westhuizen 2002). Gildenhuys (2002, 2009) states in this regard that many foreign traders, collectors and dealers cultivate contacts in local museums or pretend to be researchers, authors or members of photo safaris, and so forth, so as to gain access to reptile records, from which they then glean all the information necessary to locate and poach them.

The capture of wild organisms, apart from the ecological damage caused to the homeostasis of the larger ecosystem they inhabit, also usually spells doom for many individual organisms. Wild capture essentially involves the collection of a 'free' commodity, since collectors seldom have anything invested in these organisms in terms of costs of rearing, feeding, and general husbandry. It is, therefore, easier and less risky to capture numerous animals by techniques that could result in high mortality or impairment, than it would be to catch fewer animals with more judicious techniques, which are more time-consuming and essentially leave the poacher more vulnerable, in terms of apprehension risk, due to prolonged exposure (Herbig 2003).

It is estimated that wild-caught reptiles experience, on average, a 90 per cent mortality rate between capture and the end of their first year in captivity (Franke and Telecky 2001; Gildenhuys 2009). Franke and Telecky (2001) go on to state that just like the 'cut flower' industry, the reptile industry is based on a perishable commodity that is fully expected to die shortly after retail sale – those in the business must get their product to the marketplace and sold to the consumer before the product expires. However, unlike buyers of proteas and roses, consumers who purchase reptiles fully expect them to survive, thrive under their care, and become companion animals. The fact that the signs of reptile suffering and ill health are difficult for the average consumer worldwide to recognise enables the reptile industry to exploit both the animals and the consumers to further increase profits. Reptiles do not cry or shiver as an abused or ill cat or dog might; consequently, average consumers are unaware that they are purchasing abused or ill animals (Franke and Telecky 2001). A South African Police Service press release relating to a reptile sting operation (Operation Cobra) captured the quintessence of the damage inflicted by the intentional collection from the wild by unscrupulous traders, dealers and collectors in the following statement:

> The systematic rape of the South African environment to supply the pet trade in Europe with non-poisonous species has led to the total destruction of small ecosystems. Smugglers would target an area and literally clear it of every living animal, which could include beetles, spiders, scorpions, frogs, snakes, lizards and tortoises.

Transport, import and export

Apart from the illegal collection of wild reptiles from the environment, another essential element of the illegal trade dynamic involves the further surreptitious movement of the illegal hoard to an intermediate or final destination. Most reptiles are traded by making use of one or a combination of the following mechanisms expounded upon by Bruwer (1997), Gildenhuys (2002) and Van der Westhuizen (2002):

- Snakes are packed in empty video-cassette boxes, wrapped as parcels, and mailed to their destination.
- Snakes are placed in cotton bags, cushioned by placing tissue paper around the bags, and the bags are finally placed in sturdy cardboard/hardboard boxes (Figure 6.1). The package is then sent by mail. In both instances the packages are incorrectly marked – for example, 'children's toys' – and no return address is provided.
- Geckos and invertebrates, specifically spiders and scorpions, are packed in small, commercially manufactured, polystyrene containers to which homemade divisions are added. As many as 10 specimens can be packed into one container. These containers, up to 15 in one crate, are then packed into larger polystyrene crates and exported by ship or plane. The total package is the size of a 40-litre box.
- Exotic reptiles, specifically iguanas, are imported by adding false compartments to the bottoms of containers used for the transport

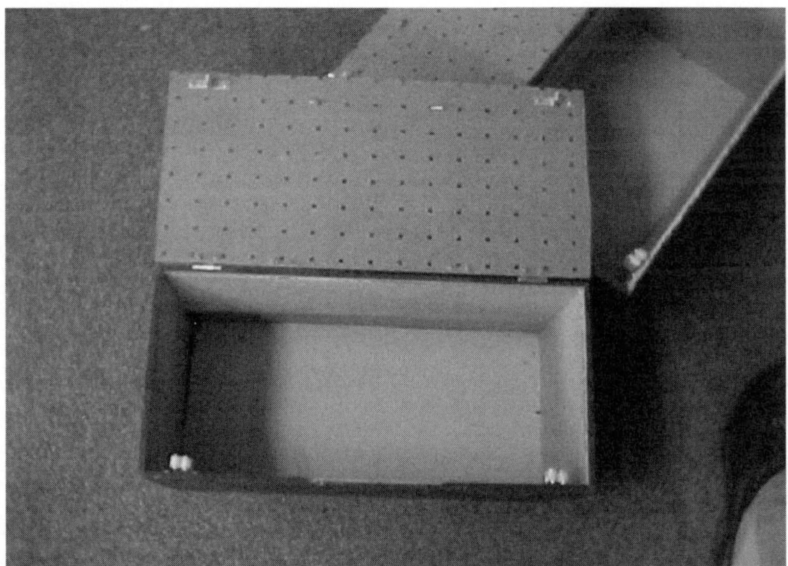

Figure 6.1 Example of containers in which an illegal consignment of snakes was smuggled.
Source: Environmental Crime Investigation Service, Western Cape Nature Conservation Board, 2001.

of tropical fish (Franke and Telecky 2001) or marine fish. Since little control is exercised over the importation of marine/tropical fish, these containers are not properly examined on arrival.

- Reptiles have been sewn into the seams of the outer garments worn by smugglers, or are simply carried in hand luggage by a compliant courier. In this regard, Makings (2002) states that the Airports Company of South Africa (ACSA) has admitted that the X-ray scanners at airports cannot easily detect animals in baggage, and if books or clothes are packed together in the luggage, the animals' outline could easily be obscured. Corroborating this submission, Kalb and Salzberg (2000) mention parenthetically that one Rodney Carrington, a pet store owner from Barbados, was arrested for bringing 55 endangered red-footed tortoises into the USA. He had stuffed all 55, 4-inch (10-cm) tortoises into his trousers – which gave him away at customs.
- Suitcases, which have been carefully modified, with a number of holes and containing several false compartments, have been used to export a variety of reptiles including tortoises. These are usually submitted as ordinary luggage to the airline authorities (Figure 6.2).

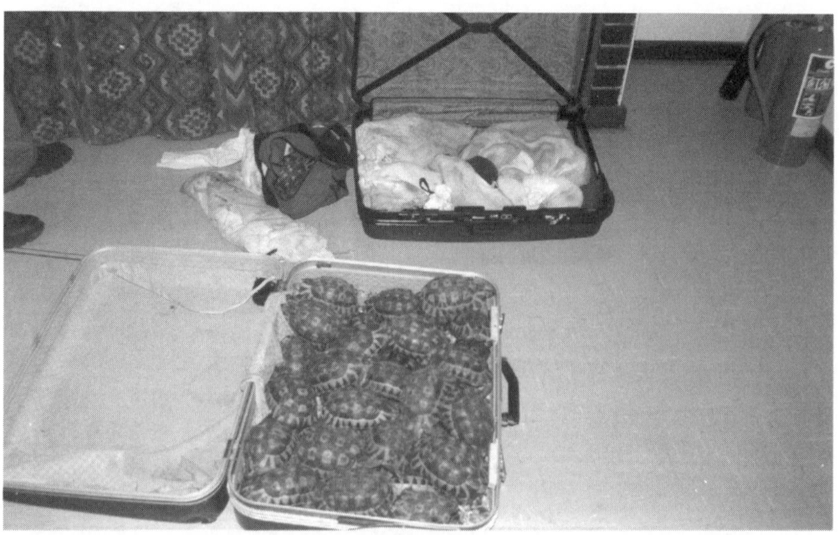

Figure 6.2 A consignment of angulate tortoises (*Chersina angulata*) ready for export in ordinary suitcases. The uppermost suitcase shows the tortoises packed in bags to facilitate transport, restrict movement and reduce sound emission.
Source: SAPS, Vredendal 2001.

- The traditional fraudulent method of adding a few illegal animals to a legal consignment is still being used.
- Another method is packaging a consignment with seemingly legal (permitted) faunal content, but replacing the content with species for which no permits have been obtained. Freight company weigh bills simply reflect what the consigner specifies as the content, and subsequently, due to paperwork ostensibly being in order, the veiled cargo arouses little further suspicion.
- Labelling illegal, non-poisonous consignments with misleading or daunting labels, e.g. 'poisonous reptiles' – so as to discourage customs or other regulating and monitoring staff from inspecting the cargo. Cargo manifests indicating only the organisms' scientific names are used to confuse the mostly (herpetologically) ignorant inspection officials.
- As a slight variation of this method, Van Dijk *et al.* (2000) report that 'turtles' (tortoises) are often shipped in Asia by openly mislabelling the consignment as fish/seafood, or even as general freight, in order to bypass more thorough inspections. This *modus operandi* is undoubtedly also utilised to import illegal batches of contraband reptiles into South Africa, and, in all probability, also to export local species to international destinations.
- Another method is shipping consignments out through harbours (under the guise of rations or victuals) on foreign vessels where very little or no control is as a rule exercised by conservation staff. A multitude of Taiwanese, Japanese, Chinese and other foreign craft sailing under Asian flags call at ports within the Western Cape Province (researcher's own observations). Since the predominantly Asian crew on these vessels are partial to chelonian (tortoise) flesh, and bearing in mind that, according to Kalb and Salzberg (2000), in China alone the volume of the chelonian food trade is measured in tens of tonnes per day and millions per year, the use of these ports, with their perfunctory control, can, all things being equal, be viewed as a most effective clandestine method of promoting what can broadly be termed 'biopiracy'. In this same vein, Franke and Telecky (2001) point out that the transportation of reptiles by speedboat, such as from the Malagasy Republic to the island of Réunion or South Africa, is becoming an increasingly common method for transporting illegal reptiles.

- Smugglers may pack highly poisonous species above other, more valuable reptile (or other) contraband concealed below, discouraging a thorough search of the consignment.

The above exposition showcases the ingenious methods used by poachers to transport their illegal bounty and provides a glimpse of the minutiae and dynamics involved in reptile poacher machinations.

Crime scenes

Crime scenes, although far less complex than *modus operandi per se*, are integrally related to reptile ecology, characteristics and harvesting methods. One or more of these factors will essentially dictate the location of, and even duration of time expended at, the crime scene. For example, a person wishing to capture and collect armadillo girdled lizards from the wild would logically locate the desired area geographically (where the species can be expected to appear most abundantly) through a global positioning system (GPS), tourist guide, regular map, or the like so as to be able to capture the greatest number of target organisms in the shortest space of time with the least effort. Since this crime scene would in all probability be in a natural setting, the *modus operandi* would be influenced accordingly; that is, target species would necessitate overt manual collection procedures, and immediate further transportation by road. From this scenario, it can be deduced that the crime scene is determined and visited in order to acquire a valuable species. The distribution range (ecology) and attractiveness (characteristics) of the particular organism are thus central factors in crime scene determination. The characteristics of the target organism in relation to its lifestyle will further determine the degree of difficulty and method by which organisms will be captured, and thus play an important role in determining time spent at the crime scene, as well as the specific *modus operandi* employed. Crystallising from the foregoing is the close relationship that exists between situational variables such as crime scene, ecology and reptile characteristics as well as *modus operandi*.

Effect and implications of herpetological crime

The illegal trade in reptiles affects the species itself not only in the context of biodiversity diminution but also in a host of other fashions. Apart from organism mortality, environmental and ecological degradation (associated with injudicious wild harvesting), and inhumane handling techniques, this illegal trade can have a deleterious effect on a host of herpetological crime variables and peripheral issues, the gist of which will be explained below.

Ecological and biodiversity ramifications

Biological diversity is currently being reduced at an alarming rate and species are disappearing, as the ecosystems they live in are destroyed. Such is the magnitude of the dilemma that it has been termed the 'sixth extinction wave' (Damm 2002). Humans and all wildlife, however, have to coexist within the limited resource base called Earth and our very existence depends on the biodiversity of the planet. Davy and Hibler (2002) assert that almost everyone agrees that humanity is in the process of squandering genetic resources that are central to our food, health and economic security.

Within a given habitat, all wildlife has individual specific living requirements, yet all wildlife is interdependent with and acts on its physical and living environment – the addition or removal of a single species from that habitat may, according to Damm (2002), create harmful reactions. Van Dijk *et al.* (2000) argue that the unsustainable and illegal trade in reptiles could lead to the loss of a group of species from peoples' daily lives, customs and conceptual world, thus leaving a culturally and emotionally poorer world for their children. These authors moot further that, financially, the short-term exploitation of a limited resource with very slow recovery is inappropriate, particularly since local collectors gain very little financial benefit from selling off a zone's resources, compromising, as it were, their options for sustainable developments such as, among others, ecotourism and reptile ranching. The conservation and biodiversity ramifications of the immense illegal reptile trade are only now becoming apparent. Franke and Telecky (2001) state in this regard that, worldwide, at least 22 reptile species are known to have become extinct in the last 400 years, and considering that 25 per cent of reptiles (more than mammals at 24 per cent, birds at 15 per cent or amphibians at 20 per cent) for which there is adequate information to assign a conservation status are threatened with extinction, the biodiversity threat starts to become abundantly clear. Notwithstanding the foregoing, reptiles also fulfil an important and often undervalued, overlooked and underestimated ecological, if not economic, role, in that they provide essential insect and rodent control services, and could in essence be saving the agricultural sector enormous amounts of revenue in prevented crop damage. They also form an important link in the food chain, as many are a major source of protein for other predatory species, construct burrows that provide shelter for a multitude of animals, and act as important dispersal agents for a variety of wild varieties of flora (Franke and Telecky 2001; Baard 2002; Van der Westhuizen 2002).

Individual organisms

It is no secret that millions of animals suffer and die in the illegal reptile trade every year; wild populations of reptiles in South Africa and abroad, including some of the rarest species on Earth are threatened by overcollection for trade by, in the main, injudicious capture, holding and transport/shipment techniques. The Humane Society of the United States (HSUS) advocates widely that each reptile sold by a pet store or trader/dealer represents depleted wild populations, damaged habitats, and individual suffering, as most pet reptiles are taken from the wild or born of wild-caught parents.

Apart from capture techniques that injure individual creatures and damage habitats, the further illegal manipulation of reptiles results in enormous physiological trauma to these organisms, more often than not, translating into high rates of mortality. Illegal reptile traders often, in order to amplify profit margins, starve and/or dehydrate reptiles prior to consignment, the rationale behind these inhumane actions being that a lighter animal utilises a lighter box when packed and, therefore, smaller shipping (freight) fees, which are assessed by weight (Franke and Telecky 2001; Gildenhuys 2002).

Transmission of diseases and parasites

According to Baard (2002), Franke and Telecky (2001) and Van der Westhuizen (2002), the illegal reptile trade poses significant health concerns for humans, domesticated animals and wildlife alike. Reptiles are known carriers of a variety of pathogens, including bacteria, parasites and viruses, some of which are highly contagious, and there subsequently exists a great opportunity for disease transmission from imported reptiles to wild populations of reptiles and other animals (Baard 1994; Franke and Telecky 2001; Baard 2002).

Pathogen transmission from organism to organism

Ticks are common on imported reptiles and there is considerable concern that they could carry zoonotic and wildlife diseases. Certain ticks are the carriers of heartwater disease, a lethal malady of cattle, deer, and other ruminants caused by the rickettsial bacterium *Ehrlichia ruminantium* (Franke and Telecky 2001; Baard 2002; De Jongh 2003; Scott 2003). Although evidence of the tick vectors of certain diseases becoming established in South Africa is still anecdotal and inferential, Franke and Telecky (2001) charge that at least eight exotic tick species on indigenous reptiles in Florida (USA), are now considered to be permanently established in the USA, in all probability via reptile imports from Africa and South America.

Potgieter (1997), Baard (2002) Hignett (2002) and Vorster (2002) also maintain that the common green iguana (*Iguana iguana*) from Central and South America carries a virus that is lethal particularly to racehorses, and that it is for this very reason not permitted to be kept or imported into South Africa. The threat is, therefore, very real and the potential of introduced pathogens to wreak havoc on native species cannot be discounted. It is, however, unfortunate that both in South Africa and abroad reptiles still receive comparatively scant attention from researchers and wildlife managers, so the state and full extent of pathogen introduction and its ramifications are still largely unknown.

Pathogen transmission from organism to humans – zoonosis

People who buy reptiles as pets often get more than they bargained for as most consumers are not aware that the majority, if not all, reptiles carry *Salmonella* bacteria (Baard 1994, Baard 2002; De Jongh 2003; Scott 2003). *Salmonella* infection (salmonellosis), which does not have to involve direct contact with a reptile, in humans manifests itself in a wide variety of conditions, ranging from asymptomatic infection to diarrhoea, fever, vomiting, abdominal cramping, arthritis, endocarditis (heart valve infection), meningitis and sepsis (Franke and Telecky 2001; Baard 2002). The HSUS states that in several cases, salmonellosis in children has resulted in severe illness or even death and that the US Centres for Disease Control (CDC) has advised that children, pregnant women, and persons with compromised immune systems avoid all contact with reptiles and amphibians. The spread of salmonellosis is, according to Franke and Telecky (2001), undoubtedly exacerbated by the unsanitary and physiologically stressful conditions in which reptiles are captured, housed and shipped, which causes imported animals to become immunosuppressed, facilitating the spread of infection.

Introduction of exotic (invasive alien) organisms/species

Apart from the disease and pathogen threat exotic species hold, the introduction of such non-native species into the natural environment can cause certain other problems for native biota (Hoover 1998). Alien species, more often than not, compete for food and space with, and to the detriment of, indigenous species, and aggressive, invasive or predatory introductions might eventually dominate habitats, forcing resident species to seek other often less suitable locales where their perpetuation might be seriously compromised (Baard 2002; Van der Westhuizen 2002). Introduced species might interbreed with indigenous/endemic species, leading to hybridisation and the eventual disappearance of the original species (biodiversity attenuation), and/or detrimentally affect ecosystem homeostasis (Baard 1994). In the Western Cape Province, little research has been done to ascertain the magnitude of exotic species presence and/or the effect that these species have had on the natural environment (Baard 2002; Stadler 2002; Van der Westhuizen 2002).

Reintroduction or release of captive reptiles into the natural environment

The removal of reptiles from their natural habitat is, according to Baard (2002), no longer considered to be the only problem relating to the illegal exploitation of reptiles. The reintroduction/release (in essence, repatriation) of reptiles, whether exotic or local in origin, into the natural environment can cause serious environmental problems. Such reintroductions/releases usually occur when people liberate their unwanted pet reptiles, pet reptiles escape, or reptile collectors, dealers or traders attempt to establish self-sustaining populations of popular species in an area from whence they may later collect (Franke and Telecky 2001; Van der Westhuizen 2002). Many of these species are not adapted to survive in hostile surroundings and either die rapidly through predation or suffer considerably, typically as a result of starvation, before eventually perishing (Baard 1994). They could also, as mentioned previously, cause major health problems for wild reptile populations and/or become established, subsequently competing for food, habitat and reproductive partners.

Crime diversification and/or intensification

Although much of the effects and implications pertaining to herpetological crime are reptile centred and biologically orientated, there are also distinctly more conventional effects and implications that could be realised by this form of conservation deviance – herpetological crime essentially acting as a catalyst/conduit for participation in other forms of crime. It is submitted that as herpetological criminals become more involved in herpetological crime, they, in all likelihood, will also become more exposed to a miscellany of criminals and criminal pursuits that might easily influence and entice the deviant to become involved in more diverse and, in all probability, more conventional forms of crime.

Conclusion

An attempt has been made in this chapter to provide an exposition of the South African and global illegal reptile trade phenomenon in order to facilitate its understanding and conceptualisation and place it in a criminological perspective. Conservation crime such as the illegal reptile trade is founded on the argument that environmental perturbation needs to be understood and addressed within the sphere of criminology, and that only through structured and focused integration of theory with practical intervention will the natural resource distortion be eliminated, achieving effective crime suppression and creative resource destiny management. Conservation criminology is dependent not only on an acute awareness and understanding of what initiates or triggers illegal exploitation, but also on an appreciation of the implications this form of deviance can have on the natural and social environment. Conservation criminology relevant to the current and next century should, therefore, develop the intellectual breadth and constitutional scope to embrace conservation and social issues holistically as related projects for the benefit of the biosphere and all its inhabitants.

References

Baard, E.H.W. (1994) *Cape Tortoises. Their Identification and Care*. Cape Town: Cape Nature Conservation.

Baard, E.H.W. (2002) Manager: Scientific Services, Western Cape Nature Conservation Board. Personal interview, 24 July, Jonkershoek, Stellenbosch.

Baasch, L. (1997) 'Please Be Fair to Reptiles', *Financial Mail*, 21 November, 17.

Branch, B. (1998) *Field Guide to Snakes and Other Reptiles of Southern Africa* (3rd edn). Cape Town: Struik.

Branch, B. (2000) *Everyone's Guide to Snakes and Other Reptiles and Amphibians of Southern Africa* (2nd edn). Cape Town: Struik.

Brown, S.E., Esbensen, F. and Geis, G. (2007) *Criminology. Explaining Crime and Its Context* (6th edn). Newark, NJ: Anderson.

Bruwer, S. (1997) 'Report on the Reptile Trade in South Africa'. Report presented to the Interpol subgroup on wildlife crime, South Africa, May 1997.

Damm, G.R. (2002) *The Conservation Game. Saving Africa's Biodiversity*. Rivonia: Safari Club International African Chapter.

Davy, B. and Hibler, M. (2002) 'Balancing Rights, Responsibilities, and Resources. The Crucible Project' in A. Wilcke (ed.), *Agriculture and Rural Development*. A. Wilcke Frankfurt: Technical Centre for Agriculture and Rural Cooperation, 38–40.

De Jongh, A.N.E. (2003) Regional environmental health officer, West Coast District Municipality. Personal interview, 14 February, Moorreesburg.

De Villiers, H. (2002) *The Biodiversity of South Africa 2002. Indicators, Trends and Human Impacts*. Cape Town: Struik.

Franke, J. and Telecky, T.M. (2001) *Reptiles as Pets. An Examination of the Trade in Live Reptiles in the United States*. Washington, DC: Humane Society of the United States.

Gildenhuys, P. (2002) Programme coordinator – ECIS, Western Cape Nature Conservation Board. Personal interview, 17 September, Jonkershoek Stellenbosch.

Gildenhuys, P. (2009) Programme coordinator – ECIS, Western Cape Nature Conservation Board. Personal interview, 3 June, Jonkershoek Stellenbosch.

Herbig, F.J.W. (2003) The Illegal Reptile Trade. PhD thesis. Pretoria: University of South Africa.

Hignett, D. (2002) Senior administrative officer, Western Cape Nature Conservation Board. Personal interview, 17 May, Cape Town.

Hoover, C. (1998) *The U.S. Role in the International Live Reptile Trade: Amazon Tree Boas to Zululand Dwarf Chameleons*. Washington, DC: TRAFFIC North America.

Kalb, H.J. and Salzberg, A. (2000) 'News Notes', *Turtle and Tortoise Newsletter. The Newsletter of Chelonian Conservationists and Biologists*, 1: 26.

Kidd, M. (1998) 'Environmental Crime: Time for a Rethink in South Africa', *South African Journal of Environmental Law and policy*, 5(2): 181–204.

Makings, R. (2002) 'Security Slip Sees Dog Carried onto SAA Flight', *Sunday Times*, 16 June, 5.

Malherbe, D.G. (2002) Proprietor – Die Vonds Snakepark. Personal interview, 2 December, Noorder-Paarl.

O'Hagan, T. (1989) *Reader's Digest. Southern African Wildlife. A Guide to Our Mammals, Birds, Reptiles, Insects, Fishes, Amphibians, Invertebrates*. Cape Town: Reader's Digest Association of South Africa (Pty) Limited.

Potgieter, D. (1997) 'n Slang in die gras na Operasie Kobra', *Rapport*, 26 October, 35.

Scott, A. (2003) Senior environmental health officer, West Coast District Municipality. Personal interview, 14 February, Moorreesburg.

South, N. (1998) 'A Green Field for Criminology? A Proposal for a Perspective', *Theoretical Criminology*, 2(2): 211–33.

Stadler, H. (2002) Assistant director, Western Cape Nature Conservation Board. Personal interview, 21 May, Porterville.

Van der Hoven, A.E. and Joubert, S.J. (1997) 'Crime Causation and Explanation' in A.E. Van Der Hoven, S. Joubert, J.J. Neser, W.J. Jacobs and C.M.B. Naudè (eds) *Criminology*. Tutorial letter 103/97 for KRM 100-5 (Crime: Causation, Explanation, Reaction and Prevention). Muckleneuk, Pretoria: University of South Africa, 1–27.

Van der Westhuizen, T., (2002) Conservation services manager, Western Cape Nature Conservation Board. Personal interview, 9 May, Stellenbosch.

Van Dijk, P., Stuart, B. and Rhodin, A. (eds) (2000) *Asian Turtle Trade: Proceedings of a Workshop on Conservation and Trade of Freshwater Turtles and Tortoises in Asia held at Phnom Penh, Cambodia, December 1999*. MA: Chelonian Research Foundation.

Van Wyk, R. (2002) Assistant nature conservation officer, West Coast District Municipality. Personal interview, 15 April, Moorreesburg.

Vorster, B.C. (2002) Proprietor – Cape Town Snake Park. Personal interview, 4 December, Ratanga Junction, Cape Town.

Chapter 7

The applicability of crime prevention to problems of environmental harm: a consideration of illicit trade in endangered species

Melanie Wellsmith

Introduction

The recent extension of criminological focus to harms against the environment and animals other than humans may be referred to as 'greening' (e.g. Beirne and South 2007). This 'environmental criminology' approach (see Box 7.1) remains small and in its infancy, and may be in conflict with mainstream criminology's distinct lack of interest in, for example, offences against animals other than humans (Cazaux 2007; Mailley and Clarke 2008). However, it would seem that conventional criminology may have something to contribute to a green agenda (White 2008). This is also recognised by some conservation scientists, as seen in this quotation from Ferraro (2005) in response to similar calls from Smith and Walpole (2005):

> Smith & Walpole point to a long-known, but persistent, problem within the field of biodiversity conservation: the appalling paucity of rigorous theory and well designed, empirical analyses of (1) the driving forces of ecosystem and species decline and (2) the relative effectiveness of interventions aimed at reversing this decline. Unless well-trained social scientists are encouraged by conservation scientists to take an interest in the global decline of biodiversity, we will make little progress in stemming this decline.
>
> (Ferraro 2005: 258–59)

This chapter, therefore, considers the benefits and problems of recent calls for the extension of situational crime prevention techniques to environmental harm, using the example of endangered species conservation.

Box 7.1 A note about terminology

Criminology: Following White (2008), I will refer to criminology dealing with environmental issues as 'environmental' (or on occasion 'green') criminology. To avoid confusion, that specific field of criminology that focuses upon the role of environments, situations and opportunity – often also called 'environmental criminology', will herein be referred to as place-based criminology, while the underpinning theories of this approach will be referred to as opportunity theories. Overall, such approaches are considered part of 'conventional criminology' (as distinct from green criminology).

Crime science: This term is often credited to journalist Nick Ross and is synonymous with the work carried out by the UCL (University College London) Jill Dando Institute of Crime Science. This approach is predominantly focused on prevention and policy-relevant analysis. It draws heavily on place-based criminology, but also many other disciplines (such as geography, psychology and physical sciences), taking a 'scientific approach' to the study of crime phenomena and ways to reduce them (UCL Jill Dando Institute of Crime Science 2008).

Philosophy: Three distinctive perspectives of ecophilosophy have been identified (Halsey and White 1998; White 2007, 2008): anthropocentric, ecocentric and biocentric. These are, respectively, human-, socio-ecological- and species-centred approaches. Connected to these, White (2008) refers to three green theoretical frameworks: environmental rights and environmental justice, ecological citizenship and ecological justice, and animal rights and species justice. These approaches will be referred to in this chapter, particularly in consideration of defining 'harm'.

Endangered species

The International Union for Conservation of Nature (IUCN) claims that:

> We are facing a serious crisis in biodiversity … . The rate that animal and plant species are becoming extinct, and the pace at which natural environments are being destroyed, are increasing every day.
>
> (IUCN 2009: para. 1–2)

Extinction of animal and plant species, then, is one element of this crisis. In order to raise awareness and intervene to prevent this, species at risk may be designated 'endangered'. The most common method of designation is the IUCN Red List of Threatened Species, which categorises species as:

- least concern
- near threatened
- vulnerable
- endangered
- critically endangered
- extinct in the wild
- extinct.

Those species listed as vulnerable, endangered or critically endangered are considered at higher risk, and this may lead to initiatives to tackle this (definitions and listed species can be found at http://www.iucnredlist.org/).

Preventing biodiversity loss and species extinction can be seen as important from all three green theoretical frameworks identified by White (2008). From an environmental justice perspective, extinction may be seen to impact upon both pleasurable activities for humans (tourism, seeing flora and fauna in their natural habitats, etc.) as well as benefits they receive from such species (e.g. medicines, food, income). From an ecological justice perspective, species extinction impacts upon biodiversity more generally, as well as the functioning of ecosystems to which they belong (Garstecki 2006). Finally, from a species justice perspective, we may argue that all species have the right to live free from interference that may otherwise threaten their existence.

Trade in endangered species

There are many reasons why species may become endangered. Although these will vary from one case, or geography, to another, the most common causes are habitat destruction followed by unsustainable trading (WWF (World Wildlife Fund) 2008). Wild flora and fauna are traded as a range of products including foodstuffs, jewellery, ornaments, clothing, pets, furniture and traditional Asian medicines (TAMs). Much trade is legal, but if it were to go unregulated, it may result in increased risk of extinction for certain species.

As a great deal of this trade is related to demand from outside the country of supply, an international dimension is introduced. In response, the international community has acted through membership of the Convention on International Trade in Endangered Species of Wild Fauna and Flora (CITES), which restricts trade in certain 'listed' species through a system of controls introduced by signatories' domestic legislation (see Box 7.2). In practice, this usually means that countries require importers/exporters to be licensed and present appropriate documentation at port. The illegal trade in endangered species, therefore, is fundamentally one of smuggling (Wellsmith 2008a). Domestic legislation may also result in a range of associated offences, such as poaching, processing or even simple possession.

The global legal trade in flora and fauna in the 1990s was estimated at around US$159 billion in exports, the majority of which (65 per cent) is timber, followed by 25 per cent relating to fisheries (Cowdrey 2002). Markets for CITES-listed species remain, however, resulting in a large illicit international trade. The nature and extent of this is difficult to establish, but a global estimate of US$9-11 billion annually (National Wildlife Crime Unit 2008) would not seem exaggerated given the often much higher (although generally unsubstantiated) claims (e.g. Ong 1998; Damania and Bulte 2001; Zimmerman 2003).

Traditional methods of enforcement

In order for legislation to effectively protect endangered species from international trade, its existence must deter potential offenders, disrupt potential markets and/or result in reductive punishment for those who transgress. Much of this relies on effective domestic enforcement in range states (to which endangered species are indigenous), in consumer states, and/or in intermediate destinations. We may question what 'effective' enforcement means, but it is clear from the literature on this topic that the dark figure of this trade is large (i.e. only a small proportion of offences come to the attention of

Box 7.2 CITES

Established in 1973, CITES provides a framework for signatories to subject international trade in endangered species to a series of controls. Import, export, re-export and 'introduction from the sea' (except App III, see below) require a system of licensing. Currently around 5,000 species of animals other than humans and 28,000 species of plants are covered by CITES. In order to reflect the degree of risk of extinction of different species, those subject to controls are listed in three Appendices, either by whole group, subspecies or geographically specified population.

Appendix I: Most at risk of extinction. Trade is only permitted in exceptional circumstances. Examples (at the time of writing) include the giant panda, tomato frog and Dalmatian pelican.

Appendix II: Not necessarily threatened with extinction, but would face a threat to survival if trade was not controlled. Examples are the hippopotamus, bald eagle and whale shark.

Appendix III: Not determined by CITES. Includes species protected by a member country which is seeking cooperation from other signatories to help control trade. This includes sea cucumber (Ecuador), two-toed sloth (Costa Rica) and the jumping pit viper (Honduras).

Many entire species are CITES-listed in either Appendix I or II, including all primates, cetaceans, cats, bears, elephants, rhinoceroses, crocodilians, sea turtles and Boidae. However, the most numerous groups include aloes, corals and frogs.

(source: http://www.cites.org, accessed 27 June 2009)

the authorities) and that punishment is usually lenient (Box 7.3), with maximum sentences rarely imposed (Garstecki 2006). This would suggest that at least two of the conditions for effective deterrence – certainty and severity – are not being achieved.

Research suggests that trade bans (such as those introduced under CITES) can be effective in reducing export of endangered species. However, there is evidence that this does not necessarily result in a corresponding reduction in poaching (thus species conservation), particularly where there are domestic (or neighbouring) unregulated markets (Cantu Guzman 2007; Lemieux and Clarke 2009) or high levels of corruption (Smith *et al.* 2003; Lemieux and Clarke 2009). Indeed, CITES-listing of a new species or its inclusion on the Red List may increase its desirability and black market value (Willock *et al.* 2004; Schneider 2008). Compounding this, enforcement remains generally under-resourced and marginalised (Fyfe and Reeves 2008).

Throughout the legal and conservation literature, there appears to be an absolute preoccupation with using enforcement and deterrent punishment to control the illicit trade in endangered species. The solutions to ineffective enforcement most often proposed are more resources (make being caught more certain) and harsher sentencing (make punishment more severe). Many criminologists would argue, however, that the lessons learned over years of studying traditional

Box 7.3 Illicit trade in endangered species – a serious crime?

In the UK, offences under COTES (Control of Trade in Endangered Species (Enforcement) Regulations 1997) have a maximum sentence of 5 years' imprisonment and/or an unlimited fine if tried in the Crown Court. The following two examples resulted in much lower sentences, despite the seriousness of harm caused to the species involved (and the profits made by the companies).

Shahtoosh shawls (Lowther et al. 2002)

The Renaissance Corporation admitted illegally dealing in these shawls, after 128 items were seized. It was estimated that 1,000 critically endangered Tibetan antelopes would have died to make them. The market value of the seized items was around £353,000. The resulting sentence was a fine of just £1,500.

Ivory and sperm whale teeth (Jenkins 2008)

A case uncovered in London involved illegal trade across Africa, China, the UK and the USA. The trader eventually pleaded guilty to seven offences (excluding importation). Remarking on the seriousness of the offence, the judge passed the maximum sentence of 2 years, but then suspended this for 2 years.

forms of crime should teach us that deterrence through punishment simply does not lead to significant reductions in offending. Instead, perhaps we could prevent offending through manipulating the environments in which it takes place.

Crime prevention

In light of the problems of controlling harmful activities (such as trade in endangered species) via regulation, criminal law, and traditional enforcement activities, methods of crime prevention may offer a suitable alternative. As a response to the possibility of extinction, the idea of acting *before* harm has occurred becomes even more appealing. Primary crime prevention seeks to achieve this, rather than relying on the general and specific deterrent effects of punishing those who have broken the law.

Closely related to crime prevention is risk management. Environmental risk management is often fraught with competing arguments and scientific uncertainty (White 2008). Thus the idea of a 'precautionary principle' has been proposed, for example, in the 1992 Rio Declaration (see White 2008: 65). This approach suggests that in the face of scientific uncertainty, the assumption of harm be reversed, so that we act to ensure safety/harm reduction unless the risk can be shown to be acceptably small. The idea of prevention, therefore, is already embedded, suggesting that there is scope for crime prevention approaches to be incorporated into environmental protection. The form this may take and the problems that may be faced will now be considered.

Situational crime prevention (SCP)

The movement towards environmental impact assessments and risk analysis (White 2008) mirrors a move in criminology in the developed Western world towards actuarial justice (Feeley and Simon 1992). Alongside this, crime control in the last two decades has embraced problem-oriented policing (POP) (Goldstein 1990) and crime science, resulting in situational measures becoming the predominant form of prevention (for a history of crime prevention in the UK, see Tilley 2002).

Situational crime prevention (SCP) is sometimes referred to as a 'theory' in its own right. However, it can more correctly be seen as a practical application of several opportunity theories; most notably rational choice, but also routine activity theory and crime pattern theory. These are summarised in Box 7.4.

Box 7.4 Opportunity theories of crime

Rational choice theory (Cornish and Clarke 1986): a form of neoclassicism in which offenders are seen as rational beings who decide to offend based on an assessment of the perceived risks, efforts and rewards of doing so. Deterrence remains an important element of preventing offending, but moves from the remote (what will the punishment be?) to the more immediate (I am more likely to get caught, it is too difficult, it is not worth it). As such, this theory can be seen as directly underpinning SCP. *Rational choice theory seeks to explain how opportunities to offend are recognised and how the choice is made to exploit them or not.*

Routine activity theory (Cohen and Felson 1979): states that for an offence to occur a motivated offender must come together in time and space with a suitable target (a person, other living being or item that may be criminally exploited) in the absence of a capable guardian. This theory can be employed at various levels of granularity. It has been used to explain macrolevel crime changes, such as the increase in burglary in the USA during the 1950s and 1960s resulting from more single-family households and women going out to work (fewer capable guardians) and the proliferation of light/weight electronic goods (suitable targets) (Cohen and Felson 1979), as well as mesolevel patterns, such as higher concentration of crimes in areas with licensed premises (e.g. Roncek and Maier 1991). In terms of crime reduction, this theory suggests we can either try to prevent offenders and targets from converging, or we can increase the capability of guardians (or the subsequently added place managers and intimate handlers (as summarised in Felson 1995)). *Routine activity theory seeks to explain how criminal opportunities are supplied.*

Crime pattern theory (Brantingham and Brantingham 1993): a combination of routine activity theory and environmental psychology. This approach states that offenders come across crime opportunities as they move about their daily lives, following regular routes or paths, with which they feel comfortable, between their routine activity nodes such as home, school/work and leisure facilities (their 'awareness space'). This theory posits that crime concentrations are the result of overlapping routines of large numbers of potential offenders and victims, which in turn are affected by the environmental backcloth (the location and nature of nodes and paths). *Crime pattern theory seeks to explain how people and things involved in crime (offenders, victims,*

SCP dispenses with the usual criminological endeavour of explaining why (some) people offend and instead takes a pragmatic, problem-solving approach to primary crime reduction, focusing on the situations of crime as opposed to the social circumstance of it (Clarke 1980). SCP seeks to identify and intervene in situations where crime opportunities are present in order to deflect offenders or targets away from one another, introduce more capable guardianship, and/or alter the thought process of potential offenders so that they make a non-crime decision. SCP can be summarised as interventions that:

- increase the perceived risk,
- increase the perceived effort,
- reduce the perceived rewards,
- reduce the perceived provocations, and/or
- remove the excuses associated with offending

at that immediate time in that specific place (in other words, it does not tackle remote causes or decisions). After various iterations, this is now presented as a matrix of 25 techniques under these five headings (Cornish and Clarke 2003: 90). Examples of such interventions include steering column locks and electronic immobilisers on cars, CCTV cameras, product identification and rapid graffiti removal.

SCP, crime science and their underpinning theories have faced a number of criticisms that are far beyond the scope of this chapter. On the other hand, there is a large and growing literature evaluating SCP, identifying 'what works' and in what contexts, and otherwise reporting on its success in reducing a broad range of offences across many countries (Clarke 1997; see also, for example, the Crime Prevention Studies series published by Criminal Justice Press and the POP Guides at http://www.popcenter.org). Of particular interest is the fact that SCP interventions tend to work quickly; a necessary feature when responding to the threat of extinction.

A further advantage of the crime science/POP approach is the strength of analysis undertaken. This demands appropriate recording of data and results in an improved understanding of the extent and nature of the problem to be tackled, the ways in which opportunities are formed and discovered, the methods used to carry out offences, and those people, situations or tools that facilitate such activities. From this, appropriate situational interventions can be suggested. In relation to the trade in endangered species, such data-based knowledge seems to be missing, except in limited examples.

It could be argued that the focus of SCP, like much of the rest of criminology, has been on 'street crime': those offences that make up the bulk of police recorded crime statistics, such as burglary, robbery, theft, criminal damage and (public) interpersonal violence. More recent discussions and use of SCP suggest that this may now be changing. Innovative areas of application include terrorism (Clarke and Newman 2006), child sexual abuse (Wortley and Smallbone 2006), and deaths of migrants at the Mexico–USA border (Guerette 2007). Additionally, there is growing interest among a number of place-based criminologists in environmental issues. Recent conference presentations (Mailley 2008; Mailley and Clarke 2008; Wellsmith 2008a, 2008b, 2008c; Clarke 2009) and publications (Schneider 2008; Lemieux and Clarke 2009; Lemieux in press) have begun to ask what role place-based criminology and SCP could play in reducing environmental harm. These papers and associated discussions suggest a particular interest in 'wildlife crime' and endangered species conservation. There is little evidence that SCP techniques have yet been applied to such problems, although a recent entry for the UK Tilley Awards (Guy 2008) and the establishment of a Partnership Against Wildlife Crime in the UK may signify a willingness to adopt such an approach in this field, but this may not be universal (Kerr and Clarke 2005).

How SCP could be used specifically to tackle the problem of endangered species is a question that requires much more consideration and collaborative work with experts in the field of conservation, ecology and environmental policy. However, Table 7.1 shows some examples of the types of intervention SCP may suggest, alongside which Schneider's (2008) call for a market reduction approach to this illicit trade can also be considered.

Table 7.1 Situational prevention of illicit trade in endangered species

	Measure	Mechanism
White (2008: 250–51; illegal fishing)	• Vessel and employee registration	Increase effort
	• CCTV and satellite photos	Increase risks
	• Fish tagging	Reduce rewards
	• Strengthen moral condemnation of over-fishing	Remove excuses
Lemieux (in press, cited in Lemieux and Clarke 2009; elephant poaching)	• Closure of logging roads	Increase effort
	• Use of pilot-less drones	Increase risks
	• DNA coding of ivory	Reduce rewards
Wellsmith (in preparation; situational conservation of endangered species)	• Secure reserves	Increase effort
	• Reward vigilance from locals/tourists	Increase risks
	• Hide targeted flora within other (non-invasive) crops	Reduce rewards
	• Compensation when endangered species destroy crops/ livestock	Remove provocations
	• More explicit customs declarations	Remove excuses

It would seem, therefore, that SCP may offer an innovative solution to reducing the illicit trade in endangered species. However, there are also significant problems associated with simply lifting SCP from traditional crime control and applying it to problems of environmental harm. It is to these that I now turn.

Issues facing situational crime prevention

There are likely to be a number of practical problems facing the use of SCP in protecting endangered species. Briefly, these include issues of funding and resources, ownership and management of implementation, set against a possible lack of political or social will to address such problems. Further, there may be a lack of expertise among criminologists in relation to issues of conservation and maybe scepticism among conservationists about the usefulness of criminology and situational prevention measures. This may be compounded by the absence of existing collaborations across such disciplines. All of these issues need to be addressed if SCP is to play a role. There are also a number of more fundamental problems that may make SCP an inadequate response to endangered species conservation.

It is difficult to see how focusing on 'crime' prevention from a conventional criminology perspective fits with the ideas of harm reduction proposed by green criminologists. This is so for three interconnected reasons. Firstly, SCP interventions would be considered successful if they led to a reduction in illegal trade in endangered species. However, these solutions may result in displacement to other species or range states. For example, poachers may start to target snow leopards if tigers are more heavily protected (Dexel 2002). While the overall number of offences may be reduced, the harm caused may increase if this displacement results in more species facing a greater risk of extinction or worse damage being caused to ecosystems or biodiversity. From a species justice perspective, regardless of the degree of risk, such activities may be seen as harmful if they result in greater human interference or other infringements of species rights. Spatial displacement may also be harmful if it leads to increased poaching or trade in countries that are less willing or able to introduce protective measures.

Displacement need be neither inevitable nor total if interventions are carefully designed. In other words, the assumption that situational measures will simply shift crime to other places, times or techniques seems unfounded, with research suggesting that well-thought-out programmes of intervention have resulted in little or no displacement, within the ability of evaluators to identify this (Eck 1993; Hesseling 1994). However, because SCP is intended to alter individuals' behaviour so that non-crime activities are chosen instead, if these are also harmful (but legal), then this cannot be seen as a green solution. This is the second reason why SCP may not fit with conceptions of environmental criminology. For example, wildlife tourism may generate revenue for antipoaching strategies, but expanding the tourist infrastructure (e.g. roads) may result in habitat destruction and associated loss of biodiversity (e.g. Lado 1992).

Finally, the solutions may result in the reduction of trade in endangered species, and even the risk of extinction they face, but unless we apply a less anthropocentric approach, it is possible that these solutions may be unpalatable or morally circumspect to those adopting an ecological or species justice perspective. In other words, the notions of 'harm' within environmental criminology may well be alien to the rational or economic solutions associated with traditional conceptions of crime and an anthropocentric application of SCP. Examples of solutions that may result in lower risk of extinction, but may be considered 'unacceptable', to varying degrees, within a green framework are shown in Box 7.5.

Also related to the issue of identifying 'harm', endangered species are not at risk just because they are (illicitly) traded. As already noted, habitat destruction, not trade, is the leading threat to species survival (WWF 2008). Further, there is a large legal market for wildlife and many species that are CITES Appendix II listed are traded, albeit within strict quotas. It must be remembered that CITES only covers international trade, not domestic markets or export of personal possessions. While domestic legislation may criminalise these activities as well, thus bringing them within the purview of SCP, there may be any number of further legal activities that negatively impact on biodiversity (e.g. local supply of bushmeat, retaliation killings for destruction of crops or livestock, and trophy hunting). Therefore, if criminologists are serious about reducing the loss of biodiversity and the number of species at risk of extinction, not only will consideration need to be given to illicit trade, but also a host of other activities, many of which may currently be legal (White 2008).

Establishing the boundaries of criminological involvement is problematic, as harm remains subjective and will be influenced by the green philosophical framework being applied. The question then is: are SCP and conventional criminology equipped to deal with defining such harms and tackling them? With its focus on practical, pragmatic and policy-oriented solutions to offending, can there be a place for SCP in reducing environmental injustice?

Conclusion: incorporating situational harm reduction into environmental criminology

In this chapter, I have considered a particular issue pertinent to considerations of global environmental criminology and the use of SCP in reducing the threat of species extinction. I have suggested that this approach of manipulating situations in order to reduce the opportunity to offend appears to offer some hope for species

Box 7.5 Solutions for species conservation that may not be 'green'

Canned hunting

Large game, often big cats, are captured or even farmed, sometimes drugged and then released in a controlled environment so that those who pay for the privilege can 'hunt' them with a greater (sometimes guaranteed) chance of success (Campaign Against Canned Hunting 2009).

Bear bile farming

Bears are intensively farmed and held in captivity to be 'milked' for bile usually twice a day to supply the TAMs market. This is done via a surgically implanted tube in their gall bladder, simply poking through the abdomen with a hollow stick, or, the now preferred method, via a permanent hole that allows bile to drip out. Not only is the notion of keeping wild animals other than humans in captivity problematic, but the conditions and procedures they undergo are degrading, painful and often result in early death from infections or other complications (Humane Society of the United States 2009), yet Damania and Bulte (2001) credit them with stabilising bear prices in China, thus reducing the demand for poached 'products'.

Hunting quotas

Quotas may lead to greater compliance than outright bans in areas where the species to be protected is considered a 'problem'. In terms of species justice, however, this still results in unnecessary killing. This approach is considered in relation to the brown bear by Knapp (2006).

Alternative supplies

Species not at risk are used to supply markets that would otherwise rely on endangered species. For example, Damania and Bulte (2001) suggest that more 'plentiful animals', such as rabbits, be used for TAMs. However, this does not fit within a species–rights approach.

conservation. However, I have also noted that there are some significant issues that need to be considered by SCP advocates before it can be successfully applied. Of these, the concept of defining harm, thus the extent of involvement and suitable measures to be employed, is the most problematic. I have asked whether SCP can adapt to this. My answer is that I believe it can, if individuals who have a passion for, and understanding of, these wider issues are able to push its frontiers. I suggest that the first step to be taken in trying to achieve this is to refer not to situational crime prevention, but rather to situational harm reduction (Wellsmith in preparation).

Another objective should be to ensure there is cross-fertilisation of criminology and SCP with wildlife conservation and environmental protection. Finally, if situational harm reduction is to be applied, then much more research needs to be carried out. This should adopt a POP-type approach to small-scale, locally identified problems, taking an holistic view of the reasons why a particular species is threatened. Resulting interventions should be subjected to quality evaluations and dissemination in order to start developing a knowledge-base of 'what works'.

However, it is clear that environmental criminology has less well-defined boundaries (in relation to harm) than many conventional approaches. Thus green criminologists will have to consider the very nature of the society in which we live, and our attitude to our environment and the other species that share it (White 2008). I contend it is this that relegates situational harm reduction to being only one of many tools required to repair environmental harm.

References

Beirne, P. and South, N. (eds) (2007) *Issues in Green Criminology*. Cullompton: Willan Publishing.

Brantingham, P.L. and Brantingham, P.J. (1993) 'Environment, Routine and Situation: Towards a pattern theory of crime', in R.V. Clarke and M. Felson (eds) *Routine Activity and Rational Choice*. Advances in Criminological Theory, vol. 5. London: Transaction Publishers, 259–94.

Campaign Against Canned Hunting (2009) *What We're About* [online]. Available at: http://www.cannedlion.org/ (accessed 28 June 2009).

Cantu Guzman, J.C. (2007) *The Illegal Parrot Trade in Mexico: A Comprehensive Assessment*. Washington, DC: Defenders of Wildlife.

Cazaux, G. (2007) 'Labelling Animals: Non-speciesist Criminology and Techniques to Identify Other Animals', in P. Beirne and N. South (eds), *Issues in Green Criminology*. Cullompton: Willan Publishing, 87–113.

Clarke, R.V.G. (1980) 'Situational Crime Prevention: Theory and Practice', *British Journal of Criminology*, 20(2): 136–147.

Clarke, R.V. (ed.) (1997) *Situational Crime Prevention: Successful Case Studies* (2nd edn). New York: Harrow and Heston.

Clarke, R.V. (2009) 'Designing Out Crime from Products', Workshop on Crime Science, University of Twente, Enschede, The Netherlands, May 2009.

Clarke, R.V. and Newman, G. (2006) *Outsmarting the Terrorists*. Westport, CT: Praeger Security International.

Cohen, L.E. and Felson, M. (1979) 'Social Change and Crime Rate Trends', *American Sociological Review*, 44: 588-608.

Cornish, D.B. and Clarke, R.V.G. (1986) *The Reasoning Criminal*. New York: Springer-Verlag.

Cornish, D.B. and Clarke, R.V. (2003) 'Opportunities, Precipitators and Criminal Decisions: A Reply to Wortley's Critique of Situational Crime Prevention', in M.J. Smith and D.B. Cornish (eds), *Theory for Practice in Situational Crime Prevention*. Crime Prevention Studies, vol. 16. Monsey, NY: Criminal Justice Press, 41–96.

Cowdrey, D. (2002) *Switching Channels: Wildlife Trade Routes into Europe and the UK*. WWF/TRAFFIC Report. Godalming: WWF-UK.

Damania, R. and Bulte, E.H. (2001) *The Economics of Captive Breeding and Endangered Species Conservation*. Centre for International Economic Studies. Adelaide: University of Adelaide.

Dexel, B. (2002) *The Illegal Trade in Snow Leopards – A Global Perspective*. Berlin: Naturschutzbund Deutschland.

Eck, J.E. (1993) 'The Threat of Crime Displacement', *Criminal Justice Abstracts*, 25: 527–46.

Feeley, M.M. and Simon, J. (1992) 'The New Penology', *Criminology*, 30(4): 452–74.

Felson, M. (1995) 'Those Who Discourage Crime', in J.E. Eck and D. Weisburd (eds), *Crime and Place*. Crime Prevention Studies, vol. 4. Monsey, NY: Criminal Justice Press, 53–66.

Ferraro, P. (2005) 'Corruption and Conservation: The Need for Empirical Analysis. A Response to Smith and Walpole', *Oryx*, 39: 257–59.

Fyfe, N. and Reeves, A. (2008) 'The Thin Green Line? The Challenges of Policing Wildlife Crime in Scotland', The Stockholm Criminology Symposium, Stockholm University, Sweden, June 2008.

Garstecki, T. (2006) *Implementation of Article 16, Council Regulation (EC) No. 338/97, in the 25 Member States of the European Union*. Report commissioned by the European Commission. Brussels: TRAFFIC Europe.

Goldstein, H. (1990) *Problem-Oriented Policing*. New York: McGraw-Hill.

Guerette, R.T. (2007) *Migrant Death: Border Safety and Situational Crime Prevention on the US–Mexico Divide*. New York: LFB Scholarly Publishing.

Guy, J.L. (2008) 'Migrants of No Return'. Unpublished application to the UK Home Office Tilley Awards 2008.

Halsey, M. and White, R. (1998) 'Crime, Ecophilosophy and Environmental Harm', *Theoretical Criminology*, 2(3): 345–71.

Hesseling, R.B.P. (1994) 'Displacement: A Review of the Empirical Literature', in R.V. Clarke (ed.), *Crime Prevention Studies*, vol. 4. Monsey, NY: Criminal Justice Press, 197–230.

Humane Society of the United States (2009) *The Unbearable Trade in Bear Parts and Bile* [online]. Available at http://www.hsus.org/wildlife/issues_facing_wildlife/wildlife_trade/the_unbearable_trade_in_bear_parts_and_bile/ (accessed 28 June 2009).

IUCN (2009) *Biodiversity in Crisis* [online]. Available at: http://www.iucn.org/what/biodiversity/ (accessed 27 June 2009).

Jenkins, C. (2008) 'Operation Charm', *Investigative Practice Journal*, 19: 6–9.

Kerr, C. and Clarke, G. (2005) 'International Enforcement Agencies', in R. Parry-Jones, J. Barnaby and S. Thiele (eds), *Proceedings of the EU Wildlife Trade Enforcement Co-ordination Workshop*, 25–27 October 2005. Bristol: Defra, 22–31.

Knapp, A. (2006) *Bear Necessities. An Analysis of Brown Bear Management and Trade in Selected Range States and the European Union's Role in the Trophy Trade*. A TRAFFIC Europe Report. Brussels: European Commission.

Lado, C. (1992) 'Problems of Wildlife Management and Land Use in Kenya', *Land Use Policy*, 9: 169–84.

Lemieux, A.M. and Clarke, R.V. (2009) 'The International Ban on Ivory Sales and Its Effects on Elephant Poaching in Africa', *British Journal of Criminology*, 49(4): 451–71.

Lemieux, A.M. (in press) 'Poaching Prevention: Lessons Learned from Protecting Africa's Elephants', in R. Mawby and R. Yarwoods (eds), *Policing, Rurality and Governance*. Aldershot: Ashgate.

Lowther, J., Cook, D. and Roberts, M. (2002) *Crime and Punishment in the Wildlife Trade*. A WWF/TRAFFIC Report. Godalming: WWF-UK.

Mailley, J. (2008) 'Situational Crime Prevention in Wildlife Crime', National Environmental Crime Conference, British Library, London, October 2008.

Mailley, J. and Clarke, R.V. (2008) 'Environmental Criminology and Wildlife Crime', Environmental Criminology and Crime Analysis (ECCA) Symposium, Izmir, Turkey, March 2008.

National Wildlife Crime Unit (2008) *Wildlife Crime* [online]. Available at: http://www.nwcu.police.uk/pages/wildlifecrime/crime.asp (accessed 2 September 2008).

Ong, D.M. (1998) 'The Convention on International Trade in Endangered Species (CITES 1973): Implications of Recent Developments in International and EC Environmental Law', *Journal of Environmental Law*, 10: 291–314.

Roncek, D. and Maier, P.A. (1991) 'Bars, Blocks and Crime Revisited: Linking the Theory of Routine Activities to the Empiricism of Hot Spots', *Criminology*, 29: 725–53.

Schneider, J.L. (2008) 'Reducing the Illicit Trade in Wildlife: The Market Reduction Approach', *Journal of Contemporary Criminal Justice*, 24: 274–95.

Smith, R.J., Muir, R.D.J., Walpole, M.J. *et al.* (2003) 'Governance and the Loss of Biodiversity', *Nature*, 426: 67–70.

Smith, R.J. and Walpole, M.J. (2005) 'Forum: Should Conservationists Pay More Attention to Corruption?', *Oryx*, 39: 251–56.

Tilley, N. (2002) 'Crime Prevention in Britain, 1975-2010: Breaking Out, Breaking in and Breaking Down', in G. Hughes, E. McLaughlin and J. Muncie (eds), *Crime Prevention and Community Safety: New Directions*. London: Sage, 12–36.

UCL Jill Dando Institute of Crime Science (2008) *Frequently Asked Questions About Crime Science* [online]. Available at: http://www.jdi.ucl.ac.uk/about/faqs/cs_faqs.php (accessed 27 June 2009).

Wellsmith, M. (2008a) 'Breeding Crime: Applying a Crime Prevention Approach to the Illegal Wildlife Trade', Environmental Criminology and Crime Analysis (ECCA) Symposium, Izmir, Turkey, March 2008.

Wellsmith, M. (2008b) 'Controlling Trade in Endangered Species: A Role for Crime Prevention?', *British Society of Criminology Conference*, University of Huddersfield, Huddersfield, July 2008.

Wellsmith, M. (2008c) 'Wildlife Crime: A Role for Criminologists?', European Society of Criminology Conference, Murrayfield Stadium, Edinburgh, September 2008.

Wellsmith, M. (in preparation) 'Situational Conservation of Endangered Species: Expanding the Frontiers of Situational Crime Prevention'.

White, R. (2007) 'Green Criminology and the Pursuit of Social and Ecological Justice', in P. Beirne and N. South (eds), *Issues in Green Criminology*. Cullompton: Willan Publishing, 32–54.

White, R. (2008) *Crimes Against Nature*. Cullompton: Willan Publishing.

Willock, A., Burgener, M. and Sancho, A. (2004) *First Choice or Fall Back? An Examination of Issues Relating to the Application of Appendix III of CITES to Marine Species*. Cambridge: TRAFFIC International.

World Wildlife Fund (WWF) (2008) *Illegal Wildlife Trade* [online]. Available at: http://www.wwf.org.uk/what_we_do/safeguarding_the_natural_world/wildlife/illegal_wildlife_trade/ (accessed 27 June 2009).

Wortley, R. and Smallbone, S. (eds) (2006) *Situational Prevention of Child Sexual Abuse*. Crime Prevention Studies, vol. 19. Monsey, NY: Criminal Justice Press.

Zimmerman, M.E. (2003) 'The Black Market for Wildlife: Combating Transnational Organized Crime in the Illegal Wildlife Trade', *Vanderbilt Journal of Transnational Law*, 36: 1657–90.

Chapter 8

The polluting behaviour of the multinational corporations in China

Yang Shuqin

Introduction

Environmental pollution has become a clear and present problem in China's economic operation in the recent years. It is akin to a time bomb, waiting to be detonated while the situation deteriorates.

The multinational corporations (MNC) spread across China are also to a certain extent playing a less than beneficial role. To everyone's surprise, after being named in the 'Pollution Blacklist', except for very few companies willing to admit the offence, many MNC excuse themselves by referring to excuses such as 'coincidence', 'accident', or 'negligence'. Some simply say that 'many local enterprises are far worse than we are', or even ignore the case entirely.

For a sizeable number of MNCs, the reason for investing in China is to evade environmental responsibility and to profit from polluting the environment. Some local governments equate 'cheap cost of pollutant discharge' with 'cheap labour force' to attract investment. Not only are the polluting MNCs protected by the local government, but some environment departments are also being kept alive by these enterprises.

On the other hand, citing commercial confidentiality, some MNCs do not disclose the information on their high-technology items to conceal the environment pollution caused. As a result, this has become the blind spot of inspection by the environmental departments.

What causes these MNCs to behave as good citizens in their home countries, but disregard their commitments and discharge pollutants recklessly in China? The first reason is the lack of monitoring by local authorities; secondly, the public are ignorant of enterprises' environmental responsibility; and, thirdly, the MNCs planted in various parts of China, while making large profits, have become the bread giver to the locals, protected by local policies and enjoying the status of supercitizens. The fourth reason is the weak public awareness of participation in environmental protection in China; the public fails to monitor effectively the polluting behaviour of the MNCs.

The condition of environmental pollution in China

As the economy of China grows rapidly, the problem of environmental pollution draws more attention from the public (Figures 8.1 and 8.2). According to the investigation by the United Nations, of the 10 most polluted cities, six are in China. The China Water Utility Department

Figure 8.1 People who live in garbage, smoke, pollution

Figure 8.2 Shanghai factories – early morning shot of one of the factory districts in Shanghai

has assessed the water quality of more than 700 rivers in China, totalling 100,000 km in length, and the result was that 46.5 per cent of rivers are currently being polluted, 10.6 per cent are seriously polluted, more than 90 per cent of the water in the cities is seriously polluted, and water of unhygienic standard is consumed by more than 300 million China residents. Seventy-four per cent of Chinese reside in areas of bad air quality, according to a World Health Organisation report. The air quality of these areas does not meet the standard, whether of any international treaty or the United Nations' Environmental and Development Convention of 1992 (http://www.eeo.com.cn/Politics/beijing_news/2008/06/05/102311.shtml).

Residents of China have few chances to read the reports in the Western media. Known to but a few, before the opening of the 2008 Olympic Games in Beijing in August of that year, *The New York Times* started discussing in a special column the pollution problems in China. The criticism by some Westerners, organisations and even government of China's environmental problem has become sharper (http://news.h2o-china.com/information/china/651411196906096_3.shtml). Therefore, another problem China is facing now is that the pollution China brings to its neighbouring countries has become the hot spot of international focus. All of a sudden, China is receiving reproaches from all around.

However, not long ago, a monthly magazine in Japan published an article entitled 'It is the World That is Polluting China'. The article stated that one of the causes of the pollution is that China, as a 'world factory', bears the burden alone of the sizeable production of the manufacturing industries of the world. The direct consequence of mass export of cheap industrial products is the massive consumption of energy and worsening environmental pollution. The price of being a world factory is to turn China into a world garbage dump.

Multinational corporations break their promise to protect the environment

Greenpeace has cast strong doubt on the international chemical industry tycoons in Beijing. It has pointed out that some developed countries imposed strict restrictions on the polluting of manufacturing locally, causing the enterprises to invest overseas directly and transfer the pollution industries offshore. Therefore, among the overseas direct investment from the developed countries, the highly polluting industries make up a high proportion. In the polluting enterprise lists publicised by the China public and the Environmental Study Centre, there are more MNCs in China breaking the environmental rules than in most other places in the world. Not only are there Top-500 enterprises such as PepsiCola, HP, and Bosch, but there are also other familiar names including Nissin, Kao and Carlsberg (http://rm.sasac.gov.cn/fxfx/swfx/200708230115.htm).

Some renowned MNCs, after being publicised, not only did not explain formally to the public, but also refused to make any statement on the rectification required for the environmental violation of its subsidiary company. A typical example is Pepsi-Cola; after its case was exposed, two of its subsidiaries were again listed (http://www.globrand.com/2009/210923.shtml). This explains from another angle that, in circumstances when the restricting system is not efficient and the punishing system is weak, even the most famous MNC, when enjoying beneficial conditions, casts aside its environmental and basic social responsibility.

The above behaviour makes the strong stronger, and the weak weaker. While the developed countries use massively the low-cost resources in China, they save massively on the expensive environmental treatment otherwise necessary. China in this case is depleting its resources, and once the resource cannot meet the demand, it is likely in the future to purchase from other countries with higher prices, and to pay the heavy price of financial and health costs as a result of the worsening environment.

The problem of potable water pollution in China

There are two prominent problems with the potable water in China. First, the water shortage problem is serious. Of the 600 cities in China, 400 are water-deficient. Second, the water contamination is as serious as the water shortage (http://www.china.com.cn/chinese/zhuanti/hjwj/1164436.htm). This is actually two sides of the same problem.

Because of the water shortage, when waste water is discharged, self-cleaning through dilution is difficult. At the same time, the waste water pollutes the only water resource left. The current state of water pollution in China is that, from city to countryside, from above ground to below ground, from ground to ocean, the water is polluted. The reason that the water pollution is not controlled is that the related rules and regulations in China are not seriously enforced; as a result, 'it is cheap to infringe, and expensive to abide by the laws'. Some enterprises would rather pay the fine than solve the pollution problem.

Figures 8.3–8.6 show some of the examples of the sort of pollution that people in China have to live with when it comes to water supply. Next we present four cases studies of MNC activities that impact upon water quality and quantity.

Case no. 1

Benma Beer Factory in Tainshui city of Gansu Province, jointly invested in by Denmark's Carlsberg Beer Company, in the early stage of construction, did not comply with the 'three-at-the-same-time' system. This meant that it did not construct the waste-water treatment facility, while it nonetheless discharged the industrial waste water directly for more than 10 years across the Grade 1 protected water source area of the eastern Tianshui city, posing a great threat to the water consumption safety of the local residents. In 1997, the Tianshui municipal government ordered rectification to be made within a certain time period; in 2004, this was officially scrutinised by the provincial government; and in 2006, the Tianshui Environment Department issued a stop-work order. Nevertheless, Benma refused to solve the problem. It paid the fine of 5,000 yuan twice a year. A treatment plant would have cost 3.9 million yuan. This is why the driving force for environmental protection measures is seriously lacking. It is easier and cheaper to pollute than to do the right thing.

Case no. 2

Noell Crane Systems (China) Limited in the Business Development Bureau's Zhangzhou Development Zone in Fujian Province, invested in by Germany's Noell Crane, was one of the 10 enterprises listed formally for provincial scrutiny because it went into production without building a waste treatment facility, caused serious pollution, and thereby threatened the safety of water consumption.

Case no. 3

Shanghai American Standard Ceramic Company did not utilise the waste-water treatment facility properly: it discharged waste water above the limit, and violated the rules of water contamination control. As a result, it was sanctioned by the Shanghai Environmental Bureau in 2006, the first batch of enterprises to be investigated and punished for its breach of environmental laws.

Figure 8.3 River completely polluted

Figure 8.4 Three pipes with water and factory background

Figure 8.5 Untreated waste water pouring into a stream

Figure 8.6 Serious water pollution in Taihu lake

Case no. 4

Shanghai Kao Co. Limited attributed its violation to an 'accident' in March 2005, when it claimed that some malfunction during production, caused the higher concentration of waste-water discharge. Its waste-water treatment facility is biologically based, so the high concentration of waste water destroyed the activity of bacteria, and it took some time for the bacteria to regain activity. Thus the water discharge did not meet the standard.

In the latest China Water Pollution Map, more than 80 MNCs in China listed. For example, BASF, Michelin, Suzhou Samsung Electronics Company, and Shanghai-Motor GM Wuling Automobile are among those on the list. Some of them have started taking measures to control the pollution of water; many, however, continue to discharge waste water. We do hope that they start to protect the water and environment in China as soon as possible.

Figure 8.7 Chemical plant

Conclusion

Environmental pollution has become a prominent problem as China's economy continues to develop, and the MNCs all around China are playing a major part in this. In the past three years in its supervision of the polluting companies, the Environment Bureau discovered that the 130 MNCs across 19 cities/provinces such as Hebei and Jilin have commonly over-discharged, violated the environmental regulations in their construction, and frequently violated their discharge application registration.

As a Chinese citizen, I have deeply felt the benefits brought by the recent economic development as I have grown up. However, it is also painful to see that the blue sky, green trees and clear water are leaving us. I sincerely wish that while investing, building factories and making profits in China, the MNCs could leave us a blue sky, and our offspring a foundation for sustainable development.

Part III

Alternative visions

Chapter 9

The indiscriminate criminalisation of environmentally beneficial activities

Avi Brisman

Introduction

Green criminology refers to the study of environmental harm by state and corporate actors, as well as individuals, and includes both specific incidents and events within defined geopolitical areas, and recurring patterns and phenomena of transboundary, transnational and global magnitude (see Carrabine *et al.* 2004; White 2008). Some green criminologists concentrate on state- and international-level environmental laws and regulations. These criminologists adopt what Halsey and White (1998: 345, 346) refer to as the 'legal-procedural approach', which 'establishes the parameters of harm by referring to practices which are proscribed by law' and that 'privileges the criminal law in the definition of what constitutes serious social injury'. Other green criminologists contemplate environmental harm more broadly, challenging prevailing definitions and ideas of 'harm' by invoking notions of environmental morality, environmental ethics, and animal, ecological, or human rights (White 1998-1999; Beirne and South 2008). These criminologists employ the 'socio-legal approach' – one that 'conceives harm in terms of damaging practices which may or may not be encapsulated under existing criminal law' (Halsey and White 1998: 345). Thus, socio-legally-oriented green criminologists consider a wide range activities and practices that may be legal, but that are nonetheless environmentally destructive (see Brisman 2008).

In this chapter, I draw on both approaches, arguing that green criminology needs to consider not just activities that hurt the environment and that are unregulated or underregulated, but also activities that are proscribed yet benefit the environment. I offer two examples of environmentally beneficial activities that are criminalised: (1) junk poaching, recyclable rustling, street scavenging, dumpster diving, and other forms of trash picking (which temper rampant production and consumption, and reduce the amount of garbage thrown into landfills and incinerators); and (2) pedicab driving (which serves as an environmentally friendly alternative to automobiles). While my focus is on the criminalisation of these activities in the USA – in multiple cities and municipalities in the case of trash picking, and in New York in the example of pedicab driving – I make reference to similar instances of criminalisation in other parts of the world. My goal is to argue that green criminology must continue to consider the ways in which environmental harms, regardless of their origin, stem from and are permitted by particular relations of power and selective criminalisation.

The first part of this chapter is devoted to trash-related activities. While a history of rubbish handling is outside the scope of this chapter, I begin with an overview of the ways in which trash, contrary to popular perception, has been and is desired and needed, including reasons why it has been and continues to be scrounged. From here, I consider the environmental benefits of certain trash-picking activities, and offer examples of and instances where such scavenging or poaching has been marginalised and criminalised. I then contemplate the reasons for such marginalisation and criminalisation, speculating that the dynamics of production and consumption, and the institutions, structures, and forces of late capitalism lie at the heart of such criminalisation.

Building from the illustration of how and why trash picking is criminalised, and how those who engage in this potentially environmentally beneficial activity are stigmatised and marginalised, I begin the second part of this chapter with a brief note about the environmental problems caused by transportation. I then discuss the benefits of pedicabs and describe the processes of criminalisation based on fieldwork conducted from August 2008 to June 2009. I conclude this chapter by offering some suggestions for future research.

Junk poaching, recyclable rustling, street scavenging, dumpster diving and other forms of trash picking

The need for garbage and trash

Garbage is frequently defined as 'refuse of any kind' (*Webster's* 2002: 935) and *trash* as 'something worth relatively little or nothing at all' (*Webster's* 2002: 2432) or as 'something we once wanted and now can't be bothered with' (Mooallem 2007: 30). Granted, there are instances in which individuals find objects of historical significance or value in the trash. For example, in 2003, a woman in Manhattan's Upper West Side discovered a painting by the Mexican artist, Ruffino Tamayo, worth more than $1 million, lying in a pile of garbage along the street (Associated Press 2007). In 2004, an old safe buried in a waste trench at the Hanford Nuclear Reservation in Washington State yielded a 1 gallon glass jug containing a batch of plutonium, among the first ever made (Fountain 2009). And in late 2004, a Queens, New York rubbish remover discovered a barrel full of dozens of ancient Mexican artefacts – bowls, figurines and jugs made between 300 BC and AD 500 – worth an estimated $16,500 (Hirshon 2009). But by definition, at least, garbage and trash would seem to have little value.

For many individuals, however, that which is labelled 'garbage' is habitually wanted and needed, and a constant source of inspiration. For example, for the anthropologists Robin Nagle, Timothy W. Jones, and William Rathje, garbage and trash serve an intellectual need and are a source of academic and scholarly enquiry (see Rathje and Murphy 1992; Shanks *et al.* 2004; Melosi 2002; see also Brown 2007; Haberman 2008; Rothstein 2008). Indeed, the entire field of archaeology is based on the detritus of earlier human endeavours (see Strasser 1999: 272).

For Dan Phillips, who uses raw materials scavenged from construction sites, as well as from contractors and companies that have ordered too much or the wrong items to build low-income housing, garbage allows him to continue his childhood pleasure of building, while reducing the landfill waste-stream. A 'master recycler' with a fierce commitment to preservation and urban renewal, Phillips employs an unskilled, minimum-wage labour force, training his workers so that they receive marketable skills that translate into larger paydays in the future (Johnson 2004; Ferrell 2006; Murphy 2009a; see also http://www.phoenixcommotion.com/mission.html).

Similarly, for 12-year-old Max Wallack, winner of the 2008 Trash to Treasure Competition (organised by *Design Squad*, a Public Broadcasting Service show, and sponsored by Intel™), in which contestants were asked to repurpose trash into practical inventions, garbage became a means for satisfying his thirst for invention, as well as a way to achieve his goal of helping homeless people and the environment. Max's invention, 'the home dome' – a round dwelling in the shape of a Mongolian yurt – is made entirely of bulky, difficult-to-dispose-of styrofoam packing peanuts stuffed into plastic grocery bags. It includes a built-in bed that anchors the dwelling to the ground by the weight of the person inside (Stone 2009).

For Dave Chameides, the Emmy Award-winning cameraman known as 'Sustainable Dave,' who has attracted attention for keeping all the garbage he has created – at home and on the road – in his house, trash has provided the impetus for his rethinking ways to cut back on the amount of things he consumed in the first place. Keeping his trash and chronicling it on his blog (http://www.365daysoftrash.com/) has allowed Chameides to call attention to growing landfills, diminishing dumping spaces, costly disposal, and the vast use of energy and carbon emissions that accompanies shipping waste long distances (Walsh 2008).

Visual artists have used cast-off objects in their works for years (see generally Zimring 2005: 137). Some of these artists (often referred to as 'folk artists' or 'outsider artists') have been self-taught and have had little or no contact with museums and galleries – their work with beer cans, bottle tops, hubcaps, and other discarded and scrounged objects often having been discovered only after their deaths (see generally Strasser 1999: 287–90; Ferrell 2006: 150–51). Other artists have gained recognition within the mainstream art world. For instance, John Chamberlain, Mark di Suvero, and Richard Stankiewicz achieved fame in the 1950s and 1960s for their 'junk sculptures' – a type of assemblage involving the welding of discarded metal into sculpture (Fineberg 1995; see also Strasser 1999: 287). In the mid-1960s, a Los Angeles-based group of African-American artists (Charles Dickson, Dale Davis, David Hammons, Elliott Pinkney, John Outterbridge, Noah Purifoy, John Riddle, and Betye Saar) began receiving attention for their Dada-inspired assemblages (Cotter 2009). More recently, Adrian Kondratowicz garnered attention for 'TRASH: anycoloryoulike', an art intervention in which the artist designed biodegradable trash bags (pink ones with white polka dots, blue ones with silver polka dots) to transform standard, everyday piles of trash into lurid sculptures of colour. Like his predecessors, Kondratowicz regards trash as both muse and medium. But for him, trash also serves as a means to convey lessons about art accessibility, urban beautification, and environmental awareness (Dembosky 2008; Jackson 2008).

Other examples of artists who use found objects in their work or whose work deals with the topic of trash abound. The SF Recycling & Disposal, Inc. runs an artist-in-residence programme 'to use art to inspire people to recycle more and conserve natural resources' (http://www.sfrecycling.com/AIR/index.php?t=d; see also Sullivan 2004). Both Tony Oursler and Mikhael Subotzky have made trash the subject of their photographs (see Rosenberg 2008), while Mark Nilsen makes 'sewer-cover paintings' – square canvases of sewer covers, made by placing a piece of canvas over a cover and then applying acrylic paint by roller so that the colors take the raised detail of the cover (Kilgannon 2003). In *I Make Maintenance Art One Hour Every Day* (1976), performance artist Mierle Laderman Ukeles cleaned floors and elevators in a Lower Manhattan office building (55 Water Street) with 300 janitors and cleaning women during regular shifts for 2 months. In *Touch Sanitation* (1978–80), she faced and shook hands with each of the then 8,500 workers in the New York City Department of Sanitation and uttered the words, 'Thank you for keeping New York City alive' (Morgan 1996, 1998; Strasser 1999: 288). In a different vein, the city of Yonkers, New York, in 2007, held a national competition to decorate six of its 45 garbage trucks in an effort to give residents something less dowdy to look at each morning, to promote environmental awareness, and to change perceptions of the Public Works Department. The winners received $2,000 and their designs were placed on the trucks. Meanwhile, the trucks have become so popular that Yonkers residents have asked to have the truck routes alternated so that they can see the other designs (Cowan 2007). At the Beginnings Nursery School in the East Village of New York City, students use a wide range of items from the schools' Material Center that they repurpose for their various art projects – objects that likely would have otherwise found their way to landfills, including bottle caps, wine corks, wood scraps, pebbles, vinyl records, CDs, and dental radiographs (Hu 2009). Finally, wreckage and rubble from the World Trade Center is now being used for memorials in towns across the USA (Wilson 2009).

These instances, however, may seem exotic or esoteric – hardly sufficient to call into question the dictionary definitions of 'garbage' and 'trash' or to contravene commonly held assumptions and beliefs about trash. But many individuals' lives and livelihoods depend on leftover, superfluous materials or by-products – that which has been rejected and thrown away. For example, in the Médina Gounass neighbourhood of Guédiawaye, Senegal, garbage is used as a building material to help raise the floors of houses that flood regularly during the summer rainy season (Nossiter 2009).

In the USA, garbage (or its containers) may not serve as a surrogate or indispensable building material (cf. Murphy 2009b; Ryzik 2009), but trash helps many people meet their economic needs. For example, 7,775 people employed by the New York City Department of Sanitation consider rubbish a means to a paycheck (e.g. Kelley 2009). (About 45 members of the Department of Sanitation are employed as 'recycling inspectors', and they make sure that New Yorkers are not mixing recycling with garbage or attempting to recycle unacceptable items (see DePalma 2005)). For Tom Szaky, founder and chief executive of TerraCycle, which collects used plastic bags, juice pouches, cookie wrappers and other items that cannot be recycled and 'upcycles' or morphs them into items such as messenger bags, tote bags, and pencil cases, trash is a raw material and the key to a multimillion-dollar, ecocapitalist (ad)venture (Belson 2008).

Unlike Szaky, who transforms trash into products that are sold, many men and women, in a tradition that dates to the early nineteenth century in the USA (and even earlier in Europe), transform garbage directly into money, hauling others' discarded items to junkyards, where they are paid based on the weight and type of materials delivered and whether they have been separated (Ferrell 2006; Farmer 2008; Khan 2009). This notion of 'trash as cash' is not an exaggeration. As Mike Powers, head of operations at TNT Scrap Metal in East Williamsburg, Brooklyn, New York, explains, there are no trash cans anywhere at the junkyard because '[w]e recycle it all. Everything you see here is money' (quoted in Khan 2009: CY4).

Garbage may be redeemable for cash – not just in the USA, but in China, Egypt, Indonesia, and elsewhere in the world (Gelling 2008; Levin 2009; Slackman 2009). But these 'do-it-yourself urban scroungers' earn far less than city waste disposal department employees, who have steady incomes with sick days and benefits, such as health insurance (Ferrell 2006: 3). And like any market, the amount one receives fluctuates (see Zimring 2005: 145). As Richtel and Galbraith (2008: A18) report, '[t]he scrap market in general is closely tied to economic conditions because demand for some recyclables tracks closely with markets for new products. Cardboard, for instance, turns into the boxes that package electronics, rubber goes to shoe soles, and metal is made into auto parts.'

Before 'trash crashed' – before the economic downturn reduced the market for recycled metals, as well as materials like cardboard, newspaper, and plastic (Richtel and Galbraith 2008) – the price of some metals on the scrap market hit record or near record highs due to rising demand from industrialising countries like China (the biggest export market for recyclables from the USA) and India (see Kurutz 2007a; Lueck 2007; Kanter 2008; Richtel and Galbraith 2008; Seabrook 2008; Urbina 2008; Vulcan 2008; Wadsworth 2008; Levin 2009; Horton n.d.). And because of the economic boom and the concomitant global demand for metal-based commodities, some individuals would not wait for items to be discarded and become trash. These thieves – 'rogue recyclers' (Wadsworth 2008) or 'criminal recyclers' as they are sometimes called (e.g. Kurutz 2007; Horton n.d.) – would pursue anything from aluminium siding on churches and houses (both those that had foreclosed and those that had not), baking racks (made of steel), beer kegs (made of stainless steel), brass vases off cemetery graves, bronze boat propellers and statues, copper wire from street lamps, electrical substations, and utility boxes, gutters and spouts to freeway guard rails, iron manhole covers, plaques from public parks, plumbing from construction sites, railroad ties, stadium bleachers, storm drains, and street grates (Ferrell 2006; Duchschere 2007a, 2007b; Havens 2007; Farmer 2008; Maag 2008; Seabrook 2008; Urbina 2008; Vulcan 2008; Wadsworth 2008; Hughes 2009; Horton n.d.). Other criminal recyclers took aim at catalytic converters ('catcons') (which contain platinum, palladium and rhodium). SUVs were favourites because they have larger catcons and offer more clearance, although all vehicles were potential targets, including police cars and low-riders (Duchshere 2007b; Pabst and Hanson 2007; Saluny 2008; Wadsworth 2008).

Such exploits were not limited to the USA. In Khabarovsk, Russia, scrap metal thieves stole a 200-tonne steel bridge, part of the only road leading to a heating plant in this city approximately 30 miles from the border with China (*Daily Mail* 2008; see also Seabrook 2008). In 2005, in Britain, the 2-tonne bronze sculpture, *Reclining Figure*, was stolen from Henry Moore's estate in Hertfordshire (north of London). Although the sculpture was never recovered, the flatbed truck and crane used in the crime were quickly discovered and evidence suggested that the work was cut up on the night of the crime. British police estimate that the sculpture, valued at $4.6 million, yielded approximately $2,300 as scrap metal (Itzkoff 2009). Elsewhere in Britain, local parish churches became victims, as thieves would tear the lead off roofs (Kanter 2008; Seabrook 2008). And because historic preservation rules require churches to replace roofs with original building materials, some churches were hit multiple times.

When the global economy slowed, demand for recyclables decreased and prices dropped. 'Even trash has become worthless,' says Tian Wengui, a Beijing resident who makes his living scouring garbage bins for soda drink bottles, soy sauce containers, and cooking oil jugs which he sells to recycling depots. In the USA, some towns and cities are curtailing the items they collect in their recycling programmes (Richtel and Galbraith 2008). Others have found it cheaper to treat everything as garbage and dump it, rather than to recycle (Richtel and Galbraith 2008; Levin 2009).

Normally, economic downturns bring with them fears of rising crime rates (Baker 2009; Monk 2009). It is unlikely, however, that 'criminal recycling' will subside simply because of the slowing global economy. While there are some indications of abatement – Richtel and Galbraith (2008) reported in December 2008 that some people who used to make a living by picking up recyclables from bins before trucks get to them have closed their operations – job loss and lack of employment opportunities have spurred others to begin 'salvaging', even with plummeting prices and even with heightened awareness of criminal recycling (see Hughes 2009). Indeed, in March 2009, vandals ripped out $1 million worth of fixtures from a 16,000 square-foot foreclosed home in southern California (Cathcart 2009).

Vulcan (2008), writing for an online investment magazine specialising in commodity equities, commodity futures and gold (the three major components of the hard-assets marketplace), hypothesises that regardless of metal prices, 'there will always be a need for scrap metal – in all its many forms, shapes and sizes.' In fact, Vulcan (2008) seems to suggest that continued or increased criminal recycling would not be such a terrible phenomenon. As Vulcan (2008) explains, using recycled metals rather than virgin ore results in a reduction in greenhouse gas emissions, water use, and water pollution, and also conserves natural resources. For example, recycling 1 tonne of steel results in an 86 per cent reduction in air pollution, a 40 per cent reduction in water use, and a 76 per cent reduction in water pollution; it conserves 54.5 kg of limestone, 1,045.4 kg of iron ore, and 636.4 kg of coal.

I cannot help but appreciate the irony that SUVs have become prime targets for catcon thieves given that these 'environmentally destructive *lusus naturae*' (Brisman 2009: 349; Brisman and Rau 2009: 267) are often purchased by individuals 'trying to look as menacing as possible to allay their fears of crime and other violence' (Bradsher

2002: 96). While the damage caused by criminal recyclers often outweighs the value of the stolen items and while taking copper from Amtrak train engines disrupts service and poses a threat to passengers (Horton n.d.) – something that I cannot condone – one could argue that the criminal recycling of SUV catalytic converters and some other metal-based items should be excused because recycling metal is more environmentally benign than the extraction of virgin ore and the tremendous amounts of pollution caused by gas-guzzling SUVs. I leave for another day a reconsideration of the legal status of rogue recycling of SUV catalytic converters and some other metal-based items (activities that cause little environmental harm, but are criminalised) and the extraction of virgin ore and the driving of SUVs (activities that cause considerable environmental harm, but have not been designated a 'crime' by state authorities). Instead, I wish to turn my attention to the individuals who pick through garbage for food and other items that they can use, as well as those who comb trash piles for items that they can sell as scrap or at garage sales and flea markets.

Living and making a living off of garbage and trash

According to Rogers (2005: 3), '[t]he United States is the world's number one producer of garbage: we consume 30 percent of the planet's resources and produce 30 percent of all its wastes. But we are home to just 4 percent of the global population' (Zimring 2005: 137, 166; Rogers 2005: 3; see generally Seabrook 2008: 48; cf. Bradsher 2009c). How do we explain the fact that the USA is the largest producer and that 'Americans remain the world's waste champions' (Worldwatch Institute 2004: 16)? These disproportionately high levels of waste are 'the product not of any natural law or strange primordial impulse,' Rogers explicates, 'but of history, of social forces ... Consumption lies at the heart of American life and economic health, and intrinsic to consumption is garbage' (2005: 9). Similarly, Kaput and Gradel (2002: 77) maintain that '[t]he principal cause of unsustainable resource use is largely a social system that promotes "conspicuous consumption" rather than intelligent, conservative resource use.' While there is some disagreement over *what* gets counted as waste and *how* waste is counted (a problem that exists in the USA and in Europe), there is little debate that a clear statistical relationship exists between waste generation and gross domestic product (GDP) per capita – in other words, 'the stronger the economy, the more trash generated' (Chertow 2002: 474).

Cognisant that growing consumption pressures have adversely affected local, regional, national, and global natural resources and ecosystem health, a growing movement of individuals in the USA (but also in Brazil, Canada, Estonia, South Korea, Sweden, and the UK) have attempted to reduce their ecological footprints by adopting alternative strategies for living based on limited participation in the conventional economy and minimal consumption of natural resources. Known as 'freegans', these street scavengers of the developed world 'liv[e] off consumer waste in an effort to minimise their support of corporations and their impact on the planet, and to distance themselves from what they see as out-of-control consumerism' (Kurutz 2007b). Drawing inspiration from the Diggers of the 1960s, an anarchist street theatre troupe based in Haight-Ashbury in San Francisco that gave away food and social services, as well as the long-haired hippies of the 1970s, who frequently foraged through supermarket dumpsters for food, clothing, and other items (Rogers 2005: 138), today's freegans comb 'through supermarket trash and eat the slightly bruised produce or just-expired canned goods that are routinely thrown out, and negotiate gifts of surplus food from sympathetic stores and restaurants' (Kurutz 2007b; see also Hoffman 1993, 2002; http://freegan.info/).

While many trash pickers and dumpster divers sift through garbage for food and other items out of necessity (e.g., Graves 2002), 'freegans' often scavenge by choice (see Bake-Paterson 2004) – intending both to actively curb the environmental degradation caused by overconsumption and to convey anticonsumerist, ecological, and political statements (e.g. Hoffman 1971; Anonymous 2003). Other individuals – often referred to as 'junk poachers' (Richtel and Galbraith 2008: A18) or 'recyclable rustlers' (Lueck 2007: A20) – are less interested in environmental ethics and trash-bin eating than in sifting through commercial and residential garbage for cardboard, paper, and, especially, metal, to sell as scrap, as well as for clothes, small appliances, tools, and other items that they might use or sell at a garage sale or flea market. But even those who scrounge for items to sell frequently regard their activities as 'running totally opposite to our egocentric, convenience-driven, disposable culture' (Mooallem 2007: 35). And an item scrounged, rather than purchased, and regardless of the motivation, is environmentally beneficial because it tempers our rampant consumption and reduces the amount of waste disposed of in landfills and incinerated (see generally Zimring 2005).

Despite this environmental boon – despite the service provided (Jacobs 2004) – freegans, junk poachers, recyclable rustlers, street scavengers, and other trash pickers across the USA and around the world (e.g. Argentina, the UK, Italy, Kyrgyzstan, Russia, and Vietnam) are stigmatised and marginalised for such activities, and, relatedly, run the risk of incurring the wrath of property owners, as well as arrest and/or fines (Zimring 2005: 4, 10, 45–46, 143, 166–167; cf. Mooallem 2007: 35 e.g. Ferrell 2006: 3, 8, 11–12, 14–15, 24–25, 28, 35, 98–99, 132, 134, 178–79, 180). For example, in 2004, the town of Trophy Club, near Fort Worth, Texas, passed an ordinance making it a crime to search through trash, with fines up to $2,000. The ordinance applied to recyclable items, reusable items, household trash, garbage and/or debris, and it prohibited opening, removing, picking up and/or searching through materials within a closed or sealed container left for kerbside collection (Ferman 2004). In October 2007, New York City Mayor Michael R. Bloomberg signed a law by which people who are caught using vehicles to 'steal' metal, paper or other recyclable material that is left on the kerb can now be fined $2,000 and have their vehicles impounded. Brokers and processors who buy stolen recyclables can also be held liable under the new law, with fines up to $5,000 for repeat offenders (New York City Administrative Code, Title 16, Sanitation, § 16–118 Littering prohibited, § 16–118(7); Rules of the City of New York, Title 15, Department of Environmental Protection, § 31–122 Sanitation Penalty Schedule; see also Lueck 2007).

While other towns and municipalities have also prohibited or attempted to prohibit trash picking and dumpster diving (e.g. 'Newark Targets "Poachers" of Curbside Recyclable Trash' 1995; cf. Bake-Paterson 2004; Graves 2002), in some localities, rustling itself is permitted (see Tinsely 2003), but codes and ordinances frustrate efforts by scroungers to make a living by scavenging. Examples include bans on possessing a shopping cart at a location other than on the premises of the retail establishment that owns the cart (Dallas City Code, Vol. II, Chapter 31, § 31–40 (Ord. No. 25439); Grabell 2004), limits to the number of garage sales one can hold during a year and the signs to promote them (Deller 2003; Tinsely 2004; Ferrell 2006: 98, 115, 132, 179), and rules regarding the accumulation of junk on one's property (Fort Worth Municipal Code, § 11A–26, 'Storage of Discarded, Used, and Broken Items' (Ord. No. 12931, 3-25-97); see also Tinsley 2004; Ferrell 2006: 115). And in the UK, a man who dived for and collected lost golf balls at courses throughout the country – and who even paid taxes on his earnings – was jailed for 6 months for theft, despite public outrage and the support of professional golfers, and companies that buy balls from divers for resale (Johnson 2002).

Why have such laws and ordinances been enacted? Why has such criminalisation occurred despite the environmental benefits of scavenging and dumpster diving? If scrounging 'operates as an essential counterforce to the ecological overload offered up by consumer society' (Ferrell 2006: 126), why have freegans and other trash pickers been punished?

The regulation and criminalisation of scrounging in the USA dates at least to the nineteenth century, when municipalities enacted restrictions on the activities of pedlars and dealers of second-hand materials due to fears of fire and disease and out of concern for public health (see Strasser 1999: 120; Zimring 2005: 34, 45–46, 157). In addition, public officials in the nineteenth century also perceived links between trade in second-hand materials, theft, and violent crime, with cities such as Boston, Chicago, New York, and Philadelphia taking measures to restrict the junk trade in an attempt to curb the theft of items that might be resold to dealers and shops (Strasser 1999: 115; Zimring 2005: 34, 68).

More recently – especially in the case of the laws and ordinances passed in the last few years – town council members and city officials have expressed concern about identity theft (see Ferman 2004; Lueck 2007). But localities have not shied away from what appears to be the main reason for such measures: economics. While cities in general often like to boast about the percentage of waste that it keeps out of landfills, which can help make a city attractive for civic-minded and environmentally conscious individuals looking to relocate, as Rathjew and Murphy (1992: 204) contend, 'recycling gets done not because it is a good thing; it gets done if it is a profitable thing.' This point is echoed by Richtel and Galbraith (2008: A18), who report that 'most recycling programs have been driven as much by raw economics as by activism.'

There are a number of ways in which economics comes into play. Cities usually make money by selling their recyclables. For example, in the mid-1990s, when Newark, New Jersey, attempted to crack down on 'poachers' of kerbside recyclable trash, Mayor Sharpe James defended the measure on the grounds that 'scavengers stealing recyclables intended for municipal collection are depriving cities of income' ('Newark Targets "Poachers" of Curbside Recyclable Trash' 1995). In 2007, New York's Department of Sanitation was paid $10-30/tonne for paper and about $190/tonne for metal. As Lueck (2007: A20) describes, 'thieves pose a particularly vexing problem ...

because they pick out the most sought-after trash – neatly bundled cardboard, or heavy pieces of metal – thereby removing the crème de la crème from the city's mix' (Lueck 2007: A20). That cities make money selling recyclables thus helps illuminate why the slowing global economy and subsequent decrease in demand for and price of recyclables lead some cities to curtail or abandon their recycling programmes altogether. It simply became cheaper for some towns and cities to treat everything as garbage and to send it to landfills and incinerators, rather than to recycle – a point noted above in the first section of this part.

Along these lines, many cities charge residents fees for garbage pick-up (because the cities, in turn, have to pay to dispose of waste). San Francisco, for example, operates under a pay-as-you-throw principle, where residents with more garbage bins pay higher monthly fees (Barringer 2008). The city tries to increase the amount of recycling it picks up so that it can sell the recyclables and decrease the amount of garbage it picks up, for which it has to pay (although it recoups some money from monthly fees). When scavengers rustle through kerbside bins, they remove items that the city would have to pay to dispose as waste – thereby reducing the city's costs – but they also remove recyclable items that the city could sell, decreasing revenue for the city.

Finally, cities make money by fining people for mixing recycling with garbage or attempting to recycle unacceptable items (DePalma 2005, 2008). New York City, for instance, frequently collects more than a quarter of a million dollars in fines for recycling violators (DePalma 2005). When scroungers pluck recyclable items from garbage or pick unacceptable items from recycling bins, they deprive New York City – and any other city with such a system of fines – of a source of income.

While cities may criminalise trash picking in order to ensure their revenue from the sale of recyclables and from fines for recycling violations, I contend that something more pervasive and systemic is afoot. We need to consider the criminalisation of junk poaching, recyclable rustling, street scavenging, dumpster diving, and other forms of trash picking as part of 'ongoing processes of criminalization' (Ferrell 2006: 6) and to examine the linkage(s) between criminalisation and capitalism.

Writing about the origins of capitalism in Britain, E.P. Thompson (1967) describes the efforts of the courts to prosecute and punish a wide variety of actions that had previously been an integral part of everyday life. New regulations made festivals, drinking, and various forms of sexual activity illegal. As Thompson explains, this process was part of a more general effort to transform a rural peasantry attuned to the schedules of farm life to the discipline of factory labour, with its demands for regular and punctual appearance and sustained, consistent labour.

Merry, in her chapter, 'The Criminalization of Everyday Life' (1998), builds off of Thompson (1967), as well as Black (1983), exploring not only efforts to regulate the behaviour of the labour force in British colonial Africa, but also the potlatch in Canada, and sexual, marriage, and labour practices in nineteenth-century Hawaii. She argues that '[a]t particular historical moments, previously accepted or at least tolerated behavior is subjected to penalties … The criminalisation of everyday life includes redefining as crimes actions already illegal but widely tolerated as well as actions routinely accepted' (Merry 1998: 15). In no uncertain terms, Merry (1998: 16) asserts that the '[c]riminalization is a fundamental part of the process of capitalist transformation and colonialism' (1998: 16).

Merry is not the only scholar to attempt to depict how law constitutes everyday social life, defines relationships, and determines cultural understandings of appropriate behaviour. For example, Hartog (1985) explores attempts to regulate pig-keeping in nineteenth-century New York City. He argues that by running their pigs in the streets of the city (where the pigs would eat garbage), the urban poor were less dependent on a cash economy for their subsistence. Garbage and pigs, then, represented competing normative orders and class struggle: 'a working class without its pigs would be that much more dependent on the market and employrs [*sic*], that much more controllable in situations of labor conflict' (Hartog 1985: 910–11).

In a different vein, Simon (2004: 137) contends that '[t]he enforcement of drug laws has always been closely tied to the social control and repression of the rights of minority groups.' In support of this proposition, he lists (1) the antiopium laws of the 1870s –the first narcotics laws in the USA – which were essentially direct attacks on the working-class Chinese immigrants on the East and West coasts; (2) the 1914 Harrison Act, which outlawed cocaine – a drug perceived as popular among African–Americans, who would commit violence and sexual assaults while high (when the truth was that it was popular among the white middle class and sold by mail order by Sears); (3) the prohibition of liquor from 1919 to 1933 – a measure promoted by white, Anglo-Saxon Protestants, who feared that the newly arrived Catholic workers would use the neighbourhood bar to foment revolution; (4) and the 1937 Marijuana Tax Act, which outlawed marijuana – a drug perceived as popular among 'lazy Mexican workers' (Simon 2004: 137–38; see also Brisman 2006). Simon (2004: 138) contends that while these antidrug laws may have originated out of a desire to control certain ethnic groups, since the 1960s, these laws have been used against anyone 'whose alternative lifestyles pose a threat to an economic system based on the work ethic, with its stress on punctuality, stability, and conformity'.

To understand the relevance of Thompson, Black, Merry, Hartog and Simon's contentions about criminalisation and capitalism to street scavenging, dumpster diving, and other forms of trash picking, let me again turn to Ferrell (2006), who quit his job as a tenured professor at Northern Arizona University and moved back to his hometown of Fort Worth, Texas, where he lived as a dumpster diver/street scrounger/trash picker for eight months. As Ferrell (2006: 28) expounds,

> America's engorged Dumpsters confirm what many already suspect: the culture and economy of consumption runs on waste. It promotes not only endless acquisition, but the steady disposal of yesterday's purchases by consumers who, awash in their own impatient insatiability, must make room for tomorrow's next round of consumption. As a result, it spawns closed communities of privileged consumers who waste each day what might sustain others for a lifetime, and landfills that clog and overflow with barely used goods, growing as big as the shopping malls from which their content not so long ago came.
>
> And yet from atop the trash heaps, from inside the Dumpsters lined up behind the shopping mall, a vast ragtag army of reconstruction emerges. Working with little more than abandoned shopping carts and their own ingenuity, urban scroungers create a complex culture of scavenging, interrupting the inexorable material from shopping mall to landfill, and undertaking to redeem contemporary U.S. society from the wreckage of its own failed arrangements. For their trouble, they regularly confront cultural and social stigmatization, and a host of legal strategies that regulate or criminalise most every moment in their redemptive dynamic, from sorting through curbside trash to distributing salvaged food to the needy. It's surely not so simple a question of law and political economy, but living the life of an urban scrounger, I began to wonder whether each statute I

> encountered, each city code, each emerging community standard regarding waste and its reuse wasn't in reality designed to eliminate any form of material acquisition and exchange except, well, shopping at the mall.

Essentially, Ferrell (2006: 162–63) argues that 'consumer culture is predicated on programmed insatiability, on the constant construction of needs and desires that can never quite be met, and so remain ready for the next new commodity. ... Corporations and their advertising agencies continually work to invent new needs and desires, layered one after the other over the basics of everyday survival, and with these new wants new markets for their consumer goods; consumers in turn acquire such goods for the emerging status they bestow, for their promise of up-to-date cultural identity.' In 'the empire of the ephemeral', to use Strasser's (1999: 200) phrase, business manufactures *consumers* as well as *products*; industry has long discouraged the repair and reuse of materials in the name of economic growth, and has 'long feared that repair and reuse might lead to lagging consumption of new commodities' (Rogers 2005: 97; see also Rogers 2005: 96, 123).

In other words, those who pick through piles of trash for food as well as for useful, functional, unused, unmarred objects with which to build and rebuild their homes (see Meyers 2009) – do not merely live off the waste of consumer society, nor do they just reject the spirit and processes of capitalism and consumer culture. Rather, they disrupt and invert such processes. Granted, the independent scrap metal haulers do not categorically or completely reject cash and consumption, but many of them – as they scrounge and salvage over time – accumulate and reuse items and parts that we are encouraged to buy, re-buy, update, and 'improve'.

To conclude this part, then, fines, penalties and other processes of criminalisation function as exercises of influence and power by the state, helping to ensure that the state, rather than individuals, makes money off of trash. In addition, such laws and ordinances benefit corporate entities, who would much rather sell you something inside their stores than have you get it for free out back or along the kerb. And finally, such laws and ordinances are, in Ferrell's (2006: 180) words, also 'designed to keep "undesirables" from fouling the consumption experiences of the city's better classes' – thus lending credence to Simon's comments regarding the correlation between criminalisation and the repression of the rights of minority groups. By reclaiming urban waste, the dumpster divers, freegans, street scavengers, junk poachers, recyclable rustlers, and other trash pickers described in this part perform an important ecological service. Yet, unfortunately, these individuals' actions are categorically, rather than selectively, criminalised.

Pedicab driving

According to Benfield and Replogle (2002: 647), 'transportation, especially our use of motorised vehicles, contributes substantially to a wide range of environmental problems, including energy waste, global warming, degradation of air and water, noise, ecosystem loss and fragmentation, and desecration of the landscape.' Unfortunately, Benfield and Replogle (2002: 648) continue, '[u]se of private vehicles has become the rule rather than the exception for those of driving age and, today, over 95% of our personal trips [in the USA] are by personal vehicles.' Although this percentage is not nearly as high in many European countries, where a greater share of trips is taken by bicycle or on foot, as China has begun to aggressively modernise its cities (e.g. Bradsher 2009a, 2009e), it has rejected European and Japanese models or urban planning, looking instead to the USA. Shortly after a bankrupt General Motors agreed to sell its Hummer division to a company from China (Bradsher and Bunkley 2009), Goodman (2009: WK3) reported:

> Like Japan – home to one of the most sophisticated rail networks on earth – China is densely populated and dependent on imported oil. As is true in Europe, China's major cities are surrounded by productive agricultural lands, making tightly clustered growth seem prudent.
>
> Instead, in a choice familiar to Americans, China has put the automobile at the center of contemporary life. China has torn down older buildings in every major city to make way for more vehicles. It has erected an impressive network of highways crisscrossing the vast country. Air quality and energy efficiency have been outweighed by reverence for the car. … China has come to embrace many of the attributes and modes of consumption that Americans may reflexively consider their own, complete with the sprawl and tangle of highways familiar to any resident of Los Angeles or Atlanta.

This absolute and per capita expansion of vehicle use in China, like that in the USA, has resulted in and will continue to result in a gluttonous appetitite for imported oil; in addition, rising carbon emissions, unhealthy air quality, runoff water pollution from transportation-related pavement, and other transportation infrastructure-related impacts are already being felt and are sure to follow (Ansfield 2009; Bradsher 2009b, 2009d; see generally Benfield and Replogle 2002; Brisman 2002, 2004).

Although China's emulation of the USA in this regard is lamentable, there are some indications that Americans' attitudes towards transportation may be shifting. For example, the new-car sales market in the USA has collapsed by 46 per cent – from levels of more than 17 million per year to below 10 million – suggesting that 'Americans' desire – and need – for new cars may be cooling' (Maynard 2009: 25; cf. Bunkley 2009). In 2008, more Americans rode public buses, underground railways, and commuter trains than in any year since 1956 (when the US government created the interstate highway system) (Cooper 2009). As of March 2009, vehicle miles travelled (also known as VMT) in the USA had declined for the thirteenth straight month (Motavelli 2009). Many cities are striving to improve bicycle paths and pedestrian walkways (e.g. Benfield and Replogle 2002) and organisations such as Transportation Alternatives are working for better-designed bike lanes, safer bridge access, more greenways, convenient and secure bicycle parking, car-free parks, congestion pricing, parking reform, and traffic justice and enforcement to ensure equal safety, respect and treatment of all street users (http://www.transalt.org/). While some of the shift away from motorised vehicle use has occurred with governmental support and/or as a result of sustainable transportation measures, the growth of pedicab driving in New York City within the last decade has occurred despite some political resistance, opposition from segments of the business community, and police harassment of pedicab drivers.

Pedicabs – for-hire, human-powered vehicles that transport one or two (and occasionally even three) passengers – offer a number of benefits to both drivers and passengers. Drivers, many of whom rent their pedicabs from owners at rates of $180–200/week, are free to set their own hours and to work as much or as little as they like, enabling them to attend college classes or pursue other interests and work opportunities (see generally Haddon 2009). Many enjoy the independence of driving a pedicab, as well as working outside, staying in shape, and the potential to make upwards of $400 a day. One driver, an aspiring musician named Garth, told me that he regards driving a pedicab as a way to meet people and network.

While pedicabs can be a more expensive means of transportation than yellow taxicabs – pedicab drivers set their own prices, but usually charge $1 per block per passenger – they can often bring their fares to their desired locations faster in rush hour than taxis. Consumers often consider them environmentally friendly alternatives to automobiles and preferable to horse-drawn carriages, which have generated controversy because of the conditions under which the horses work and live (Schirtzinger 2008; see also http://www.banhdc.org/). Pedicabs are also especially popular with tourists. Because pedicabs are open-air and move more slowly than yellow cabs, tourists can get a good look at the city and take photographs of the various sights. Many employ drivers to give them tours of Central Park. As Garth explained, 'We're like an informational center in the city.'

Currently, the pedicab industry is unregulated in New York City, meaning that anyone can drive a pedicab. Few pedicabs are insured. Licensing and safety laws enacted in 2007 – including the requirement of seat belts, turn signals, and emergency brakes, among other measures – have not been enforced because of a lawsuit challenging the licensure provisions (Baker and Grynbaum 2009; Grynbaum 2009a, 2009b; Haddon 2009).

At first blush, then, it would seem that lack of regulation would be an indication that pedicab driving is not criminalised. True, no citations or arrests have been made for driving without a licence, for driving without insurance, or for safety and inspection violations. And because citations are not being issued and arrests are not being made pursuant to pedicab-specific codes and laws, the criminalisation of pedicab driving differs from that of junk poaching, recyclable rustling, street scavenging, dumpster diving, and other forms of trash picking.

But pedicab drivers in New York City (NYC) do not conduct their business unencumbered by the law or without police harassment. Although the city does not keep track of the number of tickets issued to pedicab drivers (Haddon 2009), many have received tickets under New York Penal Law 240.20 ('disorderly conduct') and, to a lesser extent, NYC Admin. Code Section 19-176(c) ('bicycle operation on sidewalks prohibited'). (Pedicab drivers are also subject to New York City traffic regulations.) Drivers who are cited outside the catchment area of 14th Street to 59th Street and from the Hudson River to Lexington Avenue show up in court and frequently pay a fine. Those cited inside this catchment area come to the Midtown Community

Court (MCC) located on West 54th Street, where they are frequently offered something called an 'Adjournment in Contemplation of Dismissal' (or ACD), in which their cases are adjourned for a period of 6 months (sometimes a year, depending on the circumstances), after which time the cases are dismissed as long as the defendants have not been arrested again (New York Criminal Procedure Law Section 170.55). As a condition of the ACD, defendants are often required to perform community service or participate in the MCC's pedicab education programme (which lasts between 1½ and 2 hours). The pedicab education group meets once a week, four times a month for 12 months (for a total of 48 sessions per year). Since 2008, approximately 250 people have attended the group.

A typical pedicab education class begins with the facilitator – usually a licensed social worker – asking the participants to introduce themselves and state the charge listed on the ticket, the location of the infraction, and whether this was their first ticket as pedicab drivers. In the classes that I attended as part of broader, ongoing fieldwork on problem-solving courts, the great majority of drivers were foreigners – from Russia, Turkey, West Africa, and various parts of the Middle East. Many were in the USA illegally or with short-term visas. Most indicated that they were driving because it was the only job that they could obtain without paperwork – a phenomenon sure to end if and when licensing requirements go into effect. Most spoke limited English, but indicated that driving a pedicab offered the opportunity to improve their language skills. Just about all of the participants – foreigners, as well as the few US citizens – did not understand the disorderly conduct charge.

For example, when Najil introduced himself at the facilitator's request, he explained that he had received his ticket on the South Side of Central Park. 'I got this for nothing. The cop ticketed me for not going anywhere. But I was waiting for the light. He was treating me very bad.' Similarly, when Garth – a US citizen – introduced himself, he stated that he had received a ticket for blocking an entrance to the Empire State Building. 'I wasn't disorderly conducting,' Garth protested. 'I wasn't disrespectful to the police. ... The police use a lot of force with a lot of arrogance and controlling point of view. ... You can speak honorably and honestly ... without making people less of who they are.' A third driver, Johnny, from Tripoli, did not understand the facilitator's question. After Garth explained matters to him, Johnny recounted in broken English that he had also received his ticket for blocking an entrance to the Empire State Building. When asked the charge, Johnny looked at the ticket, shrugged, and handed the ticket to the facilitator, who read out loud, 'Disorderly conduct and impeding vehicular traffic'. The facilitator's statement drew a blank from Johnny.

To someone unfamiliar with the law, the charge of 'disorderly conduct' sounds much worse than it is. Many of the drivers at the pedicab education classes that I attended, as well as those that I spoke to on the streets, went to great efforts to explain that they had not been acting out of control – loudly, aggressively, disrespectfully, in a threatening manner. While fighting, cursing, or yelling in public are proscribed under New York Penal Law Section 240.20, disorderly conduct is a catch-all offence that includes obstructing vehicular traffic, and a ticket for it may be issued to a pedicab driver who has parked in a traffic lane, parked in an area marked 'No Standing Zone' or 'Loading Zone,' parked on the sidewalk, blocked a driveway, or unloaded passengers at a pedestrian crossing or bus stop.

During the course of the class, the facilitator generally tries to ascertain why the participants have become pedicab drivers, what the drivers perceive to be the advantages and disadvantages of pedicabs for drivers and customers, how the drivers determine their fees, and what the participants think about the lack of industry regulation. But the main purpose of the pedicab education programme is to instruct participants about the law. After introductions, the facilitator normally provides a little background on the MCC and its problem-solving orientation, explains the ACD process, and describes the laws relevant to pedicab drivers. This entails fleshing out the provisions of New York Penal Law 240.20 and 'reckless operation of a bicycle'. Sometimes this part of the discussion is more involved than others. For example, on one occasion, the facilitator asked the participants what they thought about the individual provisions of the disorderly conduct law. On another occasion, however, the facilitator simply asked the group what they thought the provisions meant, adding to and correcting the answers given. From what I could tell, the depth of the discussion seemed to hinge on the extent to which the participants spoke English. For instance, in one class, only one of the drivers knew what 'reckless' meant ('without thinking of our consequences … thinkless'); it should be no surprise, then, that in this class, the facilitator did not solicit the opinions of the drivers regarding the provisions of the disorderly conduct law.

While the content and dynamics of the programme can shift from class to class depending on the experiences of the drivers, during my visits to the MCC, I was able to observe a number of recurring themes. First, many of the drivers (as well as those whom

I interviewed outside the MCC) feel that pedicab drivers are held to different standards and treated more harshly than taxicab drivers. For example, Milan, from Turkey, asserted: 'Cops always double-park [in the] bicycle lane. Yellow cabs stop and unload in bicycle lanes so pedicabs can't ride there all the time or very well.'

Second, while many of the drivers feel that they are viewed positively by large swathes of the New York City population, almost all seemed to suspect that the citations and police harassment were the result of pressure from the taxi industry and horse-carriage industry, who believe that pedicabs 'steal' their business. (This sentiment was somewhat confirmed by the yellow cab and horse-carriage drivers with whom I spoke, although many of these drivers also claimed that pedicab drivers ride unsafely.) 'Generally, we're looked at as solicitors, as bad guys, as people working against the city,' Garth explained. Other pedicab drivers pointed to local businesses and theatre owners as the cause of police attention, speculating that some of the more aggressive pedicab drivers may harass shoppers and theatre-goers, adversely affecting the image of the industry.

Third, many of the drivers were resigned to the fact that they would get tickets. According to Evan from Russia, 'Regardless of what you do, you're going to get a ticket – once a month.' As a result, Evan explained, he occasionally disobeys traffic laws, such as turning right on red. 'Pedicab drivers would be more respectful of cops if they didn't crack down as much,' he suggested.

Along these lines, virtually all of the drivers recounted adverse interactions with the police officers in addition to the ones in which they received their tickets – something that was also true of the drivers with whom I spoke on the street and in Central Park. As Garth explained, 'I like just law – when the police officers … respect us as people. They [the police] talk to us like we're nobodies. … It can really put people's spirits down.' Despite comments such as these, none of the drivers with whom I had spoken indicated that they had ever filed a complaint with the city's Civilian Complaint Review Board (CCRB) (although many of the drivers recounted stories that merited the filing of a complaint and investigation). Some drivers, who were already terrified that their status in the USA had become compromised because of their citation, feared that their status might become even more precarious with a CCRB complaint. Others, such as Garth, who initially expressed interest in filing a CCRB complaint, later admitted that the programme had allowed them 'to be heard', even though the views expressed in class would not change an officer's behaviour or change New York Police Department policies the way a CCRB complaint might (see http://www.nyc.gov/html/ccrb/html/why.html).

Finally, the issue of regulation tends to divide the riders. In the abstract, most are (1) in favour of improved safety measures that would accompany regulation; (2) feel that regulation might lend greater legitimacy to their work, thereby increasing the number of customers; and (3) believe that there are too many drivers and that, at the very least, regulation would help eliminate the bad ones. But when asked whether they would vote for regulation, should such matters be put to a vote, those drivers with a better command of English – perhaps the same people less concerned about their status in working in the USA – tended to favour regulation, whereas those with more limited English did not. Many of the latter expressed fears of discrimination based on language ability, nationality, and ethnicity, and worried that regulation and its licensing tests and requirements would deprive them of one of the few ways to make a living.

Regulation does appear to be inevitable and forthcoming (Grynbaum 2009a, 2009b). While it is clear that regulation will change the dynamic of criminalisation, it is difficult to predict exactly how. With licensing, insurance, and safety requirements, drivers will encounter more ways in which they may be ticketed. However, regulation may result in fewer bad drivers, thereby potentially decreasing the number of citations for disorderly conduct. Because regulation will require the city to keep track of the number of citations issued for pedicab-related offences, overly zealous police officers may curb their enthusiasm for harassing drivers and writing under the catch-all disorderly conduct law. On the other hand, licensing requirements may offer some officers the pretext with which to stop drivers who are of a certain appearance – a potential equivalent to the 'driving while black' phenomenon in the United States.

In sum, it is difficult to conclude that the same forces that underlie the criminalisation of junk poaching, recyclable rustling, street scavenging, dumpster diving, and other forms of trash picking predominate in the context of pedicab driving (although opposition to pedicabs by the taxicab and horse-carriage industries, as well as by some business and theatre owners, does resonate with the economic reasons for criminalisation of trash-related activities). But identifying a singular root cause may be unnecessary. Private vehicle use, in general, and single occupancy vehicle use, in particular, are all too common in the USA and in New York. While pedicab driving offers an environmentally friendly alternative that should be embraced, law enforcement practices have unfortunately done the opposite, and in the process, police have harassed and contributed to the stigmatisation and marginalisation of an already struggling segment of the population.

Conclusion

In this chapter, I have argued that green criminology needs to consider not just activities that hurt the environment and that are unregulated or underregulated, but also activities that are proscribed yet benefit the environment. In support of this position, I have offered two examples of environmentally beneficial activities that are criminalised.

Beginning with junk poaching, recyclable rustling, street scavenging, dumpster diving, and other forms of trash picking, I have asserted that these activities and practices retard and oppose the dynamics and processes of environmentally unsustainable, consumption-oriented societies, but have been criminalised despite these benefits. I have suggested that the reason for such criminalisation – part of a long history that has conflated trash picking and waste handling with social standing and xenophobia – can be linked, in part, to economics: localities' desire to generate revenue from the sale of recyclables and from fines for recycling violations, and corporate entities' discouragement of repair and reuse of materials in the name of economic growth and fear that scavengers will foul the consumption experiences of the affluent.

Building off of this street scavenging example, I have next maintained that pedicabs serve as an environmentally friendly alternative to automobiles (as well as discourage the use of ethically problematic horse-drawn carriages), yet have also been unfairly and disproportionately criminalised despite their environmental benefits. Pedicab drivers – frequently immigrants to the USA – resemble, in many ways, the 'low-status', second-hand materials workers of the nineteenth century. But like the trash handlers and waste pickers of centuries past and like contemporary dumpster divers, pedicab drivers have also encountered stigmatisation, marginalisation, and criminalisation. While such attitudes towards and treatment of pedicab drivers have been far less pervasive than those encountered by urban scroungers and while the situation involving pedicab driving is still evolving with regulation on the horizon, I have posited that some of the motivations behind the stigmatisation, marginalisation, and criminalisation of pedicab driving may be similar to those underlying the stigmatisation, marginalisation, and criminalisation of trash-related activities.

These examples are but the tip of the iceberg and further research is needed to explore and expose the ways in which environmental harms stem from and are permitted by particular relations of power and selective criminalisation – what I have referred to in this chapter as the criminalisation of environmentally beneficial activities. For instance, hemp, which has a wide range of uses as food, medicine, and dietary supplement, as well as in clothes, lotions, and building materials, possesses a number of environmental benefits (Brisman 2008: 741–43; see also Strasser 1999: 90–1). It can be used in water and soil purification (i.e. as a 'mop crop' to clear impurities from sewage effluent and other waste water), and in weed control (obviating the need for herbicides and offering farmers the benefit of crop rotation); hemp seed oil can be used as fuel for vehicles and homes, providing an alternative to the fossil fuels that contribute to global warming. But in the USA, hemp is treated like marijuana because it contains tetrahydrocannabinol; it is therefore illegal to grow hemp under federal law – the Controlled Substances Act of 1970 – without a permit from the federal Drug Enforcement Administration (DEA). While some state legislatures, recognising the economic and environmental benefits of hemp cultivation, have passed bills allowing farmers to grow industrial hemp (e.g. Maine, Montana, North Dakota, Vermont, and West Virginia), farmers in these states have not yet begun to grow hemp due to fears of arrest and prosecution by the DEA (see Brisman 2008; see also www.hemp.org; www.sustainablehemp.net; www.votehemp.com). Future research might consider federal opposition to growing hemp (including the reasons why marijuana and hemp are not distinguished), the nature of state opposition, the legal status of hemp in European and Asian countries, and the evolving legal landscape in Australia, where the states of Victoria, Queensland, and New South Wales have all issued licences to grow hemp for industrial use within the last 10 years.

Other research might include an examination of bans against beekeeping, which is permitted in Chicago, Dallas, London, Minneapolis, Paris, and San Francisco, but is illegal in New York, despite the fact that bees help pollinate rooftop and community gardens, and that a single hive can produce about 27 kg of honey per harvest (depending on the keeper), thereby reducing the environmental costs of transporting honey (Cornes 2008; see also Applebome 2009; Brustein 2009; Rules of the City of New York, Title 24: Department of Health and Mental Hygiene; Title IV: Environmental Sanitation; Part

B: Control of Environment; Section 161.01 Wild animals prohibited). One might also investigate the effects of and reasons behind cities' prohibitions against raising hens and other livestock, despite the fact that such urban farming facilitates locavorism (diets based on eating foods grown only within a certain geographic radius) and allows immigrant communities to maintain aspects of their cultural heritage. For example, city dwellers in the USA may raise chickens in Chicago, Fort Collins (Colorado), Houston, New York, Oakland, Portland (Oregon), San Francisco, and Seattle (which also permits residents to have up to three goats), but not Boston (Kilarski 2003; see also Blecha 2007; Price 2007; Applebome 2009; Neuman 2009; www.madcitychickens.com; www.thecitychicken.com; http://urbanchickens.org/chicken-ordinances-and-laws).

Whether such research again demonstrates a link between environmental harm and the institutions, structures, and processes of production and consumption in late capitalist society (see White 1998–9) remains to be seen. Regardless, future research should, in the words of Beirne and South (2009: xv), attempt to 'uncover relevant sources and forms of power, including the state's willingness or reluctance to construct certain forms of harm as crimes, as well as social inequalities and their ill effects' – applicable irrespective of the specific form of criminalisation and the locus of the legal regime (or environmental harm, for that matter).

References

Anonymous (2003) *Evasion*. Atlanta, GA: CrimethInc.

Ansfield, J. (2009) 'Slump Tilts Priorities of Industry in China', *New York Times*, 19 April 19, 6.

Applebome, P. (2009) 'Envisioning the End of "Don't Cluck, Don't Tell" ', *New York Times*, 30 April, A21.

Associated Press (2007) 'Painting Found in Trash Sells for $1M', 21 November [online]. Available at: http://www.sfgate.com/cgi-bin/article.cgi?f=/n/a/2007/11/21/national/a065007S04.DTL&tsp=1 (accessed 29 November 2009).

Bake-Paterson, Z. (2004) 'The Art of Dumpster Diving', *Martlet*, 56(17): 8 January [online]. Available at: http://www.martlet.ca/old/archives/040108/feature.html (accessed 29 November 2009).

Baker, A. and Grynbaum, M.M. (2009) 'Four Hurt When a Pedicab Slams into a Taxi in Brooklyn', *New York Times*, 11 June, A27.

Barringer, F. (2008) 'A City Committed to Recycling is Ready for More', *New York Times*, 7 May, A19.

Beirne, P. and South, N. (2008) 'Introduction: Approaching Green Criminology', in Beirne, P. and South, N. (eds), *Issues in Green Criminology: Confronting Harms Against Environments, Humanity and Other Animals*, xiii–xxii. Cullompton: Willan Publishing.

Belson, K. (2008) 'Kept Out of Landfills and Reborn as a Bag', *New York Times*, 24 September, H11.

Benfield, F.K. and Replogle, M. (2002) 'Transportation', in J.C. Dernbach, (ed.), *Stumbling Toward Sustainability*. Washington, DC: Environmental Law Institute, 647–65.

Black, D. (1983) 'Crime as Social Control', *American Sociological Review*, 48(1): 34–45.

Blecha, J.L. (2007) 'Urban Life with Livestock: Performing Alternative Imaginaries Through Small-Scale Urban Livestock Agriculture in the United States', PhD dissertation, University of Minnesota. AAT 3273113.

Bradsher, K. (2002) *High and Mighty: SUVs: The World's Most Dangerous Vehicles and How They Got that Way*. New York: Public Affairs/Perseus Books.

Bradsher, K. (2009a) 'American Officials Press China on Efforts to Curb Greenhouse Gases', *New York Times*, 16 July: A10.

Bradsher, K. (2009b) 'China Outlines Plans for Making Electric Cars', *New York Times*, 11 April, B5.

Bradsher, K. (2009c) 'China's Trash Problem May Also Be the World's', *New York Times*, 12 August, A11.

Bradsher, K. (2009d) 'China Vies to Be World's Leader in Electric Cars', *New York Times*, 2 April, A1, A20.

Bradsher, K. (2009e) 'U.S. and China Agree to Study Ways to Make Buildings More Energy-Efficient', *New York Times*, 17 July, A6.

Bradsher, K. and Bunkley, N. (2009) 'Chinese Firm Acquiring G.M's Hummer Expects to Keep Operations in U.S.', *New York Times*, 3 June, B5.

Brisman, A. (2002) 'Considerations in Establishing a Stormwater Utility', *Southern Illinois University Law Journal*, 26(3): 505–28.

Brisman, A, (2006) 'Meth Chic and the Tyranny of the Immediate: Reflections on the Culture–Drug/Drug–Crime Relationships', *North Dakota Law Review*, 82(4): 1273–1396.

Brisman, A. (2008) 'Crime–Environment Relationships and Environmental Justice', *Seattle Journal for Social Justice*, 6(2): 727–817.

Brisman, A. (2009) 'It Takes Green to Be Green: Environmental Elitism, "Ritual Displays," and Conspicuous Non-Consumption', *North Dakota Law Review*, 85(2): 329–370.

Brisman, A. and Rau, A. (2009) 'From Fear of Crime to Fear of Nature: The Problem with Permitting Loaded, Concealed Firearms in National Parks', *Golden Gate University Environmental Law Journal*, 2(2): 255–72.

Brown, P. (2007) 'Highway Debris, Long an Eyesore, Grows as Hazard', *New York Times*, 11 May, A1, A17.

Brustein, J. (2009) 'Beekeepers Keep the Lid On', *New York Times*, 21 June 21, MB5.

Bunkley, N. (2009) 'New-Vehicle Sales Reach a 2009 High', *New York Times*, 3 June, B1, B4.

Carrabine, E., Iganski, P., Lee, M., Plummer, K. and South, N. (2004) 'The Greening of Criminology', in E. Carrabine, P. Iganski, M. Lee *et al.*, *Criminology: A Sociological Introduction*. London: Routledge, 313–330.

Cathcart, R. (2009) 'Vandals Strip a Vacant Villa in California', *New York Times*, 8 April, A13.

Chertow, M. (2002) 'Municipal Solid Waste', in J.C. Dernbach (ed.), *Stumbling Toward Sustainability*. Washington, DC: Environmental Law Institute, 467–78.

Cooper, M. (2009) 'Transit Use Hit Five-Decade High in 2008 as Gas Prices Rose', *New York Times*, 9 March, A13.

Cornes, S. (2008) 'Sweet Honey in the Block', *edibleMANHATTAN*, September/October (1): 53–56.

Cotter, H. (2009) 'A Life, from a Southern Farm Town to Watts, in Castoff Objects', *New York Times*, 13 May, C7.

Cown, A.L. (2007) 'Gobbling Up Garbage, and Looking Good Doing It', *New York Times*, 28 June, B1, B6.

Daily Mail (2008) 'Russian Police Hunt for Thieves Who Stole a 200-Tonne Metal Bridge', *Daily Mail*, 8 January [online]. Available at: http://www.dailymail.co.uk/news/article-506748/Russian-police-hunt-thieves-stole-200-tonne-metal-bridge.html (accessed 29 November).

Deller, M. (203) 'Sign Fine Spurs Petition Plans in River Oaks', *Fort Worth Star-Telegram*, 11 June, Metro: 7.

Dembosky, A. (2008) 'Art the Garbage Man Can Appreciate', *New York Times*, 8 September, B2.

DePalma, A. (2005) 'At the Curb, an Exercise in Confusion', *New York Times*, 12 September, A18.

DePalma, A. (2008) 'Bill to Recycle Electronics is Approved', *New York Times*, 14 February, C13.

Duchschere, K. (2007a) 'Former Employee is Arrested in Theft of Copper from Firm', *Star Tribune* (Minneapolis, MN), 10 August, 5B.

Duchschere, K. (2007b) 'Thieves Turn to Car Parts for Metal to Peddle', *Star Tribune* (Minneapolis, MN), 31 July, 1A.

Farmer, A. (2008) 'In the Metal Recycling Business, It's Loud, Dirty and Suddenly Lucrative', *New York Times*, 27 June, B7.

Ferman, D. (2004) 'Trophy Club Town Council Votes to Make Scavenging in Trash – a Crime', *Fort Worth Star-Telegram*, 20 January, 2B.

Ferrell, J. (2006) *Empire of Scrounge: Inside the Urban Underground of Dumpster Diving, Trash Picking, and Street Scavenging*. New York: New York University Press.

Fineberg, J. 91995) *Art Since 1940: Strategies of Being*. Englewood Cliffs, NJ: Prentice-Hall.

Fountain, H. (2009) 'Found in the Trash: A Jug of Plutonium (Vintage '44, Sleuths Say)', *New York Times*, 3 March, D3.

Freegan.info (n.d.) 'What is a Freegan?' [online]. Available at: http://freegan.info/ (accessed 29 November 2009).

Gelling, P. (2008) 'Trying to Stop Pollution From Killing a Lifeline', *New York Times*, 14 December, 18.

Goodman, P.S. (2009) 'What Would Mao Drive? A Little Red … Hummer', *New York Times*, 7 June, WK3.

Gopnik, A. (2007) 'New York Local: Eating the Fruits of the Five Boroughs', *New Yorker*, 3 September, 60–69.

Grabell, M. (2004) 'Homeless Find Ways to Roll with Shopping Cart Ban', *Dallas Morning News*, 8 March, 7B.

Graves, R. (2002) 'City May Tell Homeless to Move Along', *Houston Chronicle*, 14 May, 1A.

Grynbaum, M.M. (2009a) 'Safety Rules for Pedicabs Were Never Put into Effect', *New York Times*, 12 June, A20.

Grynbaum, M.M. (2009b) 'Stalled Plan to License Pedicabs Advances', *New York Times*, 15 June, A17.

Haberman, C. (2008) 'The Science of Trash, and Esteem for Its Collectors', *New York Times*, 15 January, C13.

Haddon, H. (2009) 'No Easy Ride for City's Pedicabbies', *amNew York*, 19–21 June, 03.

Halsey, M. and White, R. (1998) 'Crime, Ecophilosophy and Environmental Harm', *Theoretical Criminology*, 2(3): 345–71.

Havens, C. (2007) 'Metal Thieves Picked the Wrong Statue', *Star Tribune* (Minneapolis, MN), 2 September, 1B.

Hirshon, N. (2009) 'Professional Mover finds $16,500 in Rare Antiquities in the Trash', *Daily News* (New York), 19 July [online]. Available http://www.dailynews.com/money/2009/07/19/2009-07-19–trash_worth_16g_rubbish_guy_finds_a_little_treasure_trove.html (accessed 29 November 2009).

Hoffman, A. (1971) [1996] *Steal This Book*. New York: Four Walls Eight Windows.

Hoffman, J. (1993) *The Art & Science of Dumpster Diving*. Port Townsend, WA: Loompanics Unlimited.

Hoffman, J. (2002) *Dumpster Diving: The Advanced Course: How to Turn Other People's Trash into Money, Publicity, and Power*. Boulder, CO: Paladin Press.

Horton, J. (n.d.) 'How Criminal Recycling Works', *HowStuffWorks* [online]. Available at: http://people.howstuffworks.com/criminal-recycling.htm (accessed 29 November 2009).

Hu, W. (2009) 'Where One Man's Trash is Preschoolers' Art Material', *New York Times*, 1 June, A19.

Hughes, C.J. (2009) 'In Union Square, Copper is Easy Pickings', *New York Times*, 28 January, A27.

Itzkoff, D. (2009) 'World's Costliest Scrap Metal?', *New York Times*, 20 May, C3.

Jackson, B.K. (2008) 'Think Pink to Save the Planet', *New York Magazine*, 19 May [online]. Available at: http://nymag.com/news/intelligencer/46831/ (accessed 29 November 2009).

Jacobs, A. (2004) 'The Accidental Environmentalist: Living from One Discarded Can to the Next', *New York Times*, 23 September, B1.

Johnson, P.C. (2004) 'Leftovers Good Enough to Live in', *Houston Chronicle*, 23 May, 8.

Kanter, J. (2008) 'As Price of Lead Soars, British Churches Find Holes in Roof', *New York Times*, 8 April, C1, C6.

Kapur, A. and Graedel, T.E. (2002) 'Production and Consumption of Materials', in J.C. Dernbach (ed.), *Stumbling Toward Sustainability*. Washington, DC: Environmental Law Institute, 63–78.

Kelley, T. 92009) 'He's Sanitizing the Bronx, Block by Block', *New York Times*, 6 January, A20.

Khan, D. (2009) 'Heavy Metal', *New York Times*, 22 February, CY4.

Kilarski, B. 92003) *Keep Chickens! Tending Small Flocks in Cities, Suburbs and Other Small Spaces*. North Adams, MA: Storey Publishing.

Kilgannon, C. (2003) 'A Career in the Sewer', *New York Times*, 30 November, §14: 6.

Kurutz, S. (2007a) 'Criminal Recycling', *New York Times Magazine*, 9 December, Section 6: 64.

Kurutz, S. (2007b) 'Not Buying It', *New York Times*, 21 June, F.

Levin, D. (2009) 'Now, Just Trash: China's Recycling Market Sags as the Economy Sours', *New York Times*, 12 March, B1, B4.

Lueck, T. (2007) 'Hot Items for Thieves: Recyclables', *New York Times*, 15 October, A20.

Maag, C. (2008) 'In U.S., Metal Theft Plagues Troubles Neighborhoods', *New York Times*, 8 April, C6.

Maynard, M. (2009) 'Industry Fears U.S. May Quite New Car Habit', *New York Times*, 31 May, 1, 25.

Melosi, M.V. (2002) 'The Fresno Sanitary Landfill in an American Cultural Context', *Public Historian*, 24(3): 17–35.

Merry, S.E. (1998) 'The Criminalization of Everyday Life', in A. Sarat, M. Constable, D. Engel, *et al.* (eds), *Everyday Practices and Trouble Cases*. Evanston, IL: Northwestern University Press, 14–39.

Meyers, G.R. (2009) 'Trash House', *Green Options*, 4 March [online]. Available at: http://greenbuildingelements.com/2009/02/17/trash-house/ (accessed 29 November 2009).

Mooallem, J. (2007) 'The Unintended Consequences of Hyperhydration', *New York Times Magazine*, 27 May, 30–35.

Morgan, R.C. (1996) *Art into Ideas: Essays on Conceptual Art*. Cambridge: Cambridge University Press.

Morgan, R.C. (1998) 'Touch Sanitation: Mierle Laderman Ukeles', in L.F. Burnham and S. Durland (eds), *The Citizen Artist: 20 Years of Art in the*

Public Arena: An Anthology from High Performance Magazine 1978–1998. Gardiner, NY: Critical Press, 55–60.

Motavalli, J. (2009) 'Economy May Be Keeping Us Off the Road. *New York Times*, 15 March, AU6.

Murphy, K. (2009a) 'One Man's Trash ...', *New York Times*, 3 September, D1, D6–D7.

Murphy, K. (2009b) 'Self-Contained in Texas', *New York Times*, 16 July, D6.

Neuman, W. (2009) 'Keeping Their Eggs in Their Backyard Nests', *New York Times*, 4 August, B1, B4.

Nossiter, A. (2009) 'In a Senegalese Slum, a Building Material Both Primitive and Perilous', *New York Times*, 3 May, 10.

Pabst, L. and Hanson, E.M. (2007) 'Thieves Show How Low They'll Go', *Star Tribune* (Minneapolis, MN), 25 July, 1N.

Price, C. (2007) 'A Chicken on Every Plot, a Coop in Every Backyard', *New York Times*, 19 September, D5.

Rathje, W. and Murphy, C. (1992) *Rubbish! The Archaeology of Garbage*. New York: HarperCollins.

Richtel, M. and Galbraith, K. 92008) 'Back at Junk Value, Recyclables Are Piling Up', *New York Times*, 8 December, A1, A18.

Rogers, H. (2005) *Gone Tomorrow: The Hidden Life of Garbage*. New York: The New Press.

Rosenberg, K. (2008) 'Splitting a Gallery in Half to Focus on Social Strife', *New York Times*, 12 September, E33.

Rothstein, E. (2008) 'Nothing's Wasted, Especially Garbage', *New York Times*, 31 March, B1, B6.

Ryzik, M. (2009) 'Forget the Trash Bag, Bring a Towel', *New York Times*, 29 July, C1, C6.

Saluny, S. (2008) 'Thieves Leave Cars, but Take Catalytic Converters', *New York Times*, 29 March, A9.

Schirtzinger, A. (2008) 'Fairytale Ride or Cruel Practice?', *Our Town*, 18 September, 21–13.

Seabrook, J. (2008) 'American Scrap', *New Yorker*, 14 January, 46–59.

Shanks, M., Platt, D. and Rathje, W.L. (2004) 'The Perfume of Garbage: Modernity and the Archaeological', MODERNISM/*modernity*, 11(1): 61–83.

Simon, D.R. (2004) *Tony Soprano's America: The Criminal Side of the American Dream*. Boulder, CO: Westview.

Slackman, M. (2009a) 'Belatedly, Egypt Spots Flaws in Wiping Out Pigs', *New York Times*, 20 September, A1, A8.

Slackman, M. (2009b) 'Cleaning Cairo, But Taking a Livelihood', *New York Times*, 25 May, A7.

Stone, J.J. (2009) '12-Year-Old Makes Homeless Shelter from Trash', *Green Options*, 26 February [online]. Available at: http://greenbuildingelements.com/2009/02/26/12-year-old-makes-homeless-shelter-from-trash/ (accessed 29 November 2009).

Strasser, S. (1999) *Waste and Want: A Social History of Trash*. New York: Henry Holt.

Sullivan, J. (2004) 'Trash Turns into Treasure as New Art Form Evolves', *San Francisco Chronicle*, 22 April, E3.

Thompson, E.P. (1967) 'Time, Work Discipline, and Industrial Capitalism', *Past and Present*, 38: 56–97.

Tinsely, A.M. (2003) 'Program Offers Incentives for Glass Bottles', *Fort Worth Star-Telegram*, 2 June, Metro: 1.

Tinsely, A.M. (2004) 'City Code Watchers Are Hitting the Street', *Fort Worth Star-Telegram*, 5 May, Metro: 1B.

Urbina, I. 92008) 'Philadelphia Streets Unsafe for Manhole Covers', *New York Times*, 23 July 23, A1.

U.S. Water News (1995) 'Newark Targets "Poachers" of Curbside Recyclable Trash', October [online]. Available at: http://www.uswaternews.com/archives/arcpolicy/5curbtrsh.html (29 November 2009).

Vulcan, T. (2008) 'Thank Scrap: The Market for Recycled Metals', *Hard Assets Investor*. 22 January [online]. Available at: http://www.hardassetsinvestor.com/features-and-interviews/1/642.html?utm_source=HAI&utm_medium=article&utm_campaign=relatedItems (accessed 29 November 2009).

Wadsworth, J. (2008) 'Recycling Turns Criminal', *East Bay Express*, 23 January [online]. Available at: http://www.eastbayexpress.com/news/recycling_turns_criminal/Content?oid=627756 (accessed 29 November 2009).

Walsh, B. (2008) 'Meet Dave, the Man Who Never Takes Out the Trash', *Time*, 22 September [online]. Available at: http://www.time.com/time/health/article/0,8599,1843163,00.html (accessed 29 November 2009).

Webster's Third New International Dictionary of the English Language Unabridged (2002) Springfield, MA: Merriam-Webster, Inc.

White, R. (1998) 'Environmental Criminology and Sydney Water', *Current Issues in Criminal Justice*, 10: 214–19.

White, R. (2008) *Crimes Against Nature: Environmental Criminology and Ecological Justice*. Cullompton: Willan Publishing.

Wilson, M. (2009) '9/11 Steel Forms Heart of Far-Flung Memorials', *New York Times*, 7 September, A1, A3.

Worldwatch Institute (2004) *State of the World, 2004: A Worldwatch Institute Report on Progress Toward a Sustainable Society*. New York: W.W. Norton.

Zimring, C.A. (2005) *Cash for Your Trash: Scrap Recycling in America*. New Brunswick, NJ: Rutgers University Press.

Chapter 10

The big grey elephants in the backyard of Huelva, Spain

Lorenzo Natali

Where to begin

In this chapter we will explore a situated environmental scenario: Huelva, a town in southern Spain, heavily polluted by a huge industrial and chemical plant established during the 1960s and built in close proximity to the town, in what really is its backyard. We shall examine this case of environmental crime through a still unfolding criminological perspective, identifying the theoretical issues encountered and the methodological approaches to be taken when studying an ongoing case of conflict and of environmental crime such as the one presented here.

In the following pages we will not attempt to depict the juridical and legal intricacies of the critical situation found in Huelva. Such a task would leave no space for the specific field of empirical research I have decided to engage in. The direction of my investigation will instead develop by touching upon questions such as, which significant vocabularies and narratives concerning the problem of contamination and the empirical reality of an environmental crime circulate among the inhabitants of the area affected? And again, what decisive questions, often extending beyond the pale of environmental criminology, do such accounts raise? What demands for justice do they provoke?

In the course of our investigation, we will inevitably find ourselves observing, scrutinising and analysing the interactions between humans and the environment they inhabit just when such interactions become more dissatisfying, frustrating and increasingly fraught with risks, dangers and destruction.

As Javier Auyero and Debora Swistun (2008) remind us, there is a large amount of sociological literature interested in the study of views, sentiments and responses of people who live in polluted and health-threatening environments. Yet, these studies, almost exclusively concerned with North America, prove to be sadly inadequate – a real 'analytical and theoretical loss' (Auyero and Swistun 2008: 358) – when analysing cases characterised by disagreement, confusion, doubts, plurality and complexity of points of view about the origins, extent and effects of contamination. As a result, the sources of social perception about contamination remain under-explored.

Though based on a different tradition of thought – symbolic interactionism (Mead 1934; Blumer 1969) – my ethnographic and criminological exploration goes in the direction chosen by Auyero and Swistun for their study of the Argentine shanty town of Flammable; that is, towards the origins of social perceptions and real-life experiences of contamination.

However, my own contribution focuses on another locality, an elsewhere – the Spanish town of Huelva – fully representing a locus typical of the consequences of modernity. We shall see that many of the complex dynamics associated with the experiences of contamination described by Auyero and Swistun can also be observed in Huelva: here, too, in spite of the tireless work of a social movement fighting for the gradual reclamation of the polluted areas (Mesa de la Ria), the residents are not engaged in any large-scale collective action, nor do we find a shared knowledge of the problem or the causes, responsibilities and effects of the current contamination.

How could something (the huge, grey 'polo quimico'), originally a cause of pride for the government and a promise of increasing wealth for the population of Huelva, turn into an embarrassing elephant in the room, so that its very reality is obscured by people behaving and living as if it did not exist and as if it did not produce the degree of pollution it does? How are the residents trying to hold together the fragments of a reality that appears impossible to recompose?

These are the questions – and the underlying hypothesis – informing my research.

A critical situation: the town of Huelva – what is happening?

In this section, I will provide an overview of those aspects which

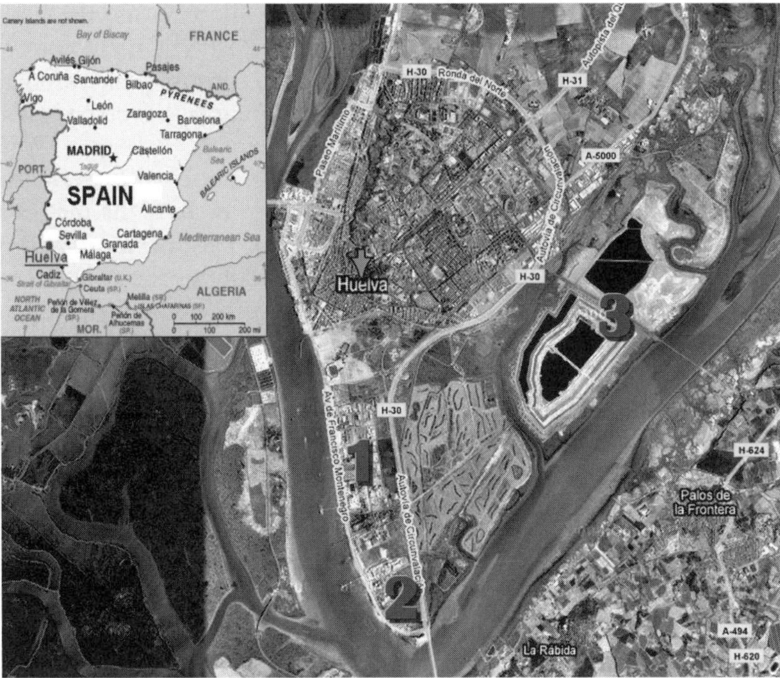

Imagery©TerraMetrics, map data © 2010 Tele Atlas.

Figure 10.1 The town of Huelva and its 'backyard': 1) the industrial and chemical plant; 2) the beach of Punta del Sebo; 3) the so-called balsas de fosfoyesos

allow us to describe the case of Huelva as an environmental crime, fully aware that the parameters used by any criminologist to decide the range of such a definition always include axiological and value aspects. In other words, 'naturalistic' data are not sufficient to assert the 'criminal nature' of certain man-made activities; it is also necessary to provide a value judgement on the facts (Forti 2000: 308).

It is well known that a broad definition of environmental crime prevails in 'green criminology', encompassing also those dimensions of damage, injustice and social harm often neglected by criminal law and by the criminal justice system (see Lynch and Stretesky 2003; Halsey 2004; White 2008; see also Barton *et al.* 2007: 205–206). It is in this wider perspective that the situation in Huelva is to be viewed.

Huelva, the westernmost town in Andalucia (Spain), lies near the sea at the junction of two rivers, the Tinto and the Odiel (Figure 10.1). Unfortunately, Huelva – as already said – is highly polluted by a huge industrial and chemical plant, built in close proximity to the town in the 1960s, under Franco. During those years, the life of the inhabitants changed dramatically: affluence had finally come to their town, but the destructive and irreversible consequences on the environment and people's health started escalating and overshadowing the promise of wealth brought by the factories.

This critical situation, compounded by the presence of industrial activities carried out by companies that already back in the 1960s were discharging their wastes into the Tinto, became more serious when some of them took to discharging phosphogypsum – a waste product of the phosphoric acid production process which contains concentrations of uranium series radionuclides and is stored in piles, the 'balsas de fosfoyesos' (Figure 10.1), covering over 1,200 hectares, just a few hundred metres from the town (Dueñas *et al.* 2007; Pérez-López *et al.* 2007; Tayibi *et al.* 2009).

Although much more needs to be done in the future, the various studies so far undertaken to scientifically assess the level of pollution in Huelva and the risks to its inhabitants' health all highlight the extreme gravity of the situation (see also Benach *et al.* 2004; Monge-Corella *et al.* 2008).

Yet, as often happens, this decidedly worrying scenario seems to be surprisingly invisible. Such a finding obviously compels us to probe further and ask ourselves: what is really happening in Huelva?

Assuming therefore that a crime does exist – at least if one accepts the wider definition of environmental crime – we return to the initial question directing our research: what indications enable the inhabitants of Huelva – the direct victims – to become aware of the existence of the crime, and which are the clues, echoed in their narratives, that can allow us, the observers, to grasp its tragically elusive 'reality'?

The construction of a look: some methodological reflections

Here is how Blumer describes the challenging but necessary process of approach and immersion in the social empirical world we have decided to investigate:

> The metaphor that I like is that of lifting the veils that obscure or hide what is going on. The task of scientific study is to lift the veils that cover the area of group life that one proposes to study. The veils are not lifted by substituting, in whatever degree, preformed images for firsthand knowledge. The veils are lifted by getting close to the area and by digging deep into it through

> careful study. Schemes of methodology that do not encourage or allow this betray the cardinal principle of respecting the nature of one's empirical world. (Blumer 1969: 39)

Obviously, this 'unveiling' is not to be read literally and with 'positivist' eyes, but as a possibly unprecedented reconstruction by the researcher of a field of observation still little understood (Ceretti and Natali 2009). This process of 'getting closer' and progressive 'visibilisation' of the social phenomenon under observation closely parallels the methods of ethnographic research. The latter is characterised by close on-site observation of the practices of the social actors and by an attempt to approach and understand the meaning of such social actions from the point of view of the protagonists themselves. The researcher, indeed, must 'have been there' and must have been in contact with the 'objects' of their study – and so, in some measure, must have allowed themself to be affected and 'modified' by them (see Denzin 1997).

The ethnographic research I present employs 'photo-elicitation interviews' (Becker 1974; Harper 2002) as a new source of qualitative data for criminology (Greek in press) applied to the environmental field. Like all ethnographic work, it is based on fieldwork and finds the limits of its observation in the field itself. However, it opens some sensitising dimensions on socio-environmental conflict and environmental crime that may also prove useful when observing the 'sensitive environments' of other realities.

The complexity in the fragments

Moving from these methodological premises, we can now enter the 'depths' of Huelva, penetrating the complexity of perspective that surrounds a radically transformed microcosm. We shall begin our immersion by intercepting and observing those significant vocabularies and narratives – created through social interaction by the very inhabitants of the polluted area – that provide descriptions, interpretations and explanations of the environmental crime being committed in Huelva and of the 'how' and 'why' it is happening. This is a level of criminological discourse about the environment deeply rooted in local reality, in the unique and 'expert' knowledge of those who live the 'experience of pollution' – knowledge that often eludes the researcher who does not carry out fieldwork.

These narratives – resulting from the collection and analysis of 50 'photo-elicitation interviews' carried out with 50 residents in 2008 – shall constantly accompany the reflections they prompt, highlighting those questions I consider central to the case examined.

I have decided to approach the interviews as a whole, as a 'vocal multitude' (though keeping the individual interviewees distinguishable) which, thus articulated and enhanced by its dissonance and contrasts, will give voice to a level of criminological competence often neglected in the study of sensitive environments that are the background to environmental crimes.

But what can actually be glimpsed through such a perspective?

Looking at an old photograph of the beach of Punta del Sebo – before and after: transformation of a territory and collective memory

Case 20: Yes, people used to bathe here ... but not now ... because it's contaminated...

Case 30: It's something I'll never forget...when I was a kid, my mother used to take us to bathe at Punta del Sebo ... we knew nothing about pollution back then.... I'll never forget going there as a teenager in my first bikini ... and when I came out of the water it was filthy ... covered in oil from the factories ... an absolute mess ... this is the memory I have.

Case 46: My husband says this [Punta del Sebo] has always been impossible ... because the Rio Tinto mines have been exploited since Roman times and all this 'shit' ... the waste from mineral washing ... has always been carried downstream.... Some people I know, they're older than me, say they used to bathe here ... but my husband says they bathed in this 'shit' ... pollution was a problem even before the factories were built.

There are some images that, more than any other, contain and awaken, in the interviewees, complex dimensions associated with the collective memory of the territory and of the radical changes it has undergone over the last 50 years. Almost invariably, these memories hark back to an idyllic, innocent past, when there was no trace of the 'evil' wrought on the local landscape by pollution. These images are old photographs, dating back to the 1950s – therefore prior to the installation of the factories – showing a beach, the so-called 'Punta del Sebo', where the Huelva residents used to bathe. The social and emotional significance of the area is increased by the presence of a monument to Christopher Columbus, a historical symbol of Huelva's identity. Those photographs are there to prove that such a time 'has really been' (Barthes 1981).

Thanks to qualitative data collected in the field, I can assert that these images of Punta del Sebo represent the 'before', 'what was there' – present in the collective memory of all the locals, either through personal experience or through the stories of those living at that time – which now no longer exists (case 20) and stands in stark contrast to what is now there, the reality of the factories. Obviously, the social perception of the place is influenced by the biographical colouring of those interviewees who have lived through such experiences (case 30).

Yet, side by side with these narratives, by far the most numerous, there are others challenging the authenticity of the version of the reality conjured by those images, going so far as to deny its existence, and labelling it as utopian (case 46), given that the area has always been polluted because of the mines dating back to Roman times. Criminological literature has already highlighted the fact that perpetrators of environmental crimes tend to skirt or downplay their responsibilities by denying the existence of the problem, blaming the victims (see Williams 1996: 319–320) or previous factors of contamination, thus making it impossible – because of the complexity of interactions developing over such an extended temporal scale (Adam 1998) – to establish responsibilities in cause–effect terms. All this works in favour of the practices of denial (Cohen 2001). Interestingly enough, these narrative repertoires are incorporated in the dialogues and the reasoning of the victims themselves. Such a development is obviously influenced by the discourses circulating in the public sphere through communication media, structured by those who have the power and the means – and not only economic means – to impose or neutralise a certain definition of reality (see Tellechea Rodríguez 2004; Luque 2006).

Looking at an image of greenwashing: from indignation to defence

Case 37: Endesa ... the combined-cycle plant ... yeah, it may well be attractive, it may well sport Huelva's colours, but ... not only it has ruined the scenery, it's also an industry which has been allowed to exist where it should never have ... what Endesa has done is use Huelva's colours as a mask, a disguise, as if to say: 'We belong to Huelva.' 'No, you are not part of Huelva.'... The plant is a source of pollution.

Case 25: Jimenez's phrase ... you could happily walk round the town ... wherever you wanted to ... pollution was unheard of. Putting that quotation up there on the façade is truly contradictory ... they are totally opposite ideas.... Those words have nothing to do with the reality of the factories.... One of the two: either they want to hide something or they don't understand what they have put up there.

Case 1: I think the idea they want to convey is that they are making an environmental improvement ... this is the meaning I see ... and I agree.

A serious interruption of the progressive restoration of the environment at the edge of the town has taken place with the construction – carried out without the municipal permit required to build it – of a new combined-cycle thermoelectric generator belonging to Endesa, Spain's largest electric utility company (Luque 2006). In building the new plant, particular attention was devoted to the 'aesthetic side': a light blue background which recalls Huelva's colours sports a quotation from an important work by the Spanish Nobel Prize winner Juan Ramón Jiménez, *Platero y yo*, which celebrates the beauty of Huelva's environs.

This is a clear instance of 'greenwashing', a communication strategy often used by corporations to render an activity that is inevitably dangerous for both environment and people more acceptable. The interviewees' answers range from indignation (case 37) to the defence of that image (case 1), and include a variety of interpretations and reflections about what is perceived as an attempt to deceive the Huelva residents, disguising an unarguably dangerous reality and generating confusion in the observers (case 25). Once again the sight of the same image aroused unique and decidedly diverse emotions, thoughts and reactions. It is exactly the uncertainty and 'symbolical ambiguity' of the places of socio-environmental conflict that greenwashers tend to exploit, in the certainty that a widespread 'labour of confusion' will have decisive consequences in creating shared (mis)understandings (Auyero and Swistun 2008: 360).

Faced with an image of conflict: work versus health and environment – an inevitable dichotomy?

Case 44: The reality is that the contamination ... the cases of cancer we have here and all the negative consequences cannot be justified by the fact that the majority of the population is working there.... It doesn't bring wealth to this area.

Case 13: 'Polo no, ria si'... everybody tells the story that's best for them.... Try saying 'plant no, river yes' to any family who eats thanks to the factories.

Case 51: 'Pole no, ria si' ... it's a battle ... between those who do not want the pole to go because that would mean risking their jobs and those who think the whole community and not the factories alone have a claim on the river.

The first factories were built in the early 1960s, and, a few years later, the inhabitants of the area started living in the aftermath of this drastic transformation of the territory. While it is true, as Mark Halsey (2006: 52) maintains, that 'structural economic power relies for its efficacy not simply on the relations between government, law and economy so much as on the flows of pleasure which invest the population at any one time' and that, consequently, 'Not only is it profitable to be environmentally destructive (in the sense of mining, manufacturing cars, clearing forests), it feels good too (in the sense of purchasing a gold necklace, driving on the open road ...)', the situation we are confronted with is decidedly more critical. Indeed, the flows of pleasure achieved with the economic development has long since been overrun and thwarted by real flows of contamination and disease, as many of the interviewees have realised, unable to decide whether the 'plant' has been more beneficial or damaging for them.

Like many socio-environmental conflicts, the one observed in Huelva (case 51) between those who are for the factories and employment (case 13) and those who speak up for health and the environment (case 44) concerns much more than the single objects of contention (employment, environment, health) and raises important questions regarding who they – the inhabitants of that territory – are (subjectivity), what they can do (power), what they can know (epistemology), and who they might become (desire) (Halsey 2006: 4). These themes run through all the stories collected in the field and reassembled in these brief fragments.

What the interviewees continually redefined, reformulated and renegotiated when they spoke of employment, environment and health was the meaning of these words – what the symbolic interactionists call social objects:

> The nature of an object [...] consists of the meaning that it has for the person for whom it is an object. This meaning sets the way in which he sees the object, the way in which he is prepared to act toward it and the way in which he is ready to talk about it. An object may have a different meaning for different individuals: a tree will be a different object to a botanist, a lumberman, a poet and a home gardener. (Blumer 1969: 11)

Being social creations, such objects form and transform continually during the process of definition and interpretation taking place in the course of social interaction and it is actually by meeting or conflicting with other people's viewpoints that anyone shapes his own significant social object. Certainly they are no mere social constructs detached from the structures of power and domination of a society; rather, dominance – just as sociality – is a constitutive part of such social objects (see Athens 2007; Ceretti and Natali 2009). Also in the environmental field, the arguments as to their value and use will be settled using the full range of domination means available to stakeholder parties (see White 2008: 50). And the ensuing uncertainty and confusion will favour those who have the power to define the different objects of contention.

The complexity and the qualitative differences emerging from the interviews also help to remove those dangerous dichotomies which still seem to paralyse any idea of a future 'disentangled from chemical industry' (Luque 2006), caging it inside the insoluble, irreconcilable and unbreakable dilemma of 'employment/factories versus health/environment'.

On environmental perceptions, denial and time-scape

Case 38: We know what is happening but when faced with this situation we see ourselves as powerless.... It's well known how dangerous phosphogypsum is but ... it's something we know is there, but it's as if we wanted to escape from it.... It's as if a curtain could be pulled in front of it so as not to see what's happening.

Case 13: Maybe because my body is used to living in such polluted air ... I hardly notice it ... our body is bound to have developed some protection against this kind of pollution, hasn't it?

Case 47: I think the reason people are not quite so worried is that since pollution doesn't kill you at once it doesn't frighten you ... it kills you little by little and doesn't look as if it's doing so, but it still kills you.

The most recurrent phrases concerning the perception of contamination and of its risks fell into the following pattern: 'We know about the pollution, but…'. This premise was then followed by various explanations justifying 'inaction' in the face of such awareness. Among them were: (1) the mechanisms of denial (Cohen 2001), which, together with habit (case 13), combine to mellow the drama of the reality endured, familiarising and adapting us to it, making it more acceptable, and ever less detectable; (2) the huge expansion of the temporal horizon concerning the contamination phenomena, which, stretching beyond human and industrial times, contributes to evaporate and disperse the perception of risk (case 47) (Adam 1998: 10); (3) the doubt and the uncertainty of the 'reality' of contamination (Auyero and Swistun 2008), which impel people to unceasingly weave the web of a vanishing reality (case 38).

During the unending process of interpreting and defining the reality of pollution, the body becomes for many the main knowledge tool (Auyero and Swistun 2008) to prove to oneself and to one's interlocutors the rationality of one's convictions about the seriousness of the situation. So we have, for example, constant references to the physical sensations attributable to air pollution; however, the shift from what is evident to our senses to what is known only through expert and technological mediation, as in the case of radiation (Adam 1998: 10) – in our case due to phosphogypsum – is rather problematic. In short, what one does not feel and see is, for many people, non-existent; it is outside their consciousness of risk (see White 2008: 59-62). Once again reality proved to be elusive, uncertain, controversial.

Popular epidemiology, different victimisation and the experience of environmental injustice

The procedures through which pollution and other forms of aggression against man and environment are interpreted, defined and valued are often the exclusive prerogative of scientific discourses (e.g. natural or medical sciences) or of extremely technical ones (such as legal ones). However, for some time now, a value has been recognised for those narratives of 'popular epidemiology' (Brown and Mikkelsen 1990) which often challenge the expert level of official science in connection with the cause–effect relationship existing between a given source of pollution and the health risks for those living near it.

If it is true that the situation in Huelva presents numerous occasions to give rise to such popular discourses (see also Brown 2003), a decisive activism on the part of the inhabitants is not to be taken for granted. It is in this respect that studies like the one by Auyero and Swistun, which go beyond a 'classical Marxist model of consciousness', prove to be particularly useful. According to such a model, confused and conflicting victims become – 'through reflection and interaction' – 'skilled' and 'expert' social actors who share a consensual view about the issue of pollution and its possible solutions (see Auyero and Swistun 2008: 358). As in the case of Huelva, the picture is far more complex, opaque and uncertain.

But let us revert to the voices of the interviewees.

While reasoning on reality and the extent of pollution-related health problems, along with the various explanations exploring the 'contamination–health problems' correlation, another significant narrative soon emerged, relating to the different forms of victimisation pollution can cause. While some people highlighted the equal distribution of the damaging effects among all the inhabitants of Huelva, regardless of proximity to the industrial area, others, instead, traced precise qualitative differences, according to individual state of health, holding that those already carrying diseases were affected more seriously by the damaging effects of pollution (see Williams 1996).

Whether this victimisation was perceived as equal or differentiated, the theme of injustice emerged all the more forcibly in the reflection that what was happening in Huelva would not have happened in another place – the recurring question being typical of any (collective) victim: 'Why us?' 'Why right here, in our backyard, and not somewhere else?'. This profile of injustice reveals a perception and awareness of being in a 'peripheral situation' – not only at a geographical level – with respect to Seville (the regional capital) and to Spanish society in general (see also Luque 2006). Other interviewees addressed more directly those experiences of environmental injustice linked to the deprivation of a right, namely that of being able to enjoy healthy surroundings, not dangerous or threatening to one's well-being.

These are some of the key questions of the debated theme of environmental justice (see White 2008: 15–16): in my qualitative research, I have focused on the deep level that such questions occupy in the real life of the people I met.

The starting point for such reflections is the conviction that the experience one lives through is the place where any knowledge we have of the world originates, and that such a world is different from that of any other person because every social actor interprets the world according to their own personal experiences, the social objects they note and the meanings they associate with them (see also Blumer 1969: 11). The experience of injustice is also part of these experiences and, as such, rooted in our biography, in our lives, and within a socially constructed and structured context.

If, in such a perspective, it is true that we do not possess a metaphysical or transcendental concept of justice – or even of environmental justice (see also Halsey 2004) – capable of generating consensus as to what is right and what is wrong, we could consider the personal experiences of injustice, including environmental ones, and the opposition to these injustices as a key starting point (see also Zagrebelsky 2006). Indeed, it is because we are all suffering subjects that even in today's fragmented and multicultural society, we can still identify categories of undesirable patterns of behaviour and achieve a certain agreement about some basic questions such as: Who suffers? Who is in need of protection? Who is the victim? (Rorty 1989; Ceretti 2000: 3).

Coming into contact with a personal experience of injustice sometimes leads one to fight against the injustice suffered, as in the case reported below. The speaker is one of the spokespersons of the Mesa de la Ria, who explains where his attachment to Huelva comes from: the origin is found in that attitude of opposition and repudiation of (environmental) injustice closely and relationally anchored to the process whereby a territory becomes alien and threatening, thus alienating itself from its inhabitants. Questioning oneself about the causes and the reasons of an injustice transforms the meaning of one's own relationship with oneself and with one's social and natural worlds.

Case A: I don't know why this land means so much to me … it's not because I met my wife here…. I already knew Huelva before meeting her…

… The fact is that simply walking around and observing what the land is … I don't know … perhaps it's from there, from those feelings, that comes the attachment that you feel towards the place you live in…

Perhaps, though, what made me truly appreciate this land was my decision to say no, to oppose an injustice … this has been a first awakening of conscience ... and then when you see the land being violated and its environment degraded and threatened you start asking yourself 'why?' If it's a rich land, how can a person be deprived of his basic right to enjoy his own environment?

... and from here, from this experience of injustice, from this becoming aware, everything comes ... little by little, as you look around, you appreciate more and more ... because ... to love you need to know.

Where does all this lead us?

As White states, although when dealing with environmental issues there is a tendency to leave the question to the experts, citizens' active participation represents 'a vital ingredient in "good practice" precautionary work' (White 2008: 78).

On the other hand, the precautionary principle eliminates neither the risks for the environment and human health nor 'the problems that the growth of knowledge and the contextual increase of scientific uncertainties introduce in our ability to decide' (Pannarale 2003: 42-43). In fact, 'the actual condition of post-normal science [...] is a situation in which (scientific and social) uncertainty becomes constitutive: [...] not only the facts or the values are uncertain but also the concrete combination of all the circumstances', within processes of 'co-production' (Tallacchini 2005: 104–105).

Notwithstanding these limitations, the precautionary principle allows us to 'subject to problematic reappraisal the distribution of risks and of their social acceptability' (Pannarale 2003: 42–43), and this 'problematic reappraisal', essential to a 'democratic re-appropriation of the determination of goals' by postmodern man (see Pannarale 2003: 44-45), certainly makes it necessary

> to broaden the base of expertise and understanding of environments and environmental issues [...]. Science can and must be a major tool in deliberations over human interventions and human impacts. But this is only one sort of knowledge.
> (White 2008: 78)

Such broadening of knowledge means introducing 'all the relevant knowledge, produced by the scientific community and by the citizens' (Tallacchini 2005: 105), including that expert knowledge consisting of the experiences the inhabitants of a place have of it and of its symbolic dimensions, of social memory, and of the depiction of possible future scenarios. As a starting point, we may take the attempt to 'give a voice' and value to those social actors who often lack the power needed to act in a significant way upon their own environment, and that is what informed the work in progress here presented.

If these desired results are to be obtained, an expansion of the democratic space is needed. This may be achieved also through forms of deliberative democracy already implemented in many local and global settings, which, even with the difficulties and uncertainties that bind them, lend value to the prospective complexity I have tried to illustrate in redrawing the democratic decision-making procedures (see also Pellizzoni 2003).

In Huelva, as elsewhere, the recognition of this plural ambiguity and multiplicity of perspectives is one of the essential requirements to overcome any dualism, to reimagine and to rewrite territory and spaces. Though more is called for, this is certainly a good beginning when attempting to pass from a prevailing passive acceptance towards a more active participation in choices concerning the place where one lives, with a view to reducing future injustices, provided that legal and law-court justice do not produce more injustices by omitting to cure existing ones.

The 'maps' drawn up by criminologists have long neglected the *terrae incognitae* we have glimpsed, more painstakingly explored in other fields of knowledge. Following the green trail blazed in the criminological field by important criminologists, we have to penetrate these unknown territories to observe from within what people see, feel, perceive, experience, notice and, therefore, think of the contested polluted environments they find themselves inhabiting willy-nilly during their lifetime. 'Solidarity,' as Richard Rorty teaches us, 'is not discovered by reflection but created. It is created by increasing our sensitivity to the particular details of the pain and humiliation of other' (Rorty 1989: xvi). If we are to seize the multiplicity of these 'sensitive' realities and narratives, we will have to (re)describe them, and redescribe ourselves, having recourse to a plurality of possible vocabularies (Rorty 1989), none excluded. In doing it so, we must be aware that 'man's experienced world is [...] only one tree in the forest' and constantly struggle to remind him that '[...] his tree is not the only one' so that he could 'yet imagine what the forest as a whole might be like' (Lowenthal 1961: 248).

References

Adam, B. (1998) *Timescapes of Modernity: The Environment and Invisible Hazards*. London: Routledge.

Athens, L. (2007) 'Radical Interactionism. Going Beyond Mead', *Journal for the Theory of Social Behaviour*, 37(2): 137–165.

Auyero, J. and Swistun, D. (2008) 'The Social Production of Toxic Uncertainty', *American Sociological Review*, 73(3): 357–379.

Barthes, R. (1981) *Camera Lucida: Reflections on Photography*. London: Vintage.

Barton, A., Corteen, K., Scott, D. and Whyte, D. (2007) 'Conclusion: Expanding the Criminological Imagination', in A. Barton, K. Corteen, D. Scott and D. Whyte (eds), *Expanding the Criminological Imagination. Critical Reading in Criminology*. Cullompton: Willan Publishing.

Becker, H.S. (1974) 'Photography and Sociology', *Studies in the Anthropology of Visual Communication*, 1: 3–26.

Benach, J., Yasui, Y., Martinez, J.M. *et al.* (2004) 'The Geography of the Highest Mortality Areas in Spain: A Striking Cluster in the Southwestern Region of the Country', *Occupational and Environmental Medicine*, 61(3): 280–281.

Blumer, H. (1969) *Symbolic Interactionism: Perspective and Method*. Englewood Cliffs, NJ: Prentice-Hall.

Brown, P. and Mikkelsen, E. (1990) *No Safe Place: Toxic Waste, Leukemia, and Community Action*. Berkeley, CA: University of California Press.

Brown, P. (2003) 'Qualitative Methods in Environmental Health Research', *Environmental Health Perspectives*, 111(14): 1789–1798.

Ceretti, A. (2000) 'Mediazione penale e giustizia. In-contrare una norma', in A. Ceretti (ed.), *Scritti in ricordo di Giandomenico Pisapia*, vol. III. Milano: Giuffrè.

Ceretti, A. and Natali, L. (2009) *Cosmologie violente. Percorsi di vite criminali*. Milano: Raffaello Cortina.

Cohen, S. (2001) *States of Denial: Knowing About Atrocities and Suffering*. Cambridge: Polity Press.

Denzin, N.K. (1997) *Interpretive Ethnography: Ethnographic Practices for the 21st Century*. Thousand Oaks, CA: Sage Publications.

Dueñas, C., Liger, E., Cañete, S. *et al.* (2007) 'Exhalation of ^{222}Rn from Phosphogypsum Piles Located at the Southwest of Spain', *Journal of Environmental Radioactivity*, 95(2–3): 63–74.

Forti, G. (2000) *L'Immane concretezza. Metamorfosi del crimine e controllo penale*. Milano: Raffaello Cortina.

Greek, C. (in press) 'Visual Criminology: Ethnographic and Documentary Photographic Research', in D. Gadd (ed.), *Sage Handbook of Criminological Research Methods*. London: Sage.

Halsey, M. (2004) 'Against Green Criminology', *British Journal of Criminology*, 44(6): 833–853.

Halsey, M. (2006) *Deleuze and Environmental Damage: Violence of the Text*. Aldershot: Ashgate.

Harper, D. (2002) 'Talking About Pictures: A Case for Photo Elicitation', *Visual Studies*, 17(1): 13–26.

Lowenthal, D. (1961) 'Geography, Experience, and Imagination: Towards a Geographical Epistemology', *Annals of the Association of American Geographers*, 51(3): 241–260.

Luque, E. (2006) 'Mobilising Memories, Evidence and Futures: Disentangling Huelva from Chemical Industry'. First draft discussion paper at ECPR Nicosia Joint Sessions 25–30 April 2006.

Lynch, M. and Stretesky, P. (2003) 'The Meaning of Green: Contrasting Criminological Perspectives', *Theoretical Criminology*, 7(2): 217–238.

Mead, G.H. (1934) *Mind, Self, and Society*. Chicago: University of Chicago Press.

Monge-Corella, S., García-Pérez, J., Aragonés, N. *et al.* (2008) 'Lung Cancer Mortality in Towns Near Paper, Pulp and Board Industries in Spain: A Point Source Pollution Study', *BMC Public Health*, 8: 288.

Pannarale, L. (2003) 'Scienza e diritto. Riflessioni sul principio di precauzione', *Sociologia del diritto*, 30(3): 21–45.

Pellizzoni, L. (2003) 'Knowledge, Uncertainty and the Transformation of the Public Sphere', *European Journal of Social Theory*, 6(3): 327–355.

Pérez-López, R., Alvarez-Valero, A.M. and Nieto, J.M. (2007) 'Changes in Mobility of Toxic Elements During the Production of Phosphoric Acid in Fertilizer Industry of Huelva (SW Spain) and Environmental Impact of Phosphogypsum Wastes', *Journal of Hazardous Materials*, 148(3): 745–750.

Rorty, R. (1989) *Contingency, Irony, and Solidarity*. Cambridge: Cambridge University Press.

Tallacchini, M. (2005) 'Scienza, Politica e diritto: il linguaggio della co-produzione', *Sociologia del diritto*, 30(1): 75–106.

Tayibi, H., Choura, M., Lopez, F.A. *et al.* (2009) 'Environmental Impact and Management of Phosphogypsum', *Journal of Environmental Management*, 90(8): 2377–2386.

Tellechea Rodríguez, J.M. (2004) 'El Conflicto 'Info-ambiental': El Caso de Huelva Información (Agosto 1983–Diciembre 1992)', *Ambitos*, 11–12(1–2): 319–340.

White, R. (2008) *Crimes Against Nature: Environmental Criminology and Ecological Justice*. Cullompton: Willan Publishing.

Williams, C. (1996) 'An Environmental Victimology', in N. South and P. Beirne (eds), *Green Criminology*. Aldershot: Ashgate.

Zagrebelsky, G. (2006) 'Giustizia. Il rifiuto dell'ingiustizia come fondamento minimo', in E. Bianchi *et al.* (eds), *Lezioni Bobbio*. Torino: Einaudi.

Chapter 11

The criticality of global environmental crime and the response of chaos criminology

Noriyoshi Takemura

Introduction

Facing a global criticality of environmental crises, humans and other species are standing on the edge of the precipice of subsistence. Protecting the environment from degradation and destruction is one of the critical challenges today because there is a possibility that this situation threatens the survival of not only our generation but also generations in the future (Beck 1986; Levin 1999; Intergovernmental Panel on Climate Change 2007; Guattari 2008).

Environmental crimes have been exerting a tremendously harmful influence on the globe and our viabilities. This harmful influence is distributed unequally and unfairly among people, between developing countries and industrialised countries. Some measures which are of benefit to people living in industrialised rich countries may inflict a loss on people living in developing poor countries. Environmental and ecological injustice is spreading from pole to pole accompanying the globalisation of different dimensions. Faced with horrible global environmental crises, some states and companies as well as people have endeavoured to overcome these difficulties in their own ways. On the one hand, some problems are made overt; on the other hand, other, more serious problems are made latent. All this time, the injustice is amplified and becomes more and more serious (Watkins *et al.* 2008).

Chaos criminology suggests that multiple theories and practices of 'social justice' may overcome the global criticality of environmental crises. Integrating critical deliberations, a new concept and method is needed, a type of 'chaos justice', which is based on non-linear thinking, and which is also based on social justice. This chapter introduces 'chaos criminology' as a perspective that provides a sound way for the theory and practice against environmental harm and for social justice.

Global warming threatens poor people

In 2008, fuel and food prices soared as never before. There could be the possibility that the ever higher cost of food will push tens of millions people into abject poverty and starvation. To a large degree, this crisis is a human-made result of misguided energy and farm policies. The most wrongheaded are perhaps the tangle of subsidies, mandates and tariffs to encourage the production of biofuels from crops in the USA and the European Union (EU). According to the World Bank, almost all of the growth in global corn production from 2004 to 2007 was devoted to US ethanol production, pushing up corn and animal feed prices and prompting farmers to switch from other crops to corn (*International Herald Tribune-Asahi*, 7 July 2008: 6). At the UN food summit meeting in Rome in June 2008, the Bush administration insisted that ethanol is playing a very small role in rising food prices. Brazil, which has an enormous sugar-based ethanol industry, also rejected demands to curb biofuel production. Argentina objected to calls to end export taxes that it and other countries have erected to slow food exports (*International Herald Tribune-Asahi*, 10 June 2008: 6).

'The bottom billion', which is a term gaining currency in the international aid community, are the poorest of the poor in developing countries living on less than $1 a day. They constitute one-sixth of the world's population. The ripple effects of skyrocketing oil and food prices are spreading worldwide. Costlier energy and food pose a grave, immediate threat to the survival of the bottom billion, who live in farming villages and urban slums in developing countries. Many of the countries at the bottom are in Africa and parts of Asia, including central Asia. World Bank President Robert Zoellick has called these multiple economic crises a 'man-made catastrophe'. Rising food and oil prices are causing more and more people to join the ranks of the poor and needy. Deepening anger and resentment among people at the bottom of society could threaten stability in developing countries (*International Herald Tribune-Asahi*, 12–13 July 2008: 20).

In Sub-Saharan Africa, four out of every 10 people live on less than $1 a day. A new demon has appeared in the form of soaring food prices: one of the ultimate consequences of economic globalisation. The great threat is global warming. The vast Sahara Desert is encroaching slowly but steadily into cropland. One-third of Sub-Saharan Africans live in drought-prone areas. The effects of global warming are serious indeed because food production relies more than 90 per cent on rainwater. For these African people, even a slight change in climate can spell the collapse of the foundations on which their daily existence rests (*International Herald Tribune-Asahi*, 26 May 2008: 26).

Former British Foreign Secretary Margaret Beckett said that since the beginning of human history, wars have been fought repeatedly over limited resources such as land, water, food and fuel. But we are now in an unprecedented situation in which almost every area on the Earth is under such pressure concurrently. Effective efforts to stem global warming are indispensable to prevent such destabilisation. What the world needs to do now is to take a big step toward eliminating the root cause of all these nagging problems (*International Herald Tribune-Asahi*, 1 July 2008: 22). Intensified oil drilling, the return to nuclear power, the pressures upon forests, the favouring of corn-based ethanol, the increased possibility of a turn to genetically modified farming, and the boost to First World agricultural protectionism – all of this must make for glum reading. Things are getting tougher, rather than better, for the advocates of a cleaner, gentler planet (*International Herald Tribune-Asahi*, 12–13 July 2008: 4). A new report by the British government cast fresh doubt on fuels made from crops as a way to fight climate change. Until recently, European governments had sought to lead the rest of the world in the use of biofuels, aiming to derive 10 per cent of Europe's transportation fuels from biofuels by 2020. The kind of the targets proposed by the European Union are contributing to deforestation, which speeds climate change, and helps force up food prices (*International Herald Tribune-Asahi*, 9 July 2008: 12).

Geopolitics of hazardous waste trafficking

The Japanese Ministry of Environment declares that we are all confronted by an increasing generation of waste and non-sustainable waste management. In recent years, the volume of discarded television sets, personal computers, refrigerators and other electrical and electronic products has also increased, and exports and imports of these for recycling or disposal have risen sharply. These discarded electrical and electronic products sometimes include lead and other harmful substances. These are being recycled under environmentally inappropriate practices in developing countries. In Japan, exports of recyclable resources to China and other Asian countries are a growing trend. With increased demand for resources associated with economic growth in China and other east Asian countries, the volume of exports to these countries in recent years has increased sharply (Ministry of Environment, Planning Division Waste Management and Recycling Department 2007: 3–4, 5–6).

Gruppo Abele-Nomos (2003) analyses the 1989 Basel Convention on the control of cross-border shipments of hazardous wastes into various African, Caribbean and Pacific countries, and other international regulatory instruments. Although these instruments have tried to end the growing flow of environmentally sensitive products from developed to developing countries, particularly in illegal hazardous waste trafficking, countries in the South continued to be the recipients of growing amounts of waste produced in the North. One side effect of increased bans on shipments of toxic substances and waste was the tremendous escalation in prices for these commodities while legal avenues for disposal were dramatically decreased (UNICRI 2000: 9). Of the around 300 million tonnes of waste produced each year in the developed world, some 50 million tonnes were shipped to Africa (United Nations 2001: 12). Both the global nature of the world economy and the inability or unwillingness of some nations to stop environmental crimes and police them effectively, have facilitated the illegal businesses of a wide range of groups and individuals who have found extremely profitable sources of illegal gain in this environment (UNICRI 2000: 9; Gruppo Abele-Nomos 2003: 15).

By the early 1980s, it was becoming increasingly difficult and costly to dispose of this enormous amount of waste in a safe and environmentally sound way. In the mid-1980s a significant North–South trend emerged, and the existence came to light of numerous contracts between Western companies and African countries. This sort of 'garbage imperialism' has been documented by several international reports and inquiries made by both institutional and non-governmental bodies. Between 1986 and 1988, at least 15 African countries were targeted by Western companies offering money for land to use as toxic waste dumps (United Nations 2001: 12; Gruppo Abele-Nomos 2003: 15). Although several African states responded to the threat of such 'waste colonialism' through the adoption of the Lomé IV Convention and the Bamako Convention, which imposed a total import ban on all hazardous wastes to African, Caribbean and Pacific countries, the threat posed by unscrupulous dumpers remained and, within a few years, shifted to other areas of the world. Both eastern Europe and southern Asia were discovered by waste traders following the ratification of the conventions closing off Africa to further waste disposal. Asia is currently considered one of the main destinations for illicit waste trafficking. According to Greenpeace reports, more than 100,000 tonnes of unauthorised waste entered India in 1998 and 1999. China is one of the biggest targets for illegally imported hazardous electronic waste, 50 per cent of which originates in the USA, which has yet to ratify the Basel Convention (Mastny and French 2002: 18; Gruppo Abele-Nomos 2003: 15–16).

Political economy of hazardous waste trafficking

Puckett and Smith (2002) critically examined the cruel situation of high-tech trashing in Asia. According to their examination, e-waste is the most rapidly growing waste problem in the world. It is a crisis not only of quantity but also a crisis born from toxic ingredients: lead, beryllium, mercury, cadmium, brominated flame retardants, and so on. Rich economies that use most of the world's electronic products and generate most of the e-waste have made use of a convenient, and until now, hidden escape valve: exporting the e-waste crisis to the developing countries of Asia. The open burning, acid baths and toxic dumping pour pollution into the land, air and water and expose the men, women, and children of Asia's poorer peoples to poison (Puckett and Smith, 2002: 1).

The export of e-waste remains a dirty little secret of the high-tech revolution. Scrutiny has been studiously avoided by the electronics industry, by government officials, and by some involved in e-waste recycling. This often wilful denial has been aided by the cynical labelling of this trade with the ever-green word 'recycling'. Although it has been a secret kept from most consumers, the export 'solution' has been a common practice for many years. e-waste exports to Asia are motivated entirely by brute global economics. A free trade in hazardous wastes leaves the poorer peoples of the world with an untenable choice between poverty and poison (Puckett and Smith 2002: 1–4).

Again, according to the analysis of Gruppo Abele-Nomos (2003), the weakness of developing countries in exercising their right to protect themselves from unwanted waste imports resulted in a continuation of the North to South waste trade and the large growth of the illegal market. Moreover, external pressures imposed by foreign waste-trading corporations often include promises of easily acquired foreign currency, increased employment, creation of waste recycling enterprises, and the transfer of new technologies (United Nations 2001: 18). Alongside the loopholes and ambiguities existing in national legislation, the disparities in domestic regulatory mechanisms and lack of effective international control, the United Nations recently emphasised that the liberalisation and deregulation of economies in developing countries have significantly encouraged the illegal export of toxic and dangerous wastes to these areas (United Nations 2001: 16; Gruppo Abele-Nomos 2003: 16).

International environmental crimes seem to be committed by a wide variety of actors, ranging from more traditional mafia-type organisations (as in La Cosa Nostra involvement in New York's garbage industry and, more recently, with the the eco-mafia in Italy) to loose networks of individuals with no criminal background belonging to various economic sectors (Gruppo Abele-Nomos 2003: 16–17). Companies in the more prosperous regions of the European Union are also outsourcing waste disposal to municipalities in poorer countries in central and eastern Europe. This process began in the early 1990s, when the change of political systems facilitated trade between East and West. The East–West trade in waste has accelerated with CEE countries' accession into the European Union (Steger 2007: 17).

Human rights and development of environmental justice

Steger (2007) develops the concept of environmental justice in relation to human rights. She mentions that a clean and safe environment and access to natural resources are basic human rights. Principle 3 of the 1994 Draft Declaration of Principles on Human Rights and the Environment establishes a foundation for environmental justice: all persons shall be free from any form of discrimination in regard to actions and decisions that affect the environment. Principle 4 states that all persons have the right to an environment adequate to meet equitably the needs of present generations and that does not impair the rights of future generations to meet equitably their needs (Steger 2007: 16).

She continues that cases of environmental injustice have to be seen in these two contexts: (1) people have the right to a clean and safe environment and fair access to natural resources; and (2) sustainable development means that the needs of some people must not be met by treating others unfairly, including future generations. The origin of the linkages between human rights and the environment derive from four streams of thought and research: (1) research showing discrimination in the distribution of environmental risks and benefits; (2) research showing that developed countries export environmental risks to developing countries; (3) the movement to establish the right to a clean environment as a universal human right; and (4) arguments claiming that environmental protection itself is enhanced when poverty is reduced, social inclusion is stressed, and citizens are armed with civil rights that ensure that they have access to information, participation, and justice (Steger 2007: 15, 17).

Steger said, moreover, that environmental justice is about the distribution of environmental harms and benefits, and access to and consideration in procedures dictating their distribution (Steger 2007: 10). In addition to the demand for equity in the distribution of environmental harms and benefits, the environmental justice movement has been characterised by a call for recognition of diversity. This means that environmental justice is not only about inequalities in how environmental goods and bads are distributed according to race or class, but also about access and participation in decision-making that affects people's lives. The World Commission on Environment and Development pleaded with governments to consider the time dimension in all their decisions and to weigh benefits in the present against losses in the future. In short, environment-related justice consists of three main spheres. It is justice towards the future generations (or intergenerational justice), ecological justice (or justice related to non-human beings), and the social dimension of distribution within the human space (intragenerational justice) (Steger 2007: 13–14).

Green criminology, environmental harm, and social justice

White (2008) argues that a distinctive, critical 'green criminology' has emerged in recent years, a criminology that takes as its focus issues relating to the environment and social harm. Much of this work has been directed at exposing different instances of substantive environmental injustice and ecological injustice. It has also involved critique of the actions of nation states and transnational capital in fostering particular types of harm, and failing to adequately address or regulate harmful activity (Lynch and Stretesky 2003; White 2005; Beirne and South 2007; South and Beirne 2006; Takemura 2007; White 2007: 33–34, 2008).

White (2007, 2008) argues that environmental justice refers to the distribution of environments among people in terms of access to and use of specific natural resources in defined geographical areas, and the impacts of particular social practices and environmental hazards on specific populations (e.g. as defined on the basis of class, occupation, gender, age, and ethnicity). Some people are more likely to be disadvantaged by environmental problems than others. There are thus patterns of 'differential victimisation' that are evident with respect to the citing of toxic waste dumps, extreme air pollution, access to safe, clean drinking water and so on. The specific groups who experience environmental problems may not always describe or see the issues in strictly environmental terms. This may be related to knowledge of the environmental harm, explanations for calamity and socio-economic pressures to 'accept' environmental risk. The environmental justice discourse challenges the dominant discourses by placing inequalities in the distribution of environmental quality at the top of the environmental agenda (Williams 1996; White 2007: 37–38).

Concerning the distribution of environmental quality, Capeheart and Milovanovic (2007) mention that, given the current global condition, social justice must include an understanding of the interactions within and among peoples. This is indeed a complex and inclusive pursuit. It is also an exciting and worthy pursuit. It requires the consideration of and sensitivity to all voices and all concerns. To talk of environmental justice is also to talk about social justice; that is, issues of fairness and quality of life are interconnected. The clearest definition of a just sustainable development is to ensure a better quality of life for all, now, and into the future, in a just and equitable manner. Antonio Negri and Michael Hardt (see Capeheart and Milovanovic 2007) hold much promise for the new global proletariat, the multitude, which will articulate new insights on justice based on global struggle. A multitude is composed of diverse people, each in their nuanced ways of being and becoming, which can never be reduced to an abstraction such as the juridic subject, or the people, or the working class. Foundational principles of justice can only be found in the processes inherent in the movement of the multitude (Capeheart and Milovanovic 2007: 2, 95–96, 138–139).

Multiple struggles for social justice

Capeheart and Milovanovic (2007) consider diverse theories and practices of social justice. Following their research, we can find multiple struggles for social justice. Some have even envisioned an environmental justice paradigm that would link environment and race, class, gender and social justice concerns. Others argue that we must deal not only with symptoms (uneven impact of environmental hazards), but also with the causes, with social injustice. Social justice includes disparate outcomes, as they are related to gender, race, class, sexual preference, and intersections. Studies show that certain groups are more likely to be adversely affected, and that this disparate impact has often been explained by two main conceptions. The first is that it is the very lifestyle of racial minorities to choose to live near waste sites. But this does not explain why they do so – only that they are likely to do so. The second is that people choose to live in neighbourhoods with toxic dump sites because they are rational economic calculators ('market dynamics'). This argument downplays available structural choices and elevates capitalist market ethos to a self-explanatory ideology (Capeheart and Milovanovic 2007: 93, 96, 100).

Postcolonial theory can be traced to the 1960s, and currently the key thinkers include Gayatri Spivak, Edward Said and others (Capeheart and Milovanovic 2007). Even though this theory has a multiplicity of meaning, it includes two key foci: (1) resistance to colonisation, and (2) attempts to break away from the strong influence of colonial thought after independence and liberation. The emphasis of postcolonial theorists is on a critical examination of history, literature, film, dominant discourse, and culture. European texts are seen as imposing and projecting their own desires and anxieties onto colonial peoples while masquerading as truth and the embodiment of rationality, logic, and objectivity. Principles of social justice emerge from struggle. Postcolonial theorists do not see formal equality as the only ideal, nor are the principles of merit and need as defined by colonial powers helpful for guidance. Rather, they seek concepts emerging from the ground up. Social justice is connected with the people yet to come (Capeheart and Milovanovic 2007: 119–120, 124).

Postmodern thought begins with a rejection of many of the core assumptions and ideologies developed during the Enlightenment period. It questions the privileging of grand narratives, the notion of the individual, a dominant and universal truth, linear logic and reasoning, possibilities of universal and stable foundations, and the neutrality of language. It suggests maintaining a sceptical eye toward the possibility of developing conceptions of justice that are grounded in self-evident truth claims as found in prevailing and dominant ideologies (Rosenau 1992; Brodeur 1993; Milovanovic 1997a, 1997b;

Baehr 1999; Milovanovic 2003; Capeheart and Milovanovic 2007: 125–126).

Halsey (2004) insists that there are a number of problematic assumptions underpinning recent efforts by criminology to theorise environmental harm: (1) the general reluctance to put into critical relief the concept of environmental damage and the associated categories of environmental crime; (2) the inability to move beyond dialectical models of society and conflict resolution; (3) the unwillingness to do away with modernist accounts of the relationship between 'words' and 'things'; (4) the incapacity to develop a nuanced account of human/environmental interaction (Halsey 2004: 845). According to him, Gilles Deleuze and Felix Guattari offer a potentially rich source for thinking through key critical issues associated with nature and its (de)regulation. They consistently conceive the world (nature) as flow rather than structure. Such a conception is critical to pulling apart what Deleuze has termed 'the image of thought' that has dominated both criminological work and state policies and practices on environmental issues to date. Their work provides a means for keeping pace with the mobility of environmental problems by considering nature and systems of environmental regulation as always already discursively produced and contested (Guattari 1995; Halsey 2004: 846, 2006; Herzogenrath 2009). Moreover, Halsey (2004) mentions that the utility of a definition of environmental crime will be the degree to which it elicits new types of existential territories, and makes possible new modes of envisioning the human/earth nexus. The task of the critic will be to draw attention to the possible by showing the contingent dimensions of the actual. The challenge is one of nurturing assemblages willing to throw the transformative weight of the acategorical behind socio-ecological struggles (Halsey 2004: 849–850, 2006).

In this connection, constitutive criminology defines crime from the point of view of harm as 'the power to deny others their ability to make a difference'. Harm is the investment of energy in injury-producing, socially constructed relations of power based on inequalities constructed around differences. Harms are actions and processes that deny or prevent us from being or becoming fully human. To be human means to make a difference in/to the world, to act on it, to interact with others, and together to transform the environment and ourselves. It is becoming and not merely existing. If this process is prevented or limited, we become less than human (Arrigo and Milovanovic 2009: 28). From the constitutive perspective in law and justice studies, justice principles can be derived from their notion of harm. That is, if we reject the legalist definition of crime and substitute the notions of harms of repression and reduction, we can also look at its reverse to discover principles of justice based on concern for the Other and specify an active role in enhancing the Other's well-being (Henry and Milovanovic 1996, 1999; Capeheart and Milovanovic, 2007: 139).

Chaos criminology

Williams (1999) offers an alternative paradigm, 'self-organized criticality theory'. It suggests that various, otherwise random, events and factors accumulate into recognisable shapes and patterns. A critical-incident perspective focuses on the 'accumulation' of variables over time to produce behaviour, as in the analogy of dropping grains of sand to form a sand pile. Both addition and subtraction are possible, as well as interaction, and all affect the composite weight of the system. These accumulated variables ultimately achieve enough weight to reach a critical point where something is waiting to happen. The next variable (perhaps one with a tiny addition to the pile) may be enough to create the behaviour. Once a behaviour is at the critical point, the effect of adding a new variable does not ensure that a particular behaviour will occur because the emission of behaviour is a weak random function. If the critical point randomly remains for an extreme period of time, it becomes supercritical. Under these conditions, the addition of each new variable is more and more likely produce behaviour. Such supercritical stress-relieving behaviour is more likely to be seen as spontaneous and potentially more harmful behaviour. Once a behaviour relieves the stress, the accumulation of variables begins again (Williams 1999: 141–152).

Young (1999), a proponent of chaos theory and chaos criminology, considers social justice as follows. Chaos theory maintains that all systems, including social systems, are based on a mixture of order and disorder, predictability and unpredictability. Non-linear dynamics or principles of chaos theory help our understanding of social justice. According to chaos theory, uncertainty, randomness, flux, absurdity, chance, and irony are a part of living and being human. A non-linear notion of social justice embodies these features of interactional life (Young 1999: 189). Complex societies in a constantly changing environment require theory and practices of law and justice that embody non-linearity. Complex adaptive systems require both order and disorder in changing mix. In such a milieu, justice must accommodate chaotic regimes in theory and practice (Eve *et al.* 1997;

Kiel and Elliott 1997; Young 1997a, 1997b, 1999: 191 and 193; Byrne 1998; Bertuglia and Vaio 2005; Taylor 2005).

Schehr (as cited in Capeheart and Milovanvic 2007) integrates chaos theory in the development of a non-linear perspective on social movement theory and justice. He places priority on subaltern modes of resistance, explaining how otherwise silenced voices redefine oppressive practice, even that seemingly small. These inputs, consistent with chaos theory, have disproportional effects on social systems: butterfly effects. His conceptual framework borrows heavily from the concepts of dynamic systems theory. Among other concepts assimilated from chaos theory, he uses the idea of non-linearity, disproportional effects, attractors, and dissipative structures. The development of more spontaneous notions of justice in context is suggested. It is a call for 'nonlinear justice systems'. Concepts of justice are emergent, arising in far-from-equilibrium conditions. It is recognition of flux, uncertainty, change, becoming, multiplicity, indeterminacy, instabilities, discovery and surprise. Postmodern ideas continue to develop, to question our understandings of justice, and to provide a challenge for further progress in ideas. Postmodern thought informs a further understanding of justice (Capeheart and Milovanovic 2007: 139, 176–177, 202).

Williams and Arrigo (2005), basing their ideas on the chaos theory and the non-linear dynamic system, suggest a way for systemic change. They mention that, in the case of environmental concerns, interrelationship and mutual dependency exist between human beings and their non-human environment. The continued endangerment of ecosystem by way of human activities is simultaneously a heightening endangerment of the welfare of human and non-human species. Both immediate and long-term problems present themselves, including such concerns as environmental degradation leading to unsafe air, water, and increasing depletion and consequent scarcity of many natural resources, including food supply. The degradation of the environment is especially problematic in low-income countries (Williams and Arrigo 2005: 58).

According to Williams and Arrigo (2005), chaos theory offers a conceptual framework for systemic change. Non-linear dynamical system displays sensitivity to initial conditions. Consequently, small input can, with time, produce drastic change within the system. Understanding fractal development provides insights, not only into the development of current forms of human interaction, but also how to use that knowledge of fractal dynamics to institute meaningful change. Using chaos to promote pro-social change at all levels and in all spheres of human interaction requires proactive strategies with transformative potential. Social change in relation to the problematic of violence is directed towards a relative reduction in the harms caused by countries, institutions, and human beings. Violence decreases as power imbalances are negated and the coexistence of individuality and difference within an atmosphere of cooperation, tolerance, and mutual aid becomes a definitive social feature (Milovanovic 1997a; Williams and Arrigo 2005: 61, 63).

In short, the exploration of chaos theory and justice contrasts greatly with modernist theories, since these latter are based on the enthusiasm of the Enlightenment for precise knowledge and tight control of both nature and society (Arrigo and Young 1996). The quest for justice becomes a quest for conformity and control, precision and predictability, reason and regulation. Contrary to modernist theories, one and only one outcome is not the natural state of a complex system, nor can theories of justice be predicated on one outcome pattern. Any notion and/or system that presumes there is only one way to do so flies in the face of the complexity of natural and social systems. In a complex world, only chaotic regimes can cope with chaos. Postmodern sensibility would take a non-linear declaration to accommodate the great variety of cultural practices now embedded in human societies around the world. Fractal and fairly autonomous social systems are the repository of such diversity (Young 1999: 190, 194–5, 199).

Deleuse and Guattari (see Taylor 2005) insist that humanity and nature are not like two opposite terms confronting each other; rather they are one and the same essential reality, the producer product. They offer a perspective on ecology as a comprehensive natural ontology of complex material systems, without falling into the trap of the Cartesian dualism of 'nature' and 'culture' (Herzogenrath). Based on the same recognition, Taylor alerts us that ecological complexity poses challenges to conventional scientific ways of knowing. Ecology is not thermodynamics, in which complexity can be simplified through statistical averaging of large numbers of identically behaving components. Whereas progress in the physical sciences depends greatly on controlled experiments in which systems are isolated from their context, this strategy is not so clearly appropriate for understanding organisms in a context of interactions with a multiplicity of hazards and resources distributed in various ways across space and time (Taylor 2005: 1).

Here some examples could be given. As a result of increased demand for biofuel as a measure against global warming, there is, on the one hand, less dependency on fossil fuel, while, on the other hand, an inflation of the corn market price has happened, with the consequence that some people are being deprived of their staple food. Similarly, although there is a tendency to welcome nuclear power plants, since these decrease carbon dioxide emissions, their proliferation much increases the danger of fatal disaster. In another case, although hazardous wastes are trafficked from industrialised countries to under developing countries in order to reduce disposal costs, this trafficking has spread much danger and disease to people all over the world. These examples contain two important points: 'non-linear relations of phenomena' and 'injustice of unequal harm distribution'. In all these cases, as they use merely a peripheral allopathy based on a modernist linear logic, lots of mostly harmful side effects have explicitly and implicitly happened, and become more and more serious. Moreover, these harmful effects concentrate on and are unequally distributed to poor people. In other words, following the capitalist logic, a cleavage in society between the rich and the poor is expansively reproduced.

As we have seen in these few examples, because the causality of environmental crime/harm is too complicated to be ascribed to only one cause–effect relation or one factor, it is necessary to introduce a nonlinear way of thinking in order to recognise this problem as a whole. In addition, if complicated relations are simplified to one linear relation, this means that other important relations and different voices are oppressed and excluded. In so doing, injustice based on a particular self-righteous interest is justified. In complex natural and social systems, a concept of 'green justice' plays a vital role in order to realise social justice. Struggles for 'green justice' are inevitably multicultural, highly diverse, and increasingly global in their methods, interests, and goals. Green justice suggests a development of more spontaneous notions of justice in context, and calls for non-linear justice systems. It is an emergent arising in far-from-equilibrium conditions. There is recognition of flux, uncertainty, change, becoming, multiplicity, indeterminacy, instabilities. These emerging principles of justice are the bases of generating political agendas for social change and for social justice (Capeheart and Milovanovic 2007: 174, 177).

Conclusion

Environmental crimes have been exerting a tremendously harmful influence. This harmful influence is unequally and unfairly distributed between developing countries and industrialised countries. Some measures which are of benefit to people living in industrialised rich countries may inflict a loss to people living in developing poor countries. Chaos criminology suggests that multiple theories and practices of 'social justice' may overcome the global criticality of environmental crises.

Since the beginning of human history, wars have been fought repeatedly over limited resources such as land, water, food and fuels. Studies have shown that the current generation of biofuels, which is reliant on food crops such as canola, corn and soybeans, helps drive up food prices by using agricultural land, as well as aggravating deforestation, and may be worse for the climate than conventional oil once the cost of production and transport are taken into account. Some people are more likely to be disadvantaged by environmental problems than others. The specificity of those placed at greater or disproportionate risk of environmental harm is reflected in literature that acknowledges the importance of class, occupation, gender, and, more recently, age. There are thus patterns of 'differential victimisation'.

E-waste is the most rapidly growing waste problem in the world. It is not only a crisis of quantity but also a crisis born from toxic ingredients that pose an environmental health threat. To date, however, industry, government and consumers have only taken small steps to deal with this looming problem. The trade in e-waste is an export of real harm to the poor communities. In recent decades, richer countries have used poor countries as a 'sink' for pollution and waste.

Chaos criminology, which is developed from chaos/complexity theory and the multiple struggle for social justice, is concerned not in the narrow focus of what is just for the individual alone, but what is just for the social whole. Given the current global condition, chaos criminology must include an understanding of the interactions among peoples. This is indeed a complex and inclusive pursuit. To talk of environmental justice is also to talk about social justice, issues of fairness and quality of life. Notions of chaos justice will always be in flux, always subject to reflection, augmentation, qualification, specification, deletion, and even replacement with a more responsive concept of social justice in context. They are ever contingent. There is no grand narrative that can encompass all of their nuances. Chaos criminology continues to develop, to question our understandings of environmental harm and social justice, and to provide a challenge for further progress in theory and practice.

References

Arrigo, B. and Young, T.R. (1996) 'Chaos, Complexity and Crime: Working Tools for a Postmodern Criminology', in B. MacLean and D. Milovanovic (eds), *Thinking Critically About Crime*. Vancouver: Collective Press, 77–84.

Arrigo, B.A. and Milovanovic, D. (2009) *Revolution in Penology: Rethinking the Society of Captives*. Lanham, MD: Rowman & Littlefield.

Baehr, A. (1999) *Bausteine einer 'postmodernen' Kriminologie*. Pfaffenweiler: Centaurus-Verlagsgesellschaft.

Beck, U. (1986) *Risikogesellschaft: Auf dem Weg in eine andere Moderne*. Frankfurt am Main: Suhrkamp.

Beirne, P. and South, N. (2007) *Issues in Green Criminology: Confronting Harms Against Environments, Humanity and Other Animals*. Cullompton: Willan Publishing.

Bertuglia, C.S. and Vaio, F. (2005) *Nonlinearity, Chaos and Complexity: The Dynamics of Natural and Social Systems*. New York: Oxford University Press.

Brodeur, J.-P. (1993) 'La Pensée Postmoderne et la Criminology', *Criminologie*, 26(1): 73–120.

Byrne, D. (1998) *Complexity Theory and the Social Sciences: An Introduction*. London and New York: Routledge.

Capeheart, L. and Milovanovic, D. (2007) *Social Justice: Theories, Issues, and Movements*. New Brunswick, NJ: Rutgers University Press.

Carrabine, E., Iganski, P., Lee, M. *et al.* (2004) 'The Greening of Criminology', in *Criminology: A Sociological Introduction*. London and New York: Routledge, 313–330.

Eve, R.A., Horsfall, S. and Lee, M.E. (eds) (1997) *Chaos, Complexity, and Sociology: Myths, Models, and Theories*. Thousand Oaks, CA: Sage.

Gruppo Abele-Nomos (2003) *The Illegal Trafficking in Hazardous Waste in Italy and Spain: Final Report*. Rome.

Guattari, F. (1995) *Chaomosis: an Ethico-aesthetic Paradigm*. Bloomington and Indianapolis, IN: Indiana University Press.

Guattari, F. (2008) *The Three Ecologies*. London: Continuum.

Halsey, M. (2004) 'Against "Green" Criminology', *British Journal of Criminology*, 44(6): 833–853.

Halsey, M. (2006) *Deleuze and Environmental Damage: Violence of the Text*. Aldershot: Ashgate.

Henry, S. and Milovanovic, D. (1996) *Constitutive Criminology: Beyond Postmodernism*. London: Sage.

Henry, S. and Milovanovic, D. (1999) *Constitutive Criminology at Work: Applications to Crime and Justice*. Albany, NY: State University of New York Press.

Herzogenrath, B. (2009) *Deleuze/Guattari and Ecology*. Aldershot: Palgrave Macmillan.

Intergovernmental Panel on Climate Change (2007) *IPCC Fourth Assessment Report: Climate Change 2007*. Geneva: IPCC.

Kiel, L.D. and Elliott, E. (eds) (1997) *Chaos Theory in the Social Sciences: Foundations and Applications*. Ann Arbor, MI: University of Michigan Press.

Levin, S.A. (1999) *Fragile Dominion: Complexity and the Commons*. Cambridge: Perseus.

Lynch, M. and Stretsky, P.B. (2003) 'The Meaning of Green: Contrasting Criminological Perspectives', *Theoretical Criminology*, 17(2): 217–238.

Mastny, L. and French, H. (2002) 'Crimes of (a) Global Nature', *World Watch Magazine*, 15(5): 12–22.

Milovanovic, D. (ed.) (1997a) *Chaos, Criminology, and Social Justice: The New Orderly (Dis)order*. Westport, CT: Praeger.

Milovanovic, D. (ed.) (1997b) *Postmodern Criminology*. New York and London: Garland.

Milovanovic, D. (2003) *Critical Criminology: Postmodern Perspectives, Integration and Applications*. New York: Criminal Justice Press.

Ministry of the Environment, Planning Division Waste Management and Recycling Department (2007) *Technologies to Support a Sound Material-Cycle Society: Development of 3R and Waste Management Technologies*. Tokyo: Ministry of the Environment, Government of Japan.

Puckett, J. and Smith, T. (2002) *Exporting Harm: The High-Tech Trashing of Asia*. Basel Action Network (BAN) and Silicon Valley Toxics Coalition (SVTC).

Rosenau, P.M. (1992) *Post-Modernism and the Social Sciences: Insights, Inroads, and Intrusions*. Princeton, NJ: Princeton University Press.

South, N. and Beirne, P. (eds) (2006) *Green Criminology*. Aldershot: Ashgate.

Steger, T. (2007) *Making the Case for Environmental Justice in Central and Eastern Europe*. Budapest: CEU Center for Environmental Policy and Law (CEPL), Health and Environment Alliance (HEAL), and Coalition for Environmental Justice.

Takemura, N. (2007) '"Criticality of Environmental Crises" and Prospect of "Complexity Green Criminology"', *Research Bulletin* (Toin University of Yokohama), 17: 5-11.

Taylor, P.J. (2005) *Unruly Complexity: Ecology, Interpretation, Engagement*. Chicago and London: University of Chicago Press.

United Nations, Economic and Social Council, Commission on Human Rights (2001) *Adverse Effects of the Illicit Movement and Dumping of Toxic and Dangerous Products and Wastes on the Enjoyment of Human Rights*.

United Nations Interregional Crime Research Institute (UNICRI) (2000) *Criminal Organizations and Crimes Against the Environment – a Desktop Study*. Rome: UNICRI.

Watkins, K. *et al.* (2008) *Human Development Report 2007/2008. Fighting Climate Change: Human Solidarity in a Divided World*. United Nations Development Programme (UNDP).

White, R. (2005) 'Environmental Crime in Global Context: Exploring the Theoretical and Empirical Complexities', *Current Issues in Criminal Justice*, 16(3): 271–285.

White, R. (2007) 'Green Criminology and the Pursuit of Social and Ecological Justice', in P. Beirne and N. South (eds), *Issues in Green Criminology: Confronting Harms Against Environments, Humanity and Other Animals*. Cullompton: Willan Publishing, 32–54.

White, R. (2008) *Crimes Against Nature: Environmental Criminology and Ecological Justice*. Cullompton: Willan Publishing.

Williams, C. (1996) 'An Environmental Victimology', *Social Justice*, 23: 16–40.

Williams, C.R. and Arrigo, B.A. (2005) *Theory, Justice and Social Change: Theoretical Integrations and Critical Applications*. New York: Springer.

Williams, F.P., III (1999) *Imagining Criminology: An Alternative Paradigm*. New York and London: Garland.

Young, T.R. (1997a) 'Challenges: For a Postmodern Criminology', in D. Milovanovic (ed.), *Chaos, Criminology, and Social Justice: The New Orderly (Dis)order*. Westport, CT: Praeger, 29–51.

Young, T.R. (1997b) 'The ABCs of Crime: Attractors, Bifurcations, and Chaotic Dynamics', in D. Milovanovic (ed.), *Chaos, Criminology, and Social Justice: The New Orderly (Dis)order*. Westport, CT: Praeger, 77–96.

Young, T.R. (1999) 'A Nonlinear Theory of Justice: Affirmative Moments in Postmodern Criminology', in B.A. Arrigo (ed.), *Social Justice/Criminal Justice: The Maturation of Critical Theory in Law, Crime, and Deviance*. Belmont, CA: West/Wadsworth, 190–200.

Chapter 12

The ecocidal tendencies of late modernity: transnational crime, social exclusion, victims and rights

Nigel South

Introduction

Criminology is seeing the rapid development of critical thinking around green issues, producing case studies and theory that meet and interweave with aspects of philosophy, political science, sociology, economics and the environmental sciences. This is reflected in the growing body of published work on 'Green criminology', to which this volume will make a significant international contribution. In this essay, I will briefly outline some of the history and agenda of this 'new' green criminology so far, but I also aim to illustrate that – unsurprisingly – this is a body of research building upon some familiar criminological foundations. As examples, I explore here transnational crime, social exclusion, and victims and rights, and conclude by signposting some emerging issues and avenues for interdisciplinary research.

A green perspective in criminology

'Criminology' can be defined in varying ways but at its simplest and in the terms most commonly accepted 'it is taken to be the study of crime, criminals and criminal justice', although there are many different approaches to the subject. In fact, criminology as a field has always been shaped by the influence of, and borrowings from, many other academic disciplines (Carrabine *et al.* 2009: 3) and has been characterised by Downes (1988) as a 'rendezvous subject'. In this sense, environmental issues provide criminology with a perfect site for engagement in interdisciplinary research on local and global issues. Just as no single theory or paradigm dominates criminology as a whole, there is no universal, prevailing theory 'of' or 'for' a green criminology, rather, it is fruitful to adopt a green 'perspective', providing a different way of examining and making sense of various forms of harm, crime and responses (South 1998).

Such a perspective is not new and the term 'green criminology' was first used by Lynch (1990: 3), who brought together the radical agenda of critical criminology with an awareness of environmental issues and activism and 'in this context ... envisioned the emergence of a "Green Criminology" '. However, to step back further, Lynch acknowledged that even this formulation did not represent 'an entirely new perspective or orientation within criminology', as environmental hazards, harms and crimes had been previously examined by criminologists with an interest in the crimes of the powerful. Whatever an explicitly green or environmental criminology may come to look like in the future, it will have been built upon a substantial amount of past work of relevance (South and Beirne 2006; White 2008).

Such work is accumulating and the mainstream of criminological study is increasingly acknowledging its importance and contribution to the vitality of the field. In her 1998 Presidential Address to the American Society of Criminology on the 'future of criminology', Zahn (1999) argued with some passion that the environment and environmental crime would become a new arena in which 'we need to test and develop theory':

> pollution of our rivers and oceans is causing global mass extinctions and a significant reduction in biodiversity. The impacts for life on this planet are far-reaching. Particulate pollution annually kills ... four times [more people than] ... homicide. ... With more focus on environmental crime will come a new definition of victims to include species other than humans and a definition of offenders to include those who pollute for convenience ... [and] for profit. Just as Sutherland's white-collar crime expanded our crime paradigm (1949) ... environmental crime will change it in the future. (Zahn 1999: 2)

In the following discussion, I will aim to identify some of the new forms and features of crime, as well as legal but ecologically injurious activities, that this expanded 'paradigm' must accommodate.

Ecocidal trends in late modernity

The *Penguin Dictionary* (2007) defines 'ecocide' as the 'destruction of the natural environment to the extent that it is unable to support life'. While I am not arguing that we have already passed a catastrophic 'point of no return', the term alerts us to our proximity to the edge of ecocide. In this respect, one of the important tasks of social and natural scientists in recent decades has been to raise awareness of prevalent late-modern tendencies to ecocidal behaviour, long established in advanced but now also a feature of many developing nations. Boekhout van Solinge (2008: 26) refers to the idea of ecocide as a 'delict' (an offence or transgression), defined by Gray (1996) as 'causing or permitting harm to the natural environment on a massive scale' and reflecting a 'breach of duty of care owed to humanity in general'. This chapter brings the idea of a 'green criminology' to bear on an examination of several indicators of such ecocidal behaviour.

Transnational crime

In a world where the process of globalisation is 'widening, deepening and speeding up ... worldwide interconnectedness in all aspects of contemporary life, from the cultural to the criminal, the financial to the spiritual' (Held *et al.* 1999: 2), trade across borders and boundaries flourishes, extends and mutates. Of course, such trading is by no means new, but recent years have seen growing acknowledgement of the corrupting influence exerted and the damage caused by both legal and illegal transnational trades in environmental goods. Instances of the former are perhaps easily overlooked, yet profoundly serious ecological damage can be carried out with official licence while being underpinned by corruption and suppression of criticism. The consequences for populations and habitats now and into the future can be deeply worrying.

One example is the clearing of forests of old growth trees in Tasmania, a rapacious process involving cutting down the trees, burning the land, introducing pesticide into water sources and polluting the atmosphere, all to provide a product for the transnational trade in woodchip for the Asian paper manufacturing industry and for other materials (Flanagan 2007). In other instances the illegal trade is diverse, enormously profitable and not simply injurious to environmental well-being and security but also to civil society, eroding trust, generating corruption and creating victims. Examples would include trading in and transportation of banned ozone-depleting substances, hazardous wastes, illegally harvested fish, timber or rare wildlife species or body parts (e.g. ivory, animal organs for certain traditional medicines), all of which will probably require organised smuggling and forged documentation and involve operations that are now found overlapping with global routes and markets involving drugs, arms and humans (French and Mastny 2001: 180; Cumming-Bruce 2003; Putt and Nelson 2008: 1). As described by the international police cooperation agency, Interpol:

> There is clear evidence that environmental criminals engage in other major areas of crime such as document and passport fraud, corruption, the possession and use of illegal weapons, murder, and other smuggling issues notably in drugs, firearms and people.
>
> (Interpol, October 2009: http://www.interpol.int/Public/EnvironmentalCrime/)

According to Elliott (2008: 9), whether 'opportunistic and informal' or 'increasingly systematic, well-financed and highly organized', such transnational environmental crime (TEC) 'is one of the fastest growing areas of criminal activity, globally worth billions of dollars'. This is an important assessment.

Nonetheless, there remain good grounds for caution about any assumptions regarding 'mafia' or cartel-type control over transnational, cross-border environmental trading and trafficking. As with forms of 'disorganised crime' (Reuter 1983) that have been described in relation to other local and international illicit markets, this is a mixed arena of sometimes distinct, sometimes overlapping, small-scale and larger-volume actors. The trading and trafficking involved can be clearly illegal but hard to prevent and penalise, or be ambiguous in terms of juridical character or the morality of proportionate responsibility (Michalowski and Bitten 2005: 139–40). Entrepreneurs involved are taking advantage of new scarcities and the commodification of naturally occurring goods, which frequently owe increases in value and price to benignly intentioned regulations and prohibitions. Hence, the two ironies of these markets are that (1) in the absence of monopolistic or oligopolistic market dominance there is uncontrolled competition without forms of profit-motivated stewardship that might have led to the exercise of some restraint and protection, and (2) regulation and prohibition help to create the scarcity and rarity of certain commodities that then drive the markets for these goods (Hayman and Brack 2002: 7).

Hayman and Brack (2002: 7) note how restrictions 'at certain points along international commodity chains' provide the inroads for familiar 'organized' crime bodies to engage in the environmental crime market, utilising experience of cross-border smuggling and moving multiple commodities according to demand, whether wildlife, weapons, drugs, or vehicles. The extent of these illegal trades is not easy to quantify or cost, but this certainly represents more than the 'occasional movements of goods' (Elliott 2008: 9) with operations involving lone smugglers as well as container-size consignments moved by ship and plane, facilitated by opportunistic use of loopholes in monitoring afforded by lax or fraudulent documentation, free-trade port arrangements, and complexity of chains of ownership and responsibility for both goods and vessels. In the analysis of Hayman and Brack (2002: 7).

> Complicated networks of interaction exist that link raw materials and producers to customers through a web of supplier relationships with the involvement of ancillary specialist services and other key actors such as legitimate business, government officials and consumers.

The next sections look in a little more detail at two such cases of supply and demand – the cases of wildlife trafficking and waste disposal – and then at how climate change and environmental disaster can also provide profitable opportunities for organised forms of crime.

Wildlife trafficking

A major form of such transnational crime is the highly profitable trade in endangered species. In 2006, it was reported that this trade is now worth around £6 billion per year:

> Whether it is slaughtering rhinos for their horns or Tibetan antelopes for their wool, smuggling snakes as pets or selling illegally felled hardwoods from the rainforest, the global illicit wildlife trade is now worth more than £6bn a year, making it the world's third-biggest source of criminal earnings after drugs trafficking and the arms trade. This alarming statistic was revealed after a meeting of the Convention on International Trade in Endangered Species of Wild Flora and Fauna (CITES), an international pact signed by almost 200 countries and top security officials. (Coonan 2006)

However, as Wyatt (2009) observes,

> the financial capital assigned to the wildlife trade does not reflect the external costs of damage to the environment nor consider other value beyond or besides the instrumental worth to humans.

National and international laws exist to protect animal and plant species, but in addition to the under-resourcing of enforcement there are other reasons why such laws can be ineffective (Naylor 2004). Among these can be genuine ignorance of restrictions, or historical and culturally grounded motives for denial of harm, as well as rejection of any reasons why such restrictions should apply or be necessary. Similar obstacles and objections can arise in relation to attempts to change and improve the ways in which society disposes of waste.

Waste disposal

The limited or ineffective regulation of waste-dumping has created highly profitable domestic and international trading in illegal disposal and dumping of 'ordinary' domestic waste but also hazardous toxic waste. Paradoxically, both weak and serious regulation can lead to illegal and dangerous disposal of waste – the former because rules are easily flouted and the latter because the costs of legitimate disposal can encourage illicit practices and services to deal with difficult waste. This has manifested itself in new forms of corporate and organised crime, and over a decade ago Ruggiero (1996) commented on how regulatory regimes can produce unintended (or at least not fully anticipated) criminogenic outcomes.

> The illegal disposal of hazardous waste has been thoroughly studied in the USA, where in some cases the involvement of organized crime reaches all aspects of the business, from the control of which companies are officially licensed to dispose of waste to those which earn contracts with public or private organizations and to the payment of bribes to dump-site owners, or the possession of such sites … Paradoxically, the development of this illegal service runs parallel with an increase in environmental awareness, the latter forcing governments to raise costs for industrial dumping, which indirectly encourages industrialists to opt for cheaper solutions.

Szasz (1986) provides a significant case study of how the US Resource Conservation and Recovery Act produced this kind of effect (Brisman 2008: 738–41), and Hayman and Brack (2002: 13) report a particularly cynical and audacious act of environmental protection racketeering that was possible only because of the impact of regulations, in which a Detroit-based company, Hi-Po, was tried in July 2000 for the deliberate contamination of rivers with toxic chemicals and diesel oil in order to profit by offering a 'clean-up service'. However, as Ruggiero (1996) and others have noted, Italy provides a case-study with particularly striking examples of this new area of criminal entrepreneurship. Indeed, it now appears that 'the transportation and illegal trafficking of toxic waste in Italy is so widely acknowledged that an Italian dictionary has an entry for 'ecomafia' to describe organised criminal networks that profit from illegally disposing of commercial, industrial and radioactive waste (Legambiente 2003)' (Walters 2007: 188). Writing in the mid-1990s, Ruggiero (1996: 139–40) described the entrepreneurialism of southern Italian organised crime groups offering waste disposal services to the industries and businesses of the north, with consequences such as those remarked upon by the Commissione Antimafia: 'The seawater of large parts of Naples province is polluted mainly because of illegal waste dumping, authorized dumping constitutes only 10% of the total waste actually disposed of in the bay of Naples.'

Just over a decade later, in 2008, the public health concerns about waste disposal in Naples had drawn international media attention with news stories of steady contamination of parts of the city and its hinterland by decades of illegal waste dumping and burning (Reuters, 17 January, 2008, 'Naples waste linked to death and disease'). The causes were reported to be 'political ineptitude, corruption and crime' that have prevented the establishment of an up-to-date and safe disposal system but maintained reliance on poorly managed landfill sites that have then been corruptly used for tipping of hazardous materials. 'An even bigger source of pollution', reported Reuters (17 January 2008),

> is the Camorra, the Naples mafia which runs a lucrative line in dumping and burning rubbish illegally. More than domestic trash, the Camorra focuses on disposal of industrial waste which it brings to Campania from Italy's rich north – one of a string of crimes against the environment earning the mafia an estimated 6 billion euros a year.

While both strong and weak regulatory regimes can produce negative outcomes, in some cases it may simply be convenience and cost reduction that has led to unquestioned practices of disastrously damaging waste disposal. The case of Love Canal (South 1998: 215–16) is one classic illustration of such circumstances, but the regionalisation of waste disposal into areas of the poor or the developing world by industry that profits the wealthy and developed world is a broader and ongoing phenomenon (South 1998: 216–19). This has both immediate impacts and profound long-lasting legacies for generations that follow. The dumping of 19 billion gallons of toxic waste and millions of gallons of crude oil in forest areas of Ecuador by Texaco during the 1970s and 1980s has led to deaths resulting from cancers (over 1,400), distress and disease among indigenous peoples, and spoiling of local water sources, fish and animal life. The claim for damages brought by the Ecuadorian government is being disputed by Chevron, the new owners of Texaco (http://www.business-humanrights.org 2008; Vidal 2009: 26–7).

Climate change, population displacement and organised crime

Organised criminal groups, corrupt legal enterprises and individual profiteers have always managed to find ways to benefit from prohibitions and scarcity (Nadelmann 1990). In the aftermath of serious environmental disasters and crises, it is likely that the conditions will provide opportunities for illegal and immoral exploitation. Loss of habitat, scarcity of food and medicines, and prohibitions regarding free movement of people will have criminogenic effects (Environmental Investigation Agency 2008: 5). Thus, loss of home and habitat leads to profound psycho-social impacts following displacement and a sense of 'loss', leaving people vulnerable to exploitation, encouragement into crime, perpetrating or being victims of human trafficking for sex and labour, or recruitment as disposable soldiers in the machinery of war. In cases of flooding, storm, fire and other emergencies, conditions of panic, crowd unrest, conflict and looting follow. Food and famine produce scarcity, which means rationing, and this, in turn, produces conditions that support corrupt diversion, illicit markets, profiteering, and food riots.

All of these developments produce profound challenges for human security, public health and crime prevention. Disasters, whether natural or unnatural, that is, those 'made more frequent or more severe due to human actions' (Abramovitz 2001: 124), also produce opportunities for legal and illegal profit generation. Corruption frequently plays a part in the scramble for contracts for reconstruction, planning and building, and even charitable aid funds can be diverted into criminal bank accounts (Popham 2009: 19). Such environmental events and immoral and illegal human behaviours that make the impact of disasters more severe while profiting from scarcity, perpetuate global inequalities and hierarchies of powerlessness and exclusion. It is these themes that the next section addresses.

Social exclusion and environmental victims

The term 'social exclusion' represents a point of convergence for several areas of policy as well as academic fields such as public health and criminology. Thus, 'The most serious threats facing human health today are deeply complex. They include economic crises, pandemics, poverty, and violence and conflict' (Costello *et al.* 2009: 1659), and within criminology, long-standing and more recent problems arise from disenfranchisement and discrimination, stigmatisation and exploitation, poverty and injustice (South 2005). Similar concerns arise in the arena of environmental politics in relation to access to sustainable resources, questions of distributive justice, and the different reasons for lack of care of and for the environment. Here the familiar criminological exercise of contrasting the circumstances and crimes of the powerful with those of the poor is mirrored in the comparison between the destructive environmental exploitation carried out by corporate bodies relative to environmental damage following actions based on need and desperation. As observed in the report of the World Commission on Environment and Development (1987: 28) (the Brundtland Commission), 'poverty itself pollutes the environment, creating environmental stress in a different way. Those who are poor and hungry will often destroy their immediate environment in order to survive.' This is just one expression of the fundamental insight at the heart of the World Commission on Environment and Development report that 'It is futile to attempt to deal with environmental problems without a broader perspective that encompasses the factors underlying world poverty and international inequality' (World Commission on Environment and Development 1987: 3).

In his discussion of these and related matters, Dobson (1998: 17) notes the intertwining of poverty, inequality, sustainability and distributive justice and how these come together in the notion of an 'environmental justice movement' (Bullard 1990; see also Szasz 1994).

Importantly, as Dobson observes, a somewhat belated but nonetheless important realisation to some in this movement was that we do not all suffer the causes and outcomes of environmental problems in fair and equal measure. In fact dynamics of inclusion and exclusion, favour and disfavour, operate in relation to exposure to good or bad environmental conditions just as they do in influencing educational, health or career expectations.

> During the early years of the movement, in an understandable attempt to build the broadest possible constituency, environmentalists often described the issue as one that affected everyone equally. ... On closer examination, however, massive inequities in environmental degradations and injustice in the policies used to correct them became evident. While created equal, all Americans were not, as things turned out, being poisoned equally. (Dowie 1995: 141)

In a world of increased scarcity, such inequalities will simply be embedded further and we will face the threat of new social constructions of hierarchies and needs emerging. The resulting competition for resources is likely to produce discrimination and violence based on ethnic, gender and other well established sources of 'difference' and discrimination. The need for vocabularies and actions defending victims and upholding rights to fairness and justice will be more important than ever. However, it would be a strange form of progress if all that was achieved was the right to equality of victimisation. There remains some unpacking to do here about the different kinds of victims affected by harms to the environment and the rights that might be pursued.

Victims and rights

Dobson (1998: 19) continues the critique of the 'equal suffering' position by noting the argument that

> the perception, and especially the suffering, of environmental risk is skewed in the direction of those least able to afford to protect themselves against it. Just as natural disasters, such as earthquakes, always cause more death and injury among poor and – and therefore poorly protected – populations, so environmental calamities of anthropogenic origin hit the poor hardest.

They also hit the least powerful hardest – the poor of minority communities and developing countries but also women. Wachholz (2007) for example, examines studies and agency reports concerning levels of violence against women after slow- and sudden-onset, climate-related natural disasters and argues that the predicted rise in natural disasters tied to climate change is likely to be correlated with increases in violence against women within the regions that experience extreme weather events.

This argument about the gender-differentiated impacts of climate change aligns with similar conclusions from the fields of migration and climate studies. Thus the International Organisation for Migration (2009: 2) reports that

> Higher death rates for women as a result of natural disasters are directly linked to the socio-economic status of women in affected societies and the degree to which women enjoy economic and social rights. Statistically, natural disasters kill more women than men, and kill women at a younger age than men. Behavioural restrictions and poor access to information and resources can directly affect a woman's chances of survival during a natural disaster or its aftermath. [see also Department for International Development, 2008]

Hence, as climate change makes new, devastating contributions to the incidence and scale of 'disasters', these occur alongside continuing inequalities that mean the impacts of such disasters have unequal and differentially distributed results: 'environmental victimology is as much about issues of race, class, poverty, trade and economics as it is about the environment' (Walters 2007: 199). Of course, human-origin crimes can combine with environmental calamity with absolutely disastrous consequences, typically where profiteering has led to conditions increasing suffering, loss of life and environmental damage or led to reduction in the amount of aid and intervention available. Green (2005) illustrates this well with her case study of the links between 'corruption, construction and catastrophe' and the consequences for victims of three major earthquakes in Turkey. The proposition here is that legislative reform in this and similar political contexts cannot have the necessary impact on human rights and prevention of the death and injury of victims without being accompanied by a process that also addresses questions of political and social organisation, authoritarianism, and corruption (Green 2005: 544). What is needed, argues Green, is a 'political criminology of natural disasters'.

Green (2005) provides an analysis here invoking the matter of rights, but how powerful and useful is the discourse of rights in current form? This has certainly been a provocative source of fresh thinking in criminology in the past (Carrabine *et al.* 2009: 430–35); nonetheless, this cannot alter the fact that the status of victims who have been denied both human and environmental rights is poorly addressed in international law although important statements on this subject do exist (Berat 1993; Bodansky *et al.* 2007). In this regard, Hulme (2008) draws attention to the 1972 Stockholm Declaration of the United Nations Conference on the Human Environment, which observes that 'Both aspects of man's environment, the natural and the man-made, are essential to his well-being and to the enjoyment of basic human rights, the right to life itself', and also to the Report on Human Rights and the Environment (1994; UN Commission on HR, Rapporteur Ksentini, Sub-commission Report), in which section 248 argues that:

> Environmental damage has direct effects on the enjoyment of a series of human rights, such as the right to life, to health, to a satisfactory standard of living, to sufficient food, to housing, to education, to work, to culture, to non-discrimination, to dignity and the harmonious development of one's personality, to security of person and family, to development, to peace, etc.

Such statements lend support to Gray's proposal that ecocide be written into international law, premised on the threat to or breach of rights to health and to life (Gray 1996: 217–22; Boekhout van Solinge 2008: 26).

In other examples of such violations of rights and what could be seen as 'offences against the person', traditional inhabitants of certain areas are forced out by incoming settlers or forcibly removed to be assimilated elsewhere. These are processes of exploitation and coercion that constitute modern ecological and humanitarian rights abuses that are often invisible but deserve exposure. The consequent loss of the ecoliteracy of cultures that can follow from such trauma and upheaval as well as from the frequently accompanying controversial practices of bioprospecting and biopatenting will result in the devastating loss of history, culture and knowledge globally (Environmental Investigation Agency 2008; Vidal 2009: 26–7). Practices described by critics as biopiracy have expanded to represent a global market for the products of ancient and tropical forests or other remote regions, as well as commercially removing and reinterpreting indigenous knowledge previously preserved and passed from generation to generation (South 2007). Various campaigning and action-research projects around the world are working with such causes and could provide opportunities for criminology to engage in fruitful interdisciplinary work. For example,

> Disconnection from nature and the local environment is causing harm to indigenous peoples who have already become marginalised by limited wealth, power and status. The consequences of such disconnection include mental and physical health problems, social pathologies and cultural collapse. As they have come to appreciate the repercussions of disconnection, many groups are now taking action to protect and support their communities and cultures through ... 'revitalisation projects'.
> (Pilgrim *et al*. 2009)

Emerging issues: natural resources, conflict and crime

Hogg (2002: 195) has drawn attention to the need for criminology to keep up with global and social change as traditional units of analysis become less material and more questionable, and asks a question relevant to times of ontological insecurities, material uncertainties and environmental challenges:

> What happens to the conceptual apparatus of criminology and how salient are its taken-for-granted terms – crime, law, justice, state, sovereignty – at a time when global change and conflict may be eroding some elements at least of the international framework of states it has taken for granted?

To put this fully into perspective, consider that in some scenarios of the future, the whole or significant parts of sovereign states may disappear due to climate change and environmental catastrophes. This has been discussed in work undertaken by Hampson (2006) for the UN Economic and Social Council (Sub-Commission on the Promotion and Protection of Human Rights, 57th session), which addressed the 'Prevention of discrimination and protection of indigenous peoples' in states and other territories threatened with extinction for environmental reasons – in other words, 'Certain States face the likelihood of the disappearance of the whole or a significant part of their surface area for environmental reasons.' This may be caused in several ways but recent disasters have followed from rising sea levels and salt water entering freshwater destroying agriculture, vulnerability to tsunamis, and the occurrence of earthquakes and volcanic eruptions. Hampson (2006) is concerned primarily with how such environmental disasters will force the evacuation of populations and give rise to a variety of human rights issues, but in the course of such a disaster and the population movement that will follow, a green criminology perspective suggests the need to consider the enormous potential for crime and injustice, conflict and injury that will follow.

It may not yet be easy to fully comprehend the consequences of climate change and environmental catastrophe, but in a recent report Abbott (2008) shows how increasing temperatures, rising sea levels and weather volatility could, by 2050, have led to

- resource wars over food and water
- the plight of up to 200 million 'environmental refugees' fleeing devastation
- an inflation of ethnic tensions and conflicts
- the prospect of the police and border services of countries closing rather than opening borders
- violent protests against polluters.

According to many commentators, conflicts of the future will increasingly be fought over environmental resources. However, although this may mean that global warming, population growth and accumulating resource poverty will all heighten existing tensions or accelerate processes of exploitation (Brahic 2008; Vidal 2009), conflicts also follow from other circumstances and conditions. In fact, conflict can occur more frequently and intensely in resource-rich states or regions. As Pearce (2002: 36) observes:

> More dangerous than environmental poverty are environmental riches. ... Particularly in poor countries, nature's bounty seems to stymie economic development, cripple governments, fill the pockets of rebels and all too often trigger protracted civil wars. Today's rebels are more interested in liberating diamonds than repressed peoples. Worse, they finance their start-up costs by promising foreign interests a share in the spoils of war.

In Angola and Sierra Leone, profits from the sale of 'conflict diamonds' have funded civil wars, and in Liberia 'conflict timber' has been similarly exploited (Boekhout van Solinge 2008).

There is some debate over the potential for conflict and criminal activity that might follow from control of water supplies (Brahic 2008), but there are already examples of popular resistance forming against water privatisation. Thus Otto and Bohm (2006: 300) report on the 1999 privatisation of water services in Bolivia that led to the expropriation of independent water and irrigation systems, the tripling of prices for some of the poorest people and subsequent resistance from a coalition of diverse groups, protests that faced police responses, with 175 protestors injured and one dead, but ultimate success as the government terminated the contract with the multinational consortium. Controlling water means controlling life, providing enormous scope for political corruption, corporate irresponsibility, and even genocide. As Pearce (2004) has recorded, from the political interests that push through great dam-building projects to the local arsenic pollution of groundwater in Bangladesh to the inappropriate hijacking of water supplies via the process of privatisation, water has always been and is becoming even more a resource intimately entwined with power and profit. The misuse of power and the criminal connections potentially associated with controlling the water supply are nicely illustrated in the movie *Chinatown* and in the James Bond film *A Quantum of Solace* where unravelling the conspiracy surrounding control of a natural resource – water – replaces the usual plot device of retrieval or destruction of 'secrets and weapons' as the objective for the mission.

Conclusion

The emergence of 'green crimes' is a feature of a late-modern 'world risk society' (Beck 2002; Aas 2007), bringing new patterns of harm, damage and conflict that could not have been easily foretold a century or so ago. The response requires a new academic way of looking at the world but also a new global politics. This is not to equate a green criminology with 'green party politics' but instead to seek the articulation of 'a position premised on the principles of environmentalism and broader issues of environmental justice' (Walters 2007: 199). Such a position should provide a standpoint going beyond the narrow boundaries of traditional criminology and draw together political and practical action to shape public policy (see

Carrabine *et al.* 2009: 452–55). As Aas (2007: 297) has argued, a global perspective is needed to force us to confront matters neglected by traditional criminology: 'If we are to grasp, and challenge, the major sources of social injustice' – and, I would add, of global insecurity – 'we need to move beyond the state-territorial principle.' This is important because it is the health of the environment globally that needs to be preserved and protected from the violence and violations of ecocide.

A 'green criminology' has much to contribute to interdisciplinary research collaboration on these themes. Let me conclude with a quotation from a report on the public health consequences of climate change, illustrating how closely shared such concerns can be:

> Management of the health effects of climate change will require inputs from all sectors of government and civil society, collaboration between many academic disciplines, and new ways of international cooperation that have hitherto eluded us. [p. 1693, col. 2] ... Climate change also raises the issue of intergenerational justice. The inequity of climate change – with the rich causing most of the problem and the poor initially suffering most of the consequences – will prove to be a source of historical shame to our generation if nothing is done to address it. (Costello *et al.* 2009: 1694, col. 1)

Acknowledgements

This chapter draws upon papers presented as a plenary address to the Dutch Society of Criminology, University of Leiden, 20 June 2008, and as part of the ASC/UNICRI panel at the American Society of Criminology meetings in St. Louis, November 2008. I am grateful to the organisers of these events and also to my colleague, Karen Hulme of the School of Law, University of Essex, for allowing me to benefit from her expertise as a lawyer and specialist in rights.

References

Aas, K.F. (2007) 'Analysing a World in Motion: Global Flows Meet the "Criminology of the Other" ', *Theoretical Criminology*, 11 (2): 283–303.

Abbot, C. (2008) *An Uncertain Future: Law Enforcement, National Security and Climate Change*. Oxford: Oxford Research Group.

Abramovitz, J. (2001) 'Averting Unnatural Disasters', in Worldwatch Institute (ed.), *State of the World 2001*. London: Earthscan.

Beck, U. (2002) 'The Terrorist Threat: World Risk Society Revisited', *Theory, Culture and Society*, 19 (4): 39–55.

Berat, L. (1993) 'Defending the Right to a Healthy Environment: Towards a Crime of Geocide in International Law', *Boston University International Law Journal*, 11: 327–48.

Bodansky, D., Brunnee, J. and Hey, J. (eds) (2007) *The Oxford Handbook of International Environmental Law*. Oxford: Oxford University Press.

Boekhout van Solinge, T. (2008) 'Crime, Conflicts and Ecology in Africa', in R. Sollund (ed.), *Global Harms: Ecological Crime and Speciesism*. New York: Nova Science Publishers, 13–34.

Brahic, C (2008) 'A Law to Stop the Wells Running Dry', *New Scientist*, 9 November: 8–9.

Brisman, A. (2008) 'Crime-Environment Relationships and Environmental Justice', *Seattle Journal for Social Justice*, 6 (2): 727–817.

Bullard, R. (1990) *Dumping in Dixie: Race, Class and Environmental Quality*. Boulder, CO: Westview.

Carrabine, E., Cox, P., Lee, M., *et al.* (2009) *Criminology: A Sociological Introduction*. London: Routledge.

Coonan, C. (2006) 'Illegal Wildlife Trade is Worth £6bn a Year', *The Independent*, 29 July [online]. Available at: http://www.independent.co.uk/environment/illegal-wildlife-trade-is-worth-1636bn-a-year-409623.html (accessed 4 December 2009).

Costello, A., Abbas, M., Allen, A., *et al.* (2009) 'Managing the Health Effects of Climate Change', *Lancet*, 373: 1693–1733.

Cumming-Bruce, N. (2003) 'Thailand Gets Tough on Wildlife Traffickers', *The Observer*, 30 November, 21.

Department for International Development (2008) *Gender and Climate Change: Mapping the Linkages*. London: Department for International Development.

Dobson, A. (1998) *Justice and the Environment*. Oxford: Oxford University Press.

Dowie, M. (1995) *Losing Ground: American Environmentalism at the Close of the Twentieth Century*. Cambridge, MA.: MIT Press.

Downes, D. (1988) 'The Sociology of Crime and Social Control in Britain, 1960–1987', *British Journal of Criminology*, 28(2): 175–187.

Environmental Investigation Agency (2008) *Environmental Crime: A Threat to our Future*. London: Environmental Investigation Agency International. [online]. Available at: www.eia-international.org (accessed 4 December 2009).

Elliott, L. (2008) 'Combating Transnational Environmental Crime: "Joined Up" Thinking About Transnational Networks', Paper to American Society of Criminology, St Louis, November.

Flanagan, R. (2007) 'Paradise Razed', *Telegraph.co.uk*, 28 June [online]. Available at: http://www.telegraph.co.uk/earth/environment/conservation/3298789/Paradise-razed.html (accessed 4 December 2009).

French, H. and Mastny, L. (2001) 'Controlling International Environmental Crime', in Worldwatch Institute (ed.), *State of the World 2001*. London: Earthscan.

Gray, M.A. (1996) 'The International Crime of Ecocide', *California Western International Law Journal*, 26: 215–71.

Green, P, (2005) 'Disaster by Design: Corruption, Construction and Catastrophe', *British Journal of Criminology*, 45 (4): 528–46.

Hampson, F.J. (2005) *The Human Rights Situation of Indigenous Peoples in States and other Territories Threatened with Extinction for Environmental Reasons*. Sub-Commission on the Promotion and Protection of Human Rights, E/CN.4/Sub.2/2005/28, 16 June 2005, United Nations.

Hayman, G. and Brack, D. (2002) *International Environmental Crime: The Nature and Control of Environmental Black Markets*. London: Chatham House.

Held, D., McGrew, A., Goldblatt, D. and Perraton, J. (1999) *Global Transformations*. Cambridge: Polity Press.

Hogg, R. (2002) 'Criminology Beyond the Nation State: Global Conflict, Human Rights and the "New World Disorder"', in K. Carrington and R. Hogg (eds), *Critical Criminology: Issues, Debates, Challenges*. Cullompton: Willan Publishing, 185–217.

Hulme, K. (2008) 'Do We Need a Human Right to a Healthy Environment?' Paper presented at Human Rights and the Environment Panel, 21 February, University of Essex, Human Rights Centre 25th Anniversary.

International Organization for Migration (IOM) (2009) *Migration, Climate Change and the Environment*. Policy Brief, May. Geneva: IOM.

Legambiente (2003) *The Illegal Trafficking in Hazardous Waste in Italy and Spain*. Rome: European Commission.

Lynch, M. (1990) 'The Greening of Criminology: A Perspective on the 1990s', *Critical Criminologist*, 2 (3–4): 11–12 [reprinted in N. South and P. Beirne, eds. (2006) *Green Criminology*. Aldershot: Dartmouth, 165–70].

Michalowski, R. and Bitten, K. (2005) 'Transnational Environmental Crime', in P. Reichel (ed.), *Handbook of Transnational Crime and Justice*. Thousand Oaks, CA: Sage, 139–59.

Nadelmann, E. (1990) 'Global Prohibition Regimes: The Evolution of Norms in International Society', *International Organization*, 44: 479–526.

Naylor, R.T. (2004) 'The Underworld of Ivory', *Crime, Law and Social Change*, 42: 261–95.

Otto, B. and Bohm, S. (2006) ' "The People" and Resistance Against International Business: The Case of the Bolivian "Water War"', *Critical Perspectives on International Business*, 2 (4): 299–320.

Pearce, F. (2002) 'Blood Diamonds and Oil', *New Scientist*, 29 June, 174, 2349: 36–41.

Pearce, F. (2004) *Keepers of the Spring: Reclaiming Our Water in an Age of Globalization*. Washington, DC: Island Press.

Pilgrim, S., Samson, C. and Pretty, J. (2009) 'Rebuilding Lost Connections: How Revitalisation Projects Contribute to Cultural Continuity and Improve the Environment', Interdisciplinary Centre for Environment and Society Occasional Paper 2009-01. University of Essex, UK [online]. Available at: http://www.essex.ac.uk/ces/esu/occ-papers.shtm (accessed 5 December).

Popham, P. (2009) 'Mobsters "Out to Make a Killing from the Quake" ', *The Independent*, World News, 15 April, 19.

Puut, J. and Nelson, D. (2008) 'Crime in the Australian Fishing Industry', *Trends and Issues in the Crime and Criminal Justice*, 366: 1–10.

Reuter, P. (1983) *Disorganised Crime: Illegal Markets and the Mafia*. Cambridge, MA: MIT Press.

Ruggiero, V. (1996) *Organised and Corporate Crime in Europe: Offers That Can't Be Refused*. Aldershot: Dartmouth.

South, N. (1998) 'A Green Field for Criminology?: A Proposal for a Perspective', *Theoretical Criminology*, 2 (2): 211–34 (special issue).

South, N. (2005) 'Inequalities, Crime and Citizenship', in M. Romero and E. Margolis (eds) *The Blackwell Companion on Social Inequalities*. Blackwell, Malden, MA: 350–71.

South, N. (2007) 'The "Corporate Colonisation of Nature": Bio-prospecting, Bio-piracy and the Development of Green Criminology', in P. Beirne and N. South (eds), *Issues in Green Criminology: Confronting Harms Against Environments, Humanity and Other Animals*. Cullompton: Willan Publishing, 230–247.

South, N. and Beirne, P. (eds) (2006) *Green Criminology*. International Library of Criminology, Criminal Justice and Penology. Aldershot and Brookfield, VT: Dartmouth.

South, N. and Wyatt, T. (forthcoming) 'Comparing Illicit Trades in Wildlife and Drugs: An Exploratory Exercise'.

Sykes, G. and Matza, D. (1957) 'Techniques of Neutralization: A Theory of Delinquency', *American Sociological Review*, 22: 664–73.

Szasz, A. (1986) 'Corporations, Organised Crime and the Disposal of Hazardous Waste: An Examination of the Making of a Criminogenic Regulatory Structure', *Criminology*, 24 (1): 1–27.

Vidal, J. (2009) 'We Are Fighting for Our Lives and Our Dignity', *The Guardian*, 13th June, 26–27.

Wachholz, S. (2007) 'At Risk: Climate Change and Its Bearing on Women's Vulnerability to Male Violence', in P. Beirne and N. South (eds), *Issues in Green Criminology: Confronting Harms against Environments, Humanity and other Animals*. Cullompton: Willan Publishing, 161–185.

Walters, R. (2007) 'Crime, Regulation and Radioactive Waste in the United Kingdom', in P. Beirne and N. South (eds), *Issues in Green Criminology: Confronting Harms Against Environments, Humanity and Other Animals*. Cullompton: Willan Publishing, 186–205.

White, R. (2008) *Crimes Against Nature: Environmental Criminology and Ecological Justice*. Cullompton: Willan Publishing.

World Commission on Environment and Development (1987) *Our Common Future*. Oxford: Oxford University Press.

Wyatt, T. (2008) The Illegal Wildlife Trade and Deep Green Criminology: Two Case Studies of Fur and Falcon Trades in the Russian Federation. PhD thesis, University of Kent, UK.

Wyatt, T. (2009) Personal communication.

Zahn, M. (1999) 'Presidential Address — Thoughts on the Future of Criminology', *Criminology*, 37 (1): 1–16.

Index